# PAVEL BURE

# PAVEL

CONTENTS


Preface   *vii*

# Preface

I WAS TOLD EARLY ON that I had quite a mountain to climb when I
set out to write a biography of Pavel Bure. It was all too true. Trying to
track down the real story about anything involving the National Hockey
League is a daunting task. In the professional hockey realm, paranoia
and secrecy rule. The task is made doubly difficult when your subject is
shadowed by controversy.

The voices and views of many key individuals are missing in this book.
Pat Quinn, Arthur Griffiths, George McPhee, Ron Salcer, Mike Gillis,
former Bure teammates and certain journalists either refused interviews
or made themselves unavailable. Lacking their cooperation, I was forced
to rely on a number of secondary sources. To clarify, the comments I
collected are in the present tense; those largely derived from press confer-
ences or multiple sources that aren't credited are in the past tense.

Why so many people refused to talk about Bure is open to speculation. For those close to him, cooperating with an unauthorized biography could be regarded as a betrayal of trust; for others, the motivations
might be indifference, resentment, arrogance or, in some cases, perhaps
even fear. When he heard I was doing a book on Bure, one hockey writer

said to me, "If Bure finds out, he'll have somebody break your legs." He wasn't smiling when he said it. Whether or not his belief has any basis in truth, it does indicate one unsettling aspect of the way Bure is regarded. He is definitely not your ordinary hockey player and his still-evolving story is complex. To tie up all the loose ends would require more time and ammunition than I was given. This effort is only a start, but hopefully a good one.

Finally, I would like to extend my thanks to the following: the staff at Greystone Books; publisher Rob Sanders, for his faith; editor Michael Carroll, for his poise under pressure; designer Peter Cocking, for his artful eye; my wife, Anne Rose, and my daughter, Riley, for their patience; my brother, Brian, for his long-distance aid; Miles Davis and John Coltrane, for their inspiration; and various hockey writers, for graciously sharing their insights.

# CHAPTER ONE

# Out of the Night

*The knife dreams of a hand to deliver it from oblivion.*
*But all depends on what the man with the hand decides.*
JORGE LUIS BORGES, "THE KNIFE'S MILONGA"

HE WORE BLACK, the color of the night he was leaving behind, the color of the hired gun he had become. Like most of the other passengers on this transatlantic flight from Moscow to New York City, he was Russian. He had the trim and solid physique of an athlete, but no one seeing him for the first time would ever guess he was a professional hockey player. His nose had never been broken, there were no scars on his face, no missing teeth. Instead, his features were of a type more commonly associated with fashion models or movie stars: perfect cheekbones, coiffed blond hair, slate-blue eyes and full red lips. At 27, Pavel Bure, a warrior in one of the world's most violent games, still possessed the angelic look of a choirboy.

Sitting beside Bure in the first-class cabin was Yuri Ushakov, bound for Washington, D.C., to begin his new appointment as Russia's ambassador to the United States. The two men conversed for hours. Perhaps they talked about their motherland and the dramatic changes that had transformed it forever. Perhaps they discussed fresh beginnings. Like Ushakov, Bure was also about to assume a new posting; he was headed to New York to rendezvous with the National Hockey League's Florida Panthers. Two days before, on January 17, 1999, the Panthers had acquired Bure from the Vancouver Canucks in a blockbuster seven-player trade that had made headlines in sports pages across North America.

The transaction was the culmination of a five-month standoff that began when Bure left the Canucks in September 1998 and returned to Russia, stubbornly refusing to honor the final year of a contract that would have earned him a whopping US$8 million. Demanding to be traded, he had spent the first half of the hockey season in limbo, suspended without pay, while Brian Burke, the Canucks' newly appointed general manager, attempted to find a buyer for his disgruntled superstar. When no one would meet Burke's asking price, the frustrated GM threatened to let Bure sit out the entire year.

It was a peculiar impasse; no NHL player had ever walked away from a contract of this magnitude before. The situation was made even odder by the fact that Bure refused to discuss the reasons for his trade ultimatum, saying only that it was a personal issue and that he was motivated by principles, not money.

Although few could appreciate the logic, Bure's agent, Mike Gillis, insisted that his client's tight-lipped attitude made good sense. "He wants to leave for a number of different reasons that, if they are made public, are going to do nothing but create ill will toward a bunch of different people. I don't think an explanation is advisable, good business or necessary."

But Bure's unexplained desire to escape Vancouver, a city where he had been worshipped with a passionate devotion for seven years, did create ill will. There was a public backlash that intensified as the stalemate dragged on and as the Canucks, crippled by key injuries and the absence of their marquee player, slipped ever lower in the NHL standings. Bure was called an ingrate millionaire, a petulant prima donna and worse. The former poster boy had become a whipping boy.

The Russian's silence only fueled speculation about his true motivations. According to some stories, Bure couldn't stomach his coach, Mike Keenan. According to others, he was at odds with Canucks captain Mark

Messier. It was said that he disliked the fish-bowl atmosphere in Vancouver, that he craved the anonymity afforded by a larger city. Bure's mother, Tatiana, evidently as much in the dark as everyone else, weighed in with her own opinion, saying she thought her son just wanted to play for a better team, one that had a realistic chance of winning the Stanley Cup.

But there were also darker rumors: lurid tales involving blackmail, drug deals, death threats and gangsters. The news reports about Bure's life in Moscow—detailing a swirl of high-society parties, fashion shows, public meetings with controversial Russian politicians and trips to nightclubs in luxury sedans accompanied by stone-faced bodyguards with bulges in their overcoats—merely added to the intrigue.

But then intrigue was nothing new with Bure. There had been a sense of mystery about him ever since his much-disputed drafting by the Canucks in 1989, a draft that some NHL general managers still insist was illegal. The precise details of his sudden and unexpected exit from Russia to join the NHL in the fall of 1991 were unclear, as were the circumstances surrounding his marriage to an American woman shortly after his arrival in North America—a woman whose identity he refused to reveal, a woman no one had ever seen.

Not only did Bure have film-star looks, he attracted the racy, tabloid-style attention normally reserved for Hollywood celebrities. Throughout his career, unconfirmed stories linking him with one controversy or another repeatedly surfaced in the media. In 1993 it was reported that Bure had made payments totaling thousands of dollars to Russian extortionists. During the Canucks' run to the 1994 Stanley Cup finals, several sportswriters claimed that Bure had made his own extortion demands, threatening to refuse to play in a key game unless his new contract was finalized. The charge was never substantiated, but despite denials by Bure's agent and Canucks management it became widely accepted as truth.

Controversy of a more sinister nature followed during the 1996–97 season, when Bure attempted to revive a family watchmaking business in Europe. Although Bure denied it, FBI sources claimed that his partner in the venture was a Russian mafiya boss involved in extortion, drug dealing and money laundering.

Later that season, with the Canucks still vying for a playoff spot, Bure left the lineup with a neck ailment. The resulting debate over the actual severity of the injury evidently enflamed his simmering discontent. During the summer of 1997, he abruptly fired both his longtime agent, Ron Salcer, and his father, Vladimir, who was his personal trainer. (His split with his father was more than simply the end of an athletic partnership—he severed all ties.) Bure then made it known he was seeking a trade. Typically he offered no explanation.

Finally, in June 1998, after the most tumultuous season in Canucks history, Bure's name hit the front pages again when police wiretaps revealed he had been dating the niece of Gillian Guess, a Vancouver woman who had become the focal point of one of the most publicized murder trials in Canadian history.

Yet, while the details of Bure's life off the ice were a source of perpetual conjecture, there was never any dispute about his value as a player and as a gate attraction. In an era that had become increasingly dominated by stifling defensive systems and conservative play, Bure was a virtuoso, a dazzling offensive force blessed with explosive speed, superb stickhandling skills and a blistering shot. His acceleration was electrifying, his creativity startling. The charismatic Russian not only put fans in the seats, he could lift them out of them. He was hockey's version of the proverbial magician and his hat: you never knew for sure what he was going to pull out of it.

But beyond simply being an exciting player, Bure was a game-breaker. He scored goals that came against the flow of the play, goals created out of nothing, timely goals that turned games around, goals that were sudden dagger thrusts to the heart.

It was this lethal artistry that the Florida Panthers, a colorless club that ranked near the bottom of the NHL in offense, sought when they made the trade for Bure. The Panthers were in a battle to make the playoffs, and they hoped the Russian gunner would supply the spark needed to propel them into the postseason. His services wouldn't come cheaply: a six-year contract worth an astounding US$47 million. In terms of total dollars, it was, at the time, the largest contract ever signed by an NHL player.

Florida fans were thrilled by the trade and eager to see what impact the baby-faced sniper would have on their team's anemic offense. But

Panthers general manager Bryan Murray was willing to wait a few games before inserting his pricey new acquisition into the lineup. After all, Bure hadn't played a minute of competitive hockey in nine months, an eternity in the fleeting career of a professional athlete. Although he had been holding daily workouts in Moscow, skating laps in an empty arena was no substitute for the high-tempo action of the best league in the world. He was coming in cold, with no time to acquaint himself with his new teammates, no opportunity to recover from jet lag.

It was generally assumed that Bure would sit out the next two games in Florida's schedule, a pair of back-to-back encounters against the New York Islanders and the New York Rangers. That way, with the NHL All-Star Game following immediately afterward, he would have seven full days to prepare for his debut with the Panthers.

But Bure had other ideas. After a 10-hour flight from Moscow, he arrived in New York and stayed up until midnight to adjust to the time difference. He then slept until 9:00 A.M. and reported to the rink the next day in time for a brisk morning skate with his new team. After the session, Bure pronounced himself ready to play in that night's contest against the New York Islanders. The news sparked a flurry of media attention, and a special news conference was arranged to introduce the newest Panther to reporters. Interest was high. The Islanders received three times the usual number of requests for media credentials for the game.

"I have to start to play, anyway," Bure told reporters. "So I'll start tonight. I really want to play. The sooner I start the better. It was pretty hard, especially the last five months. I was missing it a lot. Finally it's over and I'm glad."

Florida cautiously limited the Russian's ice time to about 12 minutes, half of what he normally logged in a game. Even a dozen minutes was enough to make a difference, though. Early in the second period, with the score tied 1–1, while cruising outside the Islanders' blueline, Bure pounced on a long pass from Panthers defenseman Robert Svehla. Accelerating quickly, he darted through an opening between defensemen Scott Lachance and Zdeno Chara and burst in alone on goalie Felix Potvin. Bure, a left-handed shot, moved the puck to his backhand and began angling to his right. Potvin took the bait, committing himself to the move and leaving his feet. The instant he did, Bure cut sharply back to his left and smoothly slipped the puck past the sprawling netminder into the open side of the net.

In its execution, the play bore an eerie resemblance to the most famous goal of Bure's career: the dramatic breakaway winner he had scored in double overtime against goalie Mike Vernon during the first round of the 1994 Stanley Cup playoffs, the one that deep-sixed the Calgary Flames.

Bure's goal spelled doom for the Islanders. The suddenly inspired Panthers went on to pop in three more unanswered goals, with their new winger adding a second marker on the power play, and cruised to a 5–2 win. Bure was voted the game's first star. It was only one game and one victory but, as omens go, it was an auspicious one.

Yet an amazing detail from the game went unreported in the next day's newspapers. By a strange coincidence, Brian Burke, who was in New York to deliver a speech at an international sports summit, was also in attendance at the Nassau Coliseum. At the precise moment that Bure was deking Potvin out of his underwear, high above the ice in the media box, the Canucks' general manager was being interviewed about the Bure trade by a reporter from a Florida television station. The timing of the goal, the manner in which it was scored, the converging images of past and present, and the buzz of the crowd interrupting Burke in midsentence combined to make this a karmic moment.

That January night in Uniondale, Long Island, one chapter in Bure's life closed and another opened, and in the turning of the page the Russian Rocket had delivered a message. He was back and he had brought his dagger.

# CHAPTER TWO

# The Beautiful Machine

*The Child is the father of the Man.*

WILLIAM WORDSWORTH, "MY HEART LEAPS UP"

PAVEL BURE WAS BORN in Moscow on March 31, 1971, the first child of parents Vladimir and Tatiana. From the beginning, Pavel was an extremely active child. As Vladimir recalls, "He was always a very fast boy. It was not possible for him to sit still, even for a minute. He runs around, zoom! zoom! Every time, it's 'Where's Pavel? Where's Pavel? Look out, here comes that crazy Pavel.'"

Although Pavel is a Russian, his family on his father's side has German ancestry. The Bures hailed from the town of Furna, Switzerland, near the Austrian border. They were watchmakers by trade, and one of Pavel's ancestors, who was also named Pavel, moved to Russia in 1815 and became the watchmaker to the Russian royal family. Because of his appointment, he became an honorary nobleman and all of his relatives were also considered nobility. The watchmaking company was passed down from Pavel to his son, Maxim, and in turn to his son, Vladimir, who was the company director when it closed in 1917, following the

Russian Revolution. It is said that Czar Nicholas II took two Pavel Bure watches with him when he left the Winter Palace forever.

If genetics is destiny, then Pavel was fated to be an athlete. Both his father, Vladimir, and his grandfather, Valeri, were world-class athletes. Valeri was a goalie with the Soviet Union's national water-polo team, but his athletic aspirations were brutally shattered when he was exiled to a Stalinist labor camp in the wilds of Siberia. The reason is lost in time, but then reason was unimportant during this dark era. An estimated 20 million people, most of them innocent of any crime, vanished into the gulags during Joseph Stalin's reign of terror. Athletes were frequently victims of Stalin's purges because they had contact with Westerners. In Valeri's case, his family's former links with the czar would have been enough to make him suspect.

Valeri endured 18 years in captivity. After his release, he became an accomplished swimming coach and was known affectionately as Father Bure. He died of a stroke in 1975 at a swimming competition, but he lived long enough to see his son, Vladimir, who was one of his pupils, become a champion swimmer and fulfill the Olympic dream that had been denied him. Vladimir won numerous European champion-ships and competed in three Olympics for the Soviet Union, winning four medals. In Mexico City in 1968, he earned a bronze medal in the 4 x 200-meter freestyle relay. In Munich in 1972, he won a bronze medal in the 4 x 200-meter freestyle relay and a silver medal in the 4 x 100-meter freestyle relay. He also placed third in the 100-meter freestyle behind American Mark Spitz, who captured a record-setting seven gold medals. In Montreal in 1976, Vladimir finished fourth in the 4 x 100-meter relay and seventh in the 100- and 200-meter freestyle. In recognition of his ath-letic achievements, Vladimir was awarded the Order of Lenin, the Soviet Union's most prestigious sports honor.

Vladimir met Tatiana Lvovana, a pretty blond, in 1969. She was an 18-year-old university student studying chemistry in Minsk, the capital of the Republic of Belarus. Tatiana came to watch a swimming competition one day and was attracted to Vladimir at first sight. They were married two years later. After the wedding, Tatiana abandoned her studies accord-ing to her husband's wishes and became a homemaker. "I need a wife, not a professional," he told her.

Pavel was an Aries child, the sign of the ram, a symbol of offensive power. Those born under this zodiac sign are said to be impetuous, restless, high-energy people, risk takers who chafe at restrictions and who perform best in a competitive atmosphere. Candid and direct in personal relationships, they are self-reliant but also self-centered—often concerned with their personal advancement and physical satisfaction to the point of greed. They have an attraction to speed, danger and noise.

Bure's March 31 birth date is shared by a number of famous people, including philosopher René Descartes, composer Franz Joseph Haydn, actor Richard Chamberlain, boxer Jack Johnson, and one notable Canadian hockey player, a guy named Gordie Howe. On the day Bure entered the world, Howe was in his 25th NHL season.

Pavel was only three months old when Vladimir began teaching him to dog-paddle in the bathtub of their Moscow apartment. Vladimir harbored ambitious goals for his first son: "When I started Pavel in swimming, it was with only one thought—making the national team and winning gold medals." Pavel could swim before he was able to walk, but to the dismay of his father, it wasn't the chlorinated water of the swimming pool that drew him, but rather the frozen water of the skating rink.

Pavel's first love was hockey, the game he and his childhood pals played on the frigid Moscow streets until their feet became numb. Even inside the family apartment, the little boy was focused on hockey. He had a small plastic stick and would run up and down with it, imagining himself deking defensemen and scoring fantastic goals.

"I played lots, but without skates. And no puck, just ball," Bure told interviewer Iain MacIntyre of the *Vancouver Sun*. "I played after school. When I was young, there were not many hockey practices. After that you were free. We go and play hockey in the street. Lots of kids, lots of teams. If you win, you stay on and play another team. If you lose, you wait maybe 40 minutes before your next turn. And it was cold. If you lose, you are very upset."

Igor Larionov, the great Russian center, fondly recalled playing similar street-hockey games in his 1990 autobiography *Larionov*: "It is wonderful when a young boy, hardly conscious yet, gets used to the game in the open spaces, outside in the fresh air, without instructions and shouts from the coach. You just go outside and chase the puck until your legs give out."

Larionov, who comes from the whimsically named Voskresensk (Sundayville), a factory town of 60,000 located 140 miles outside of Moscow, credited those early games with providing the foundation for his later success. "One of the reasons I advanced through the ranks to the top Khimik team was the confidence learned in the streets," he says in his autobiography. "When I stepped on the artificial ice I did not feel like a newcomer. I knew about competition. I'd learned it in the school yards."

During Larionov's formative years, the Soviet Union had just begun to assert its dominance on the international hockey scene. By the time of Bure's birth in 1971, the Red Machine had reached the peak of its supremacy, having won its ninth consecutive world championship. The national team's success helped to establish hockey as the second most popular sport in the Soviet Union, next to soccer.

In Pavel's mind, hockey, with its tactics and team play, possessed an excitement and glamor that swimming couldn't approach, and the older he got the more convinced he became that his destiny was on the rink and not in the pool. Swimming was too lonely a pursuit, its training too monotonous. As Bure confessed to sportswriter Mike Beamish of the *Vancouver Sun*, "I can swim very well, but it is not something I wanted to do every day. It's boring. Jump, swim. Jump, swim. So what? There are many more interesting situations in hockey."

Pavel was six when Vladimir took him to his first hockey tryout at the Central Army Sports Club (CSKA) school. He had no equipment other than a stick and a pair of girl's figure skates. "There were more than 100 kids there," Vladimir recalls. "They all skate and the coach watches them and then he calls out their names, the best skaters first." Pavel waddled around on his ankles and kept falling. He spent most of the practice clinging to the boards. "You know when the coach calls Pavel's name?" Vladimir asks. "Last!"

It was an embarrassing situation for both father and son, as Vladimir was one of the nation's most accomplished sports heroes. After the tryout, he took his son aside for a chat. "Look, it is not possible for you to be last," he told him. "You are a Bure. You must be first. You have a choice. If you want to be a sportsman, then sports must become your life. If we come back in two months and you are last, I'll take you out. You'll never play hockey again. Understand?"

Pavel understood. He practiced hard, watching closely and trying to copy the style of the better skaters. Vladimir constantly reminded him that hard work and dedication were the keys to success, and Pavel heeded his advice. Even as a youngster, he diligently put himself to bed early so he would be sharp the next day. Pavel improved rapidly. Two months later he wasn't last. By the end of one year, he was the best.

In the Soviet system, all of the major clubs in the country's elite hockey league maintained their own schools. Beginning at age six, boys would be brought by their parents to tryouts where they were evaluated by coaches. Those thought to show promise were invited to attend the special school. The young hockey hopefuls began their day with training from 7:00 to 8:30 A.M., then attended regular classes at another school.

Tatiana took Pavel to practice. They would get up at 5:00 A.M. to take two buses and a train to reach the rink. His mother encouraged him not to waste time, but rather to read during the long commute. Books became his companion while traveling, and reading became a lifelong habit. Pavel was especially interested in history, and for a time he wanted to be a journalist. But his major preoccupation was always athletics, not scholastics. Unlike his brother, Valeri, who excelled at school, Pavel was a C student.

The Soviet hockey system was designed not only to produce excellence, but also to create a consistent style, since players would usually remain with one team throughout their careers, advancing up the ladder of various age groups until, finally, if they were skilled enough, they graduated to the elite team.

The two most successful sports schools in the Soviet Union were the Central Army Sports Club and the Dynamo Sports Society, both founded in 1923. Their hockey teams were assembled in 1947 to participate in the first official season of the Soviet hockey league, which lasted one month and consisted of seven games. Of the 12 teams involved in that first year of competition, eight were connected with either military or police organizations.

The Dynamo Sports Society was founded by Feliks Dzerzhinsky, the head of the Cheka, or secret police, which later became the KGB. Until the collapse of the Communist system in the early 1990s, virtually all of the players on the Dynamo hockey team were required to become officers in the KGB or the Soviet militia. In his book *The Red Machine*, Lawrence Martin notes:

> This secret police affiliation has remained largely unknown to Canadians, whose players have often shown wariness or paranoia about the possibility of being followed around by KGB agents when they have visited the Soviet Union. What they didn't realize was that they were actually playing against them—secret agents on defense, at center, on the wings. It happened every time they played Dynamo and most times when they played the Russian national team, some of whose players were usually from Dynamo.

Because of its KGB connection, Dynamo enjoyed access to the best sports facilities and equipment the Soviet Union had to offer, but it couldn't compete with Central Army in sheer numbers. As Martin points out, "If Central Army isn't developing stars at the army sports schools, it can spot them during their compulsory two years in the army. If it misses them there, it can lure them away from other hockey clubs later on." The power of the Soviet Army was aided by the fact it could also offer employment to a player, the rank of an officer, that would continue after he finished his hockey career.

Central Army won 32 Soviet league titles from 1948 to 1990. In the other 11 years, it finished second 10 times and third once. From 1977 until 1989, the club's dominance was absolute. Making a mockery of the competition, Central Army captured 13 consecutive championships.

The sports school (Number 707) that Bure attended produced several prominent Russian champions, including figure skaters Ekaterina Gordeeva and Sergei Grinkov and tennis players Andrei Chesnokov and Andrei Olkhovski. The school was located near Central Army's home arena and adjoining sports complex, and Pavel would sometimes visit the rink with his father and watch the senior players practice. Father and son had divergent hockey tastes. Pavel rooted for Central Army; Vladimir favored Moscow Spartak, the trade-union team, the people's team. During the late 1960s and early 1970s, Army-Spartak games were the Soviet version of the Toronto Maple Leafs–Montreal Canadiens rivalry, drawing 100 million TV viewers.

Pavel's childhood hockey heroes were Central Army stars Boris Mikhailov and Valeri Kharlamov. Along with center Vladimir Petrov, they formed CSKA's dominant line of the 1970s. At the 1973 World Championships, they spearheaded a Soviet juggernaut that won 10 games without a defeat and outscored its opponents 100 to 18. The troika combined for a stunning 43 goals and 86 points.

It is no mystery why Bure admired Kharlamov. Although small in stature at five feet six inches and 155 pounds, Kharlamov possessed exquisite physical skills and, like Bure himself, was an explosively quick skater. In a hockey system that emphasized team play, his blend of artistry and daring made him stand out as a rare talent.

Kharlamov so flummoxed the Canadians with his inventive play in the 1972 Summit Series that Team Canada assistant coach John Ferguson eventually instructed Bobby Clarke to "break his ankle." In Game 6, Clarke did just that, delivering a wicked two-hand slash to Kharlamov's ankle that knocked him out of Game 7 and rendered him lame for the decisive Game 8.

Kharlamov was unable to play in the first Canada Cup competition in 1976 because of injuries he had suffered in an automobile accident. Five years later, after he was left off the Soviet roster for the second Canada Cup, Kharlamov was involved in another crash with more serious consequences. On August 27, 1976, on a rain-slick highway outside Moscow, he was killed when his wife, Irina, lost control of their Volga sedan and it skidded into a speeding truck. He was just 33.

Mikhailov was also talented, but not as flashy as Kharlamov. Bure admired Mikhailov's spunk. He was a tireless worker and was willing to stubbornly plant himself in front of the net and absorb hits in order to collect "garbage" goals. As the Canadian team discovered in 1972, Mikhailov could also be an extremely irritating and noisy presence on the ice. When the Canadians tried to intimidate him with physical abuse during the 1972 series, he responded by kicking a hole through Gary Bergman's shin pads with his skate blades. By the time Mikhailov retired in 1981, he was the top goal scorer in Soviet hockey history.

Kharlamov and Mikhailov were small men by North American standards, but then size was never a major criterion in cultivating hockey talent in Russia, because the Soviet style put a premium on speed and skill.

Bodychecking and aggressive physical play were less effective on the large international ice surface. As Bure once recalled, in an interview in Stan Fischler's *Hockey Stars Speak*, "A big guy without much skill could play pro in North America on the smaller rinks. With us it was different. I grew up with a couple of huge guys, and they were tough but slow. The coach told them, 'We don't need you. We need playmakers with skills.'"

The emphasis on speed, intricate passing and puck control can be traced to the origins of the Soviet game. Most accounts of the rise of Russian hockey begin in 1946 when the Soviets first began to play six-a-side hockey. According to this scenario, in an astonishing triumph of Stalinist-inspired totalitarianism, the u.s.s.r. magically emerged eight years later on the international scene to win the 1954 World Championships, stunning the favored Canadian team 7–2 in the decisive game of the tournament. Although it is true the Soviets made rapid strides in hockey, the tale is mostly myth.

As Robert Edelman writes in his book *Serious Fun: A History of Spectator Sports in the USSR*, "The Soviets did not start from scratch, as many accounts have suggested. In fact, Soviet hockey players simply adapted to a different version of a game that they had played for decades." That game was known as bandy.

Bandy is played outdoors on a sheet of ice the size of a soccer field rimmed by six-inch-high boards, with 11 men on each side, using a small orange ball rather than a puck. The nets are about midway between the dimensions of a hockey net and a soccer net. One of the crucial differences between bandy and hockey is that there is no bodychecking. Because of the size of the rink and the rules, the emphasis is on skating and passing. Offensive strategy is similar to soccer: intricate passing patterns, designed to set up one player for a clear, close-in shot. As Boris Mayorov, captain of the Soviet national team during the 1960s, recalled in a 1999 article by Jack Todd in Montreal's *Gazette*, "I grew up playing bandy, all day, every day, every winter. That's why we could skate so well. I don't think the Canadians ever understood that."

Bandy has a long tradition in Russia and Scandinavia, and in the early 1900s there were organized leagues operating in Moscow and St. Petersburg. An indication of how quickly Soviet bandy teams adjusted to conventional hockey can be judged by three exhibition games the

Soviets played in February 1948 with LTC Prague. Although the Prague club was composed almost entirely of players from the Czechoslovakian national squad (the winner of the 1947 World Championships), the Soviets proved to be their equals, winning 6–3, losing 5–3 and tying 2–2.

The guru of early Soviet hockey was Anatoli Tarasov, an air-force officer who coached Moscow's Central Army team from 1947 to 1975. Along with co-coach Arkady Chernyshev, Tarasov would guide the Soviet national team to nine straight world and Olympic titles between 1963 and 1972. Rather than simply copy the Western hockey model as Soviet officials urged, Tarasov was intent on developing a unique game style. A theatrical, complex, intelligent individual, he brought a scientific and analytical approach to hockey. As Roy MacSkimming notes in his book *Cold War*: "Unimpeded by a hockey tradition, he was able to see tactics and training afresh. Unencumbered by nay-saying experts at home, he was—paradoxically—free under Soviet Communism to be inspired, to start at ground zero, to experiment with new, untried methods that would have been laughed out of the rink in Canada."

Ironically one of Tarasov's major influences was a Canadian—coach and fitness expert Lloyd Percival. Percival's 1951 book, *The Hockey Handbook*, with its revolutionary ideas on training, conditioning and tactics, virtually ignored in Canada, was hungrily devoured by Tarasov.

Tarasov aimed to develop an all-round athleticism in his players through intense conditioning. He had them engage in gymnastics, running, swimming, rowing and weight lifting for strength and conditioning, and soccer, basketball and volleyball for tactics and teamwork. Some of this was a reflection of the Soviet philosophy of "physical culture" and the concept of the body as a "beautiful machine," but some of it was simply born of necessity.

Until 1956, there wasn't a single indoor ice rink in the Soviet Union, a country so massive it spanned 11 time zones. As late as 1985, the Soviet Union had only 102 indoor rinks, compared to more than 9,000 in Canada. Because they had no choice, the Russians took dry-land training to the limit. When *Montreal Star* journalist Jock Carroll visited Moscow in the summer of 1964, he was shown the off-season training of Soviet hockey players by Tarasov. "The exercises resumed with a warm-up period of running around the open-air basketball courts," Carroll wrote.

"The players ran perhaps a half mile, meanwhile tossing heavy medicine balls back and forth across the volleyball net, passing the ball behind their backs or under their legs before returning it. One group stood in a circle, seeing how long they could keep a soccer ball in the air, at one point using only their feet, another time using only their heads."

Carroll also observed two teams playing a combination of soccer and basketball simultaneously, using a soccer ball and a basketball, with the added complication of bodychecking. The players competed for more than two hours, then ran off to play tennis. "Once you start skating," Carroll asked Tarasov, "will there be as much exercise and calisthenics as this?"

"More," responded Tarasov, "this is only the appetizer. During the hockey season, we go in for much more extensive exercise."

On the ice, Tarasov preached "attacking hockey," a game based on speed, mobility, puck control and teamwork. He contrasted this to the Canadian style, which he termed "power hockey," a game built on body-checking and intimidation. As Tarasov wrote in his book *Road to Olympus*, "The attacking style of hockey actually eradicates power hockey, because it requires speedy manouevres, it requires profound thought, decisions which contain more craftiness, common sense, coordinated actions, superior technique than brute force. The future is with this type of hockey."

Tarasov had left the scene by the time Bure rose to prominence, but in many respects the future superstar was the Tarasovian ideal, a player who embodied the traits the Soviet hockey sage prized most highly. Even though Bure would later come to symbolize the new Russia, he was, at heart, old Russian in his playing style and many of his attitudes.

In addition to his hockey workouts, Bure also received personal conditioning training from his father, who based his methods on his experience as a swimming coach. Whereas most other children were allowed to do nothing but enjoy themselves in the summer, Pavel was only permitted a three-week holiday before Vladimir sent him off to train with his swimmers.

At 11, Bure was already considered a promising talent. As a result, in July 1982, he was blessed with a rare opportunity. That summer Wayne Gretzky traveled to Moscow with his family, girlfriend Vikki Moss and a camera crew to tape a television special with Soviet goaltending great Vladislav Tretiak. Bure was one of three young Russian players picked to practice with Gretzky. Little did the Great One realize that a decade later he would be competing against one of the youngsters he was introduced to that day.

When he was 11, Bure won an award as the best forward in his league. "Congratulations," Vladimir said. "But it's no big deal. You may be the best player here, but there are lots better than you. You have to get better."

Vladimir insisted that his son live up to daunting standards. He had a rule. Pavel had to score a third of his team's goals. "If the score was 6–2, then he had to score two goals," he says. "If he does, he plays good. If he scores only one goal, that's not good enough. If his team scored 12 goals, he had to score four. A hat trick would not be good enough. He'd be a bad boy."

Vladimir was aware that his approach was extreme, but he made no apologies for it. After all, his father had been even tougher on him. Years later, when Pavel was in the NHL, Vladimir told author Roy MacGregor, as quoted in *The Home Team*: "Sure I'm a little bit crazy, like every father who dreams that his son is the best. Pavel, he is my son. I have lots of work with my kids. Now, when he scores a goal, I know it is my score. Pavel's work is my work."

Pavel, on his part, seemed willing to accept the bargain. From an early age, his ultimate goal was to win an Olympic gold medal, the color that had eluded his father in three Olympics. "My biggest dream is to go to the Olympics and win a gold for the family," Bure once said.

Pavel understood the psychological dynamic that drove his career. In MacGregor's *The Home Team*, he said, "Dad always came second. He wanted me to win over everybody. It's true he couldn't beat Mark Spitz. He really work hard but he still couldn't beat him. Maybe he dream about how his son is going to beat everybody. He just remind me all the time I must work hard. Even if I win MVP trophy I must work harder."

Because of Vladimir's status as a champion swimmer, the Bures lived well. They had money for fine clothes, they owned a car and could afford annual vacations. But this life of privilege changed in 1979 when Vladimir retired from competitive swimming. He found work as a swimming coach, but the wages were modest in comparison to what he had earned as an athlete. Within a few years, the family savings had vanished and the tougher financial conditions put an added strain on an unraveling marriage.

When Pavel was 12, his parents separated. Vladimir moved out, and Tatiana, who had never worked before, had to find a job. She worked as a manager of a supermarket, where she earned 180 rubles a year, which at the time was equivalent to about $900. Tatiana later returned to her studies, completing a degree in business by taking correspondence courses at the Commerce and Trade Institute. She eventually found work as an economist and became head of planning for her company.

At 14, Pavel began to earn money for the first time when he joined Central Army's junior team. His annual salary was 40 rubles, or about $8. The next year he made 70 rubles. At 16, his salary was boosted to 120 rubles. In comparison, the average citizen's annual salary at the time was about 150 rubles.

In December 1986, Bure traveled to Canada with a touring national Soviet midget team that played games in Ottawa, Peterborough, Kitchener, Toronto, Winnipeg, Regina, Edmonton, Vancouver and Trail. The game in Vancouver was held at the Pacific Coliseum, which means that, contrary to popular belief, Bure's first game as a member of the Vancouver Canucks in November 1991 wasn't actually his debut on Coliseum ice.

Mike Murray, the public-relations director with the Canadian Amateur Hockey Association, was the tour's organizer, and he spent a lot of time with the Soviet team. Murray, who had a working knowledge of Russian, developed a friendship with Bure. Murray says there was no doubt about Bure's star potential. "Even though he was the youngest player on the tour, he dominated games. He was faster than anyone and had so many skilled moves."

The trip was Bure's first exposure to Western society, and he admitted in a later interview on the NHL's Web site that it was an eye-opening experience. North American society didn't resemble the harsh, poverty-stricken wasteland depicted in Soviet propaganda. "I met a Russian guy who had just moved here and I asked him how he was doing and he told me about his work," Bure said. "I thought that was impossible. There are no jobs here. He told me it was easy—you just go out and look for them. I then started riding the bus looking for all the people who were sleeping in the street and cardboard boxes, but I couldn't find them. It was then I realized what was happening. We were shown only the parts of the country the government wanted us to see. Perhaps they thought if they made the rest of the world look bad, we would all feel good about where we were living."

Murray says the Soviet teenagers were astounded by the variety and amount of food that was available to them. "Before the first game in Ottawa, we had a buffet. We thought they were going to eat for three hours. The hotels would put out fresh fruit and the Soviet kids would take it to their rooms and hoard it."

When the Soviets played at Northlands Coliseum in Edmonton, Bure asked Murray if it would be possible to meet some of the Oilers. "I knew Kevin Lowe and he got Gretzky and [Paul] Coffey to come in before the game and sign autographs. When they saw them, those kids' chins dropped to their knees. Pavel told me it was the highlight of his hockey career."

At the end of the tour, each Soviet player was given $200 spending money. Murray says the players brought him their money and asked if he would go out and buy them 15 ghetto blasters. "That's what they were most interested in: ghetto blasters, blue jeans and muscle magazines."

Prior to the 1987–88 season, coaches from the Central Army senior team had Bure scrimmage with the veterans, but they decided he was too young and small to make the jump to the big team. Despite Bure's insistence that he was ready, they didn't promote him from the junior squad until a number of Central Army regulars left in September 1987 to play in the Canada Cup tournament. To fill the void, the coaches let Bure suit up with the older players for an exhibition game.

As Bure recalled in Fischler's Hockey Stars Speak, "They put me on the fourth line, and the first time I stepped on the ice, I was circling around, when all of a sudden, one of my teammates intercepted the puck and we had a two-on-one. The other fellow carried the puck all the way down the ice. Then, at the last split second, he passed to me and I had an empty net to shoot at. I touched the puck for the first time and it went into the net."

Despite this remarkable debut, Bure spent most of the 1987–88 season with the Central Army junior team. He saw action in only five league games with Central Army's senior squad, counting one goal and one assist. He didn't make the national junior team that year, but he did play with the victorious Soviet under-17 team in the Esso Cup tournament in Quebec City.

Bure became a regular with Central Army's senior team in 1988–89, at age 17. Central Army had always prided itself on developing successive waves of talent, and with his veterans getting long in the tooth, coach Viktor Tikhonov was grooming Bure and other rising young stars to step into the breach. The stable also included defensemen Vladimir Malakhov, Igor Kravchuk and Sergei Zubov and forwards Viacheslav Kozlov, Andrei Kovalenko, Alexander Mogilny and Sergei Fedorov. In Mogilny and Fedorov, Tikhonov had two-thirds of what he envisioned as the team's next great line, the successor to the Larionov–Makarov–Krutov combo.

Fedorov, an agile, swift-skating center from Pskov, the historic town where Czar Nicholas II was forced to abdicate his throne, was a two-way threat, adept at both offense and defense. Lean and rangy with a regal profile, the blond, blue-eyed Fedorov had graduated to the Central Army team at age 17 in 1986 and had been one of the U.S.S.R.'s top performers at the 1988 World Junior Championships in Czechoslovakia, posting five goals and seven assists in seven games.

Mogilny, dark, curly-haired and intense, was from Khabarovsk, a Siberian city on the Chinese border, a distant eight-hour flight from Moscow. Mogilny's path to Central Army was pure serendipity. At age 15, while visiting Moscow for a national youth-hockey camp, Mogilny stopped in at Central Army's arena to deliver a gift to forward Andrei Khomutov. He stayed to watch an Army practice, lost track of the time and missed his flight home. The next flight to Khabarovsk wasn't scheduled for three days. During the interval, Mogilny became acquainted with the Central Army junior coach and got an invitation to try out with the team. He made the squad and took up residence at the Central Army barracks.

At 17, Mogilny was promoted to the senior team where he scored 15 goals and one assist in 28 games. Mogilny was so gifted that Tikhonov • is said to have convulsed with joy watching him play. His personality was as unique as his talent. He had a rebellious, independent streak and an affinity for Western music and clothes.

Mogilny soon became unhappy with the strict and sheltered life of the Red Army. As a lowly private, he had no privileges. The team refused to give him an apartment of his own and he had to live at the club's camp in the countryside. Mogilny frequently clashed with the autocratic Tikhonov. The antagonism between the two came to a head at the 1988 Olympics in Calgary. During the last game of the tournament, an inconsequential contest against Finland, Tikhonov began to berate Mogilny for taking a penalty. Mogilny responded with a few choice words of his own. Tikhonov flew into a rage and punched Mogilny in the stomach.

Shortly after the team returned home with a gold medal, Tikhonov told Mogilny he would be awarded the military rank of an officer. Mogilny surprised Tikhonov by informing him that he had no desire to become a military man. Tikhonov tried to bully Mogilny into compliance, threatening to remove him from the new top line he had formed with Fedorov and Yevgeny Davydov. Eventually Mogilny became a junior lieutenant.

While the Soviet national team under Tikhonov was riding high, the junior squad slipped off its pedestal during the late 1980s. The Soviet junior team hadn't won a world title in four years, though it had come frustratingly close in Moscow in 1988. After going unbeaten through the first six games of the tournament, the U.S.S.R. met Canada in the gold-medal game. Despite dominating play and outshooting the Canadians 40–18, the Soviets were repeatedly thwarted by goaltender Jimmy Waite and lost 3–2.

The U.S.S.R. arrived at the 1989 World Junior Championships in Anchorage, Alaska, hungry for revenge. Soviet coach Robert Cherenkov had a lot of heavy artillery in his arsenal. The mercurial Mogilny was back, along with Fedorov. Joining them on the number-one line was Bure. Although his name wasn't widely known in the West yet, Bure had been turning heads in his first full season with Central Army. By the end of the season, he would rack up 17 goals and nine assists for 26 points in 32 games and would be voted rookie of the year.

United for the first time in Anchorage, the three speedsters proved to be a devastating force. Toronto *Globe and Mail* sports columnist Grant Kerr, who covered the event for Canadian Press, says, "Their line dominated pretty much every shift they played and they were facing some pretty stiff competition. A lot of future NHLers played in that tournament." The top-caliber talent included Americans Jeremy Roenick, Mike Modano, John LeClair and Tony Amonte; Canada's Rod Brind'Amour, Eric Desjardins, Andrew Cassels and Mike Ricci; Czechoslovakia's Bobby Holik and Robert Reichel; and Finland's Teemu Selanne.

"Bure was much more slender then and a lot us wondered how he would stand up when he hit the pros," Kerr says. "But there was no mistaking his talent. He had those magic feet." What made Bure's performance doubly impressive was his age. At 17, he excelled in a tournament usually dominated by 19-year-olds. Bure scored eight times to tie Roenick for the most goals, led all Soviet players with 14 points and was voted the top forward in the tournament.

As in 1988, the championship was decided on the final day of competition. After six games, Sweden and the Soviet Union were tied for first with identical 5–1–0 records, but because the Soviets had defeated the Swedes 3–2 in their one head-to-head meeting, they only needed to win their last game against Canada to clinch the title. Led by Mogilny, who counted a hat trick, the Soviets erupted for five goals in the second period, blowing open a tight 2–1 game and cruising to a 7–2 victory. Revenge and the gold medal were theirs.

Bure was ecstatic. He had won a gold medal in his first world junior championship and had played brilliantly. Even Vladimir was impressed. "The first time my dad was really happy," Pavel told interviewer Jim Taylor in a 1995 interview in *Sports Only*, "was when I got the best forward on the junior team in Anchorage. 'You're almost there,' he told me, 'but it's another step to be on the national team.'"

The next year, back in Russia, Bure took that big step up. But before he did, a series of events transpired on the other side of the world that would have a major impact on his hockey future.

# CHAPTER THREE

# Risky Business

*Fortune brings in some boats that are not steered.*
WILLIAM SHAKESPEARE, *CYMBELINE*

THE STORY OF HOW the Vancouver Canucks came to draft Pavel Bure defies easy explanation, largely because the people involved have never been able to agree on the precise details. Why conflicting accounts exist is something of a mystery in itself, but the fact that they do merely underscores the widespread suspicion that something underhanded occurred. Certain elements of the tale sound as if they were lifted from the pages of a spy thriller; others simply read like bad fiction. Although truth in this matter may be a slippery commodity, one thing is certain: Bure's selection at the 1989 Entry Draft was the most disputed in NHL history. To understand why, it is necessary to return to the point where fact and fiction first collided: June 17, 1989, on the floor of the Metropolitan Sports Center in Bloomington, Minnesota.

Created in 1963, the NHL Entry Draft, or Amateur Draft as it was known until 1979, is the main organ of the league's reproductive system, the gateway to the big time for young players from around the globe. In

1980, after 17 years of being held in Montreal hotels and office buildings, this private event moved to the Montreal Forum and opened its doors to the public for the first time. Today the draft has evolved into a much-hyped phenomenon, attracting live television coverage and extensive media analysis and fan interest. It has become the hockey version of TV's *Wheel of Fortune*. The futures of players and teams are decided here, multimillion-dollar deals brokered, jackpots won, dreams dashed.

Each team arrives for the draft with scads of statistical and biographical data on all the available prospects. Top-ranked players will have been interviewed, their friends, family members and former coaches questioned, and the game films studied in detail. Yet despite all the time and effort invested, the process of selecting future NHL players is far from an exact science. Players who excel in the junior ranks aren't always able to make the transition to the pros. Raw talent alone is no guarantee of success at the NHL level. Other intangibles such as character, desire and self-discipline figure in the equation. Some prospects can't handle the pressure, some get injured, some develop personal problems. The younger the player, the more opportunity a team has for making an error. Since the NHL expanded the draft to include 18-year-olds in 1980, the task of crystal ball–gazing has been made even more difficult.

Anyone who doubts the fallibility of NHL scouts need only spend some time thumbing through the roll call of previous Entry Drafts. There have been many overlooked gems. NHL teams believed there were 47 players better than Mark Messier in 1979, 116 better than Brett Hull in 1984, 124 better than Rick Tocchet in 1983, 133 better than Doug Gilmour in 1982, 165 better than Theoren Fleury in 1987 and 198 better than Dominik Hasek in 1983. Some future stars were never drafted and only made the NHL as free agents, a list that includes Curtis Joseph, Ed Belfour, Adam Oates, Dino Ciccarelli, Steve Duchesne, Joe Mullen, Tim Kerr and Geoff Courtnall.

By the same token, the history of first-round picks is littered with the names of blue-chip prospects who failed to make an impression and vanished without a trace. Names such as Frank Spring, Greg Vaydik, Fred Williams, Neil Brady and Daniel Dore are now only remembered by trivia buffs.

In some years, the depth of talent is deeper and the chances of a team making an embarrassing gaffe in the opening round decreases, but even in the best of years, less than a third of the players drafted after the first three rounds make it to the NHL, much less rise to stardom. The potential to improve a team may be significant in the Entry Draft, but the window of opportunity is a small one.

The draft is arranged so that teams select in the reverse order of their standings, an attempt to maintain a semblance of competitive balance and give hope to the NHL's downtrodden franchises. Despite its good intentions, however, the system doesn't always achieve the desired effect. Bad teams don't get bad by accident. As with most corporate enterprises, excellence begins at the top. Incompetent management produces inferior coaches and mediocre players. For some teams, the draft is not a blessing, but a torment.

During the 19-year period from their inaugural NHL season in 1970 through to 1988, the Vancouver Canucks enjoyed a better cumulative drafting position than any other team in the league. In that time span, the Canucks had nine picks in the top five and 16 selections in the top 10. Despite this bounty, the Canucks missed hitting the bull's-eye with amazing consistency. In fact, with most of its first-round picks, the club barely made contact with the target.

In 1970 the Canucks drafted Dale Tallon ahead of Darryl Sittler, Reg Leach and Rick MacLeish. In 1971 they opted for Joceyln Guevremont over Rick Martin or Larry Robinson. In 1972 they chose Don Lever, ignoring Steve Shutt and Bill Barber. In 1973 Dennis Ververgeart got the nod over Lanny McDonald, Bob Gainey and Rick Middleton. In 1977 the Canucks jumped on Jere Gillis instead of Mike Bossy or Doug Wilson. In 1979 they selected Rick Vaive over Ray Bourque. In 1985 they selected Jim Sandlak instead of Joe Nieuwendyk or Mike Richter. In 1986 they nabbed Dan Woodley when Brian Leetch and Adam Graves were up for grabs.

Although other teams have made their share of regrettable first-round picks, they could also point to triumphs. The Canucks' sorry history permitted no such fond reflection. Of the 190 players drafted by Vancouver up until 1989, only one had attained superstar status —

winger Cam Neely, chosen ninth overall in 1983. Yet even Neely was an embarrassing reminder of the Canucks' ineptitude.

Vancouver drafted Neely because of his striking combination of size, aggression and scoring skill. As a 17-year-old rookie in 1982–83, he had posted 120 points in 72 games for the Portland Winter Hawks of the Western Hockey League and had helped lead Portland to the Memorial Cup title. But after pulling Neely out of the junior ranks the following year and rushing him into the lineup at age 18, the Canucks rapidly lost patience with his slow progress as a scorer and instead began to focus on developing the aggressive aspect of his game. With his hands perpetually banged up from brawling, Neely lost his scoring touch. In a terrible miscalculation, the Canucks gave up on him at age 21, trading him to the Boston Bruins in June 1986, along with Vancouver's first-round pick in the 1987 draft (which turned out to be defenseman Glen Wesley), in exchange for center Barry Pederson.

In Beantown, Neely soon regained his confidence, blossoming into a 50-goal scorer and becoming one of the NHL's premier power forwards. Wesley, in turn, developed into a solid rearguard. When the Bruins later traded Wesley to the Hartford Whalers in 1995, they received a package of three first-round draft picks. With two of those picks, they hit pay dirt, snagging defenseman Kyle McLaren and winger Sergei Samsonov, the 1998 NHL rookie of the year. For the Bruins, the Neely trade was a gift that kept on giving.

Pederson turned in a couple of adequate seasons in Vancouver before fading badly. In 1990 he was dispatched to Pittsburgh along with Tony Tanti and Rod Buskas in return for Andrew McBain, Dave Capuano and Dan Quinn. None of those players had any real impact with the Canucks. From such turning points, mediocrity is maintained.

But in Bloomington on June 17, 1989, there was reason to believe the Canucks might finally be primed to turn the corner. In 1987 the team had hired Pat Quinn, a respected hockey man, as president and general manager. A big, lumbering defenseman known for his toughness, Quinn had played nine years in the NHL, including a stint with Vancouver in its first two seasons in 1970–71 and 1971–72. His career was highlighted by a thundering check he had delivered to Bobby Orr during the 1969 playoffs, a hit that rendered Orr unconscious and sparked a mini-riot at

Boston Garden. After retiring, Quinn earned a law degree and enjoyed success as a coach in Philadelphia and Los Angeles.

Quinn's hiring by Vancouver was widely perceived as a positive move, but the method of its handling was badly bungled. The big Irishman had taken the coaching post with the Los Angeles Kings in 1984 on the understanding that he would eventually succeed Rogatien Vachon as general manager. But early in the 1986–87 season, when the Kings failed to offer him the GM's job, Quinn began to contemplate a move. He had an escape clause in his contract that stated if Los Angeles didn't renew his contract by September 30, 1986, he was free to seek future employment elsewhere. To facilitate that option, his contract wasn't registered with the league so that prospective employers couldn't be charged with tampering.

The Canucks made a pitch for Quinn in December 1986, offering him a lavish contract and total control of the club's hockey operations, with the twin portfolios of president and general manager. The contract called for Quinn to join Vancouver for the 1987–88 season. However, when Quinn signed the deal on December 24, 1986, he was still coach of the Kings, meaning he was being paid by two rival clubs in the same division. To seal the deal, Vancouver gave Quinn a $100,000 signing bonus. Arthur Griffiths, the Canucks' vice chairman, placed the check in a sealed envelope and had the Canucks' trainer deliver it to Quinn during a practice when the Kings were in Vancouver on January 2, 1987.

The pact was meant to be kept secret, but word soon leaked to the media. When NHL president John Ziegler got wind of it, he contacted Canucks chairman Frank Griffiths and asked him to destroy Quinn's contract. If Griffiths had complied, the matter would have been closed and the story about Quinn being committed to Vancouver would have been publicly denied. But Griffiths refused, insisting he had every legal right to sign Quinn.

In response, Ziegler expelled Quinn from the NHL for "dishonorable conduct" and fined the Canucks $310,000–$10,000 a day for each day that Quinn coached the Kings after he reached an agreement in principle with Vancouver on December 11 until his expulsion on January 30. Ziegler also fined the Kings $130,000 for not reporting Quinn's signing to the league when first informed of the development.

A subsequent investigation by NHL general counsel Gil Stein led to Quinn's reinstatement in May, but banned him from coaching for three years. Quinn and the Canucks appealed the ruling in British Columbia's Supreme Court. In November 1987, Justice Patrick Dohm reduced the Canucks' fine to $10,000, stating Ziegler had no authority to impose fines on the basis of each day the offense continued. But the court upheld Quinn's coaching suspension. Quinn also failed to have Ziegler's charge that he had acted dishonorably overturned. It was a bitter blow. "A man works his whole life to establish a reputation for honesty. This has been tough on me," he admitted at the time.

On September 15, 1987, as his first significant move as Canucks general manager, Quinn acquired goalie Kirk McLean and winger Greg Adams from the New Jersey Devils in return for center Patrick Sundstrom and a fourth-round draft pick. His second major achievement came in the 1988 Entry Draft when, with the second pick overall, he chose Trevor Linden, a hardworking, long-striding forward who led the Canucks with 30 goals in his rookie season. Linden was a character player you could build a team around, and Vancouver fans were hopeful Quinn could find another key piece of his assembly project among the youngsters at Bloomington's Metropolitan Sports Center.

Unfortunately the crop of junior players in 1989 wasn't considered impressive, and unlike the 1988 draft, in which a spirited debate had raged over the relative merits of the top two junior prospects—Linden and Mike Modano from the Western Hockey League—there was little consensus or drama about who would be taken first overall.

The situation would have been different had all of the available prospects been on an equal footing. But three of the most enticing talents—Pavel Bure, Bobby Holik and Mats Sundin—all carried large question marks. In its 1989 draft preview, *The Hockey News* had described Bure as "without question the best player eligible for the 1989 Entry Draft. He is not, however, the best available player." Bure was obviously not the most recognizable player, either—his thumbnail biography was accompanied by a photograph of Sergei Fedorov.

*The Hockey News* reference to Bure's availability spoke to the risk involved in drafting young Soviet players. Although there were signs in the spring of 1989 that the Soviets would soon permit some of their older players to play in the NHL, the possibility of them releasing any of their best young players was considered extremely remote. At the time, only one Soviet had been given permission to play in the NHL: Sergei Priakin, who signed with the Calgary Flames on March 29, 1989. Although Priakin had played for the Soviet national team, he wasn't one of the nation's top talents. Most hockey observers believed that the earliest the Soviets would permit Bure to leave would be after the 1994 Olympics, if at all.

Holik, a six-foot-one, 205-pound winger from Czechoslovakia's Dukla Jihavla team in Prague, had an impressive hockey pedigree. His father, Jaroslav, was a coach and former player, and his uncle, Jiri, had been one of the top scorers in Czech history, having played in four Olympics and 14 world and European championships. But like Bure, Holik's availability was foggy. The Czechoslovakian Hockey Federation had shown no willingness to part with its best young players, either.

Although Sundin, a gangly six-foot-three-inch forward from Bromma, Sweden, wasn't from an Iron Curtain country, the 18-year-old still had to serve a year of military service and was under contract with Djurgardens Stockholm of the Swedish elite league through the 1990–91 season, making him a long-range proposition, as well.

The Quebec Nordiques, who owned the first pick, were expected to choose Dave Chyzowski, a high-scoring left winger from the Kamloops Blazers of the Western Hockey League. Instead, Quebec opted for Sundin. The Nordiques liked the Swede's skating ability, his quick hands, his puck sense and his size. Even if he was still several years away from making the NHL, Sundin, Quebec's scouts felt, had the potential to make the wait worthwhile.

Sundin's selection was a historic one—he was the first European player to be chosen first overall—and a harbinger of change. In the early 1990s, as the Iron Curtain disintegrated and the process of acquiring young European stars became less problematic and less expensive, more and more of the NHL's top prospects would come from overseas. All told, 38 Europeans were snapped up in the 1989 draft, 15 per cent of the total number of players drafted. By 1992, the number of Europeans drafted would rise to 80 players, or 34 per cent of the total selections.

But the most noticeable change among the European draft picks in 1989 was their country of origin. No longer were the majority of these players from Scandinavia or Czechoslovakia. Instead, 18 of the 38 foreign imports picked in Bloomington came from the Soviet Union, though none were selected in the first three rounds of the draft. The NHL teams with the keenest insight into the European talent base scored biggest at the 1989 draft. Of all the NHL clubs, none profited as much as the Detroit Red Wings. In the third round (53rd overall), Detroit took Swedish defenseman Nicklas Lidstrom, in the fourth round (74th overall) they selected Sergei Fedorov of the Soviet Union, and with their second-last pick (221st overall), they nabbed Soviet defenseman Vladimir Konstantinov. All three would become NHL All-Stars and key components of Detroit's future Stanley Cup–winning teams.

In a bold move, Holik was taken 10th overall by the Hartford Whalers. Bure wasn't picked during the first three rounds which, according to popular belief, disqualified him from being drafted in any of the later rounds. In 1986 the NHL had adopted a policy that limited underage selections (younger than 19) to the first three of the 12 draft rounds. The league believed this strategy would give older players, overlooked in their first year of eligibility, a second chance to be drafted. However, under certain circumstances, underage players could still be drafted after the third round. The rules governing the eligibility of these players were specific. They included: those who had played at least one year of U.S. college hockey; those with three seasons of major junior experience; those with three seasons in a registered U.S. high school; those with two seasons of European First Division experience. In each instance, 11 games was considered the minimum requirement for a season.

Bure, who was 18, had played 32 games with Central Army in the Soviet elite league in 1988–89. However, according to NHL records, he had played only five games with Central Army in 1987–88, six fewer than the required quota for a season. But Canucks management believed the NHL's figures were inaccurate. It was convinced Bure had played enough games in 1987–88 to be eligible.

Why were the Canucks so confident? This is where things gets murky. According to the commonly accepted version, the Canucks had a hockey spy in Moscow, someone with inside knowledge of the Soviet system, who had kept a tally of Bure's record. It was on the basis of the spy's information that the Canucks believed the NHL stats were incomplete. This story received its first public airing during the 1994 Stanley Cup playoffs when *New York Times* columnist Dave Anderson tackled the topic. The upstart Canucks were giving the favored New York Rangers all they could handle in the Cup final and Bure, the leading goal scorer in the playoffs, had fully emerged in the eastern media's consciousness. Curious to learn how the flashy Russian had wound up in a Canucks uniform, Anderson interviewed Burke, who at the time was the NHL's vice president of hockey operations, the same portfolio he held with the Canucks in 1989.

"Our man in Moscow," Burke told Anderson, "kept telling us Pascha, which is what everyone there called him, had played 11 games; nine league games and two exhibition games. We planned to take him in the eighth round, but when I heard that Edmonton also planned to take him in the eighth round, we took him in the sixth round." Burke refused to divulge the informant's identity, saying, "Only three people know his name. Pat Quinn, Mike Penny [head scout] and myself."

In a March 1999 interview, Burke confirmed Anderson's account of events for me, and also admitted that obtaining the details about Bure's eligibility "cost them a lot of U.S. dollars." Once again, despite the fact that 10 years had passed, Burke declined to identify the Canucks' Moscow informant.

But when I spoke with Penny, he outlined a slightly different version of events. Penny says there was no mysterious Moscow informant. Instead, he claims he was aware—from his overseas scouting trips—that Bure had played other games. Four of the extra games were with Central Army. The other two were a pair of exhibition games played in Finland between the Soviet and Finnish national teams in December 1987. Penny saw those two games in person. "One of the games was in Vierumaki, a little town in Finland where the Finns had a training center," Penny recalls. "I rented a car and drove up there just prior to Christmas. Bure played again in the next game in Helsinki." Penny says he and Mike Murray, from the Canadian Amateur Hockey Association, were the only North Americans who witnessed the games.

Although Bure wasn't playing with the Central Army team, but rather with the Soviet national squad, Penny believed that because those games were sanctioned by the International Ice Hockey Federation, they should rightfully count as part of Bure's official record.

Murray, however, says Penny's memory is faulty. The visit to Vier-umaki actually happened in 1988, just prior to the World Junior Championships in Anchorage, Alaska. If this is true, then those two games wouldn't be relevant because they hadn't occurred during the 1987–88 season when Bure's record was in dispute. Murray says he is sure of this because he was in Moscow in December 1987 with Canada's national junior team and had visited Bure on Christmas Eve. "Pavel hadn't made the Soviet national junior team and he was just getting ready to leave for the Esso Cup tournament in Quebec," Murray says. The fact that Bure was only 16 at the time (he wouldn't turn 17 until March 1988) and hadn't been chosen for the world junior team casts even greater doubt on Penny's recollection that the Russian was playing with the Soviet national team in December 1987. Bure was simply too young.

Because of previous trades, the Canucks had only three draft picks in the first five rounds of the 1989 draft, not the ideal scenario for a team in dire need of immediate help. The Canucks used their first pick (eighth overall) to select Jason Herter, a defenseman from the University of North Dakota in the Western Collegiate Hockey Association. Herter never played for the Canucks—his entire NHL career would consist of one game for the Toronto Maple Leafs. Vancouver's second pick, Robert Woodward, never played a single minute in the NHL. The Canucks' third pick, defenseman Bret Hauer, would enjoy a somewhat longer NHL career: 29 games.

In the interval between the fourth and sixth rounds, the Canucks' management team discussed strategy. Quinn asked for input and Penny pushed for picking Bure. Penny says the decision was a "no-brainer. Bure was by far the best player available. He had a tremendous amount of skill and ability. He could skate and had great puck sense. He was playing with men and playing well, and he was still just a boy. The only question was, did those extra two games count? I thought they did." Penny believed the potential benefits were worth the risk. "What was the worst-case scenario? If someone challenged the pick and it was denied, then we'd lose a sixth-round pick. But if we were right, we get a hell of player. I said to Pat, 'Let's take Bure.'" Penny says Quinn stared at him and growled, "Jesus Christ, I hope you're right on this one."

Although the Canucks were unaware of it, a similar discussion was taking place at the Detroit Red Wings' table. After selecting Fedorov in the fourth round, Detroit's European scout, Christer Rockstrom, urged the club to pick Bure, too. New York Rangers GM Neil Smith, who was then Detroit's director of player personnel, said he didn't think Bure had played enough games to be eligible. Smith checked with NHL vice president Gil Stein, who informed him that Bure hadn't played the required 11 games. Smith returned to the Red Wings' table and relayed Stein's message. Rockstrom, however, was adamant that Bure had actually played 11 games, although he didn't have the evidence on hand. Smith returned to Stein and told him his European scout said Bure should be eligible. Stein still said no. When Smith returned to the table, Detroit's fifth pick was coming up. With the issue still unresolved, the club decided to select Shawn McCosh, a center from Niagara Falls of the Ontario Hockey League. But Rockstrom persisted, and by the time the sixth round was at hand, he had convinced Smith to risk a pick on Bure.

Bure's eligibility was also a topic of discussion in the Edmonton Oilers' camp. As the sixth round began, Oilers head scout Barry Fraser was quizzing Goran Stubb of European Scouting about Bure's status. "There were a lot of stories about how many games he had played," Fraser says. "Some said 11, some said 20. We had similar information to the Canucks, but we didn't know if it was legitimate or not. You have to realize that they didn't keep very good records in those days and the Soviets didn't want people to know. We hadn't actually made a decision what we were going to do at that point."

Neither Edmonton nor Detroit got the chance to roll the dice. Vancouver, picking three slots in front of the Red Wings and seven before the Oilers, moved first. NHL vice president Brian O'Neill announced, "The Vancouver Canucks select Pavel Bure of the Soviet Union." The words were barely out of O'Neill's mouth when Rockstrom began angrily pounding his fist on his table. Representatives from several teams raced up to the head table and protested vehemently. What was normally an uneventful portion of the draft had suddenly become animated. As Burke recalls, "The other teams were tossing expletives at me and everyone else on the Canucks."

Winnipeg Jets general manager Mike Smith was similarly stunned by the Canucks' move. Smith says he made a visit to Moscow prior to the 1989 draft with the intention of working out a deal with the Soviet Ice Hockey Federation to obtain Bure's services. Smith's proposal involved paying a substantial transfer fee to the Soviets over a three-year period, during which time Bure would continue to play with Central Army, but also visit Canada to train with the Jets. At the end of the three years, Bure would then join Winnipeg. The arrangement would have allowed Bure to continue to develop his skills and join the NHL as a relatively mature 21-year-old. Smith's scheme never got off the ground. "The Soviets rejected the idea," he says, "and like fools we didn't draft him." Of course, like most everyone else, Smith believed Bure was ineligible.

Order was eventually restored and the draft continued. Having made their one venture into the European ranks, the Canucks returned to familiar ground, selecting seven North Americans in the remaining rounds. Only one of them—Sandy Moger—would ever make the NHL, and when he did, it wasn't with Vancouver, but rather as a member of the Boston Bruins.

The Vancouver papers made only a brief mention of Bure in their summation of the draft. The majority of the ink was reserved for the Saskatchewan-born Herter, who was billed as the top-rated junior defenseman. But the Bure case wasn't closed. As a result of complaints from the Hartford Whalers and Washington Capitals, the NHL's head office launched an investigation into the legitimacy of Bure's drafting. The Capitals and Whalers argued that the NHL's own stats had indicated that Bure was ineligible. Even if the Canucks could prove he had played enough games to qualify, the Capitals and Whalers believed it was unfair to allow the Canucks to draft Bure when everyone else had been told he was off-limits.

The NHL's inquiry into the matter was clearly not top priority. It took league president John Ziegler 11 months to render a decision. Finally, on May 17, 1990, Ziegler declared in a news release that the Canucks' selection of Bure was illegal. The Russian winger would be tossed back into the 1990 draft and any of the 21 NHL teams could draft him in any round.

The Canucks' brass wasn't pleased. "I don't agree with the result, obviously," Quinn said to reporters. "But I want to meet with Ziegler and find out what appeal procedures, if any, are open to us." However, Quinn didn't sound hopeful that a solution could be found. "I would expect if we were given a chance to appeal, we'd have to go before the Board of Governors. The problem is how do you get the board together before the draft?" Quinn had a point. The Entry Draft was scheduled for June 16 in Vancouver. The Board of Governors meeting wasn't slated to convene until June 17.

Burke was less diplomatic. "I'm just astounded by the decision. I'm outraged," he told reporters. "There are some hard questions to be asked about the people we pay to tell us whether a player is eligible or not." Burke was referring to the Central Scouting Bureau, the talent-seeking organization run by the NHL to identify and evaluate the best juniors around the globe. Burke said that NHL officials assured him on draft day that Bure was fair game in the sixth round. "The NHL's own stats indicated he was eligible," Burke fumed. "Never again are we going to rely on accuracy from Central Scouting as it relates to drafting a European player."

Burke's outburst appears to have been designed to deceive reporters. He now admits the word he actually received from NHL officials regarding Bure's eligibility was: "You draft at your own peril." Besides, Vancouver's decision to draft Bure wasn't based on information supplied by Central Scouting.

The Canucks decided to contest Ziegler's verdict, but with the 1990 Entry Draft less than a month away, they had to act quickly. Quinn placed a call to Igor Larionov in Moscow and asked him to see if he could get his hands on documents that would establish the validity of the Canucks' claim to Bure.

Larionov contacted Soviet journalist Igor Kuperman, an editor of the Soviet magazine *Sports Games*. Kuperman had 15 years of experience covering Soviet and international hockey in Moscow. He had served as a statistician with the Soviet hockey league and was a member of the NHL's European branch of Central Scouting. As Kuperman recalls, "Igor came to me and asked if I could find any other senior games that Bure had played in. I knew Igor and said I would be happy to help him, but I warned him that even if I did find something, it probably wouldn't count. Igor said, 'Don't worry about that. Just do it.' "

Kuperman sifted through the relevant files. The material was all handwritten and the research took some time. To Kuperman's surprise, in addition to the five games with Central Army already credited to Bure, he discovered others. "I found six games. Not five or seven, but exactly six."

The extra games were from exhibition contests Bure had played in with Central Army during a preseason tournament and a club tournament at the midseason break when the Soviet national team was on tour. "In one of those games," Kuperman says, "Bure played only one shift. But it still counted as a game and it made the total 11." Eleven games was, of course, the magic number, if exhibition games qualified as league games.

Kuperman made copies of the game sheets and took them to Central Army assistant coach Boris Mikhailov, who confirmed their accuracy. Kuperman then got a letter from the Soviet Ice Hockey Federation to authenticate the findings, and met with Larionov. The pair went to the Canadian embassy in Moscow, where Larionov had the documents faxed to the Canucks' office in Vancouver. With the assistance of Goran Stubb of Central Scouting, Penny says he obtained documentary evidence of the two games with the national team that Bure had played in Finland. The entire package was then forwarded to Ziegler.

However, if Murray's memory is accurate, then those two games in Finland had no bearing on Bure's eligibility and Burke and Penny's account of nine league games and two exhibition contests becomes suspect. In fact, it makes it seem as if Bure's drafting by the Canucks was based on erroneous data. On the other hand, Kuperman claims to have found six extra games in which Bure appeared, two more than Burke or Penny attribute to him. But the games Kuperman found weren't league games, but exhibitions, putting their validity into question, as well.

Whatever was in the documents the Canucks sent to NHL headquarters, they provoked no quick response. The club was still waiting for an answer on June 15 on the eve of the 1990 draft. As Burke recalls, "We were gathered in a suite at the Four Seasons Hotel. We had already decided if the decision went against us, we would use one of our two first-round picks to draft Bure again." Later that night, Brian O'Neill knocked on the door and asked Quinn and Burke to come down to the NHL's executive suite. "When we got there," Burke says, "Ziegler handed us a press release." The NHL president had reversed his earlier ruling. The Canucks' pick would stand—they owned the negotiating rights to Bure.

The timing of Ziegler's announcement, just before the 1990 draft, appears to have been designed to limit the opportunity for protest from other GMs and owners, who were predictably irate. Some of them would make their feelings known to Ziegler behind closed doors at the NHL's Board of Governors meeting on the day following the draft.

In response to reporters' questions about the controversy and the anger of rival teams, Ziegler tried to play down the flap. "They're a competitive lot. Part of the problem is a failure to understand the information on which I based my decision. I don't think the feeling is widespread. I make some difficult decisions that people don't always agree with."

Ziegler didn't elaborate on the information on which he based his decision. Presumably he was referring to Kuperman's detective work. But some suspected there was more to the story. In the spring of 1992, by which time Bure was a rising NHL star, Vancouver *Province* sports columnist Tony Gallagher cited an anonymous NHL owner and a general manager who alleged that Ziegler changed his ruling in the Canucks' favor not because of any statistical evidence, but rather because Quinn offered to drop a pending lawsuit against Ziegler that he had initiated in response to his earlier suspension.

Was there any substance to Gallagher's allegations? Not according to Arthur Griffiths, who vigorously denied the charge, as reported by Gallagher: "This is an out-and-out lie. The two issues do not line up in time. John released a statement softening his position on Pat and we all signed agreements that there would be no legal action from either side on Pat's matter almost a year before Bure was drafted."

Gallagher, however, remains convinced that a backroom deal occurred. "I know it's a fact," he insists. Gallagher also believes that widespread dissatisfaction at Ziegler's handling of the affair contributed to his eventual ousting as league president in 1992.

Whatever the truth about the Moscow research and Ziegler's sudden about-face, it had no effect on the historical record. To this day, *The National Hockey League Official Guide and Record Book* lists Bure as playing five games with Central Army in 1987–88. No reference to any international games is mentioned.

# CHAPTER FOUR

# Mutiny in Moscow

*It is impossible to predict the time and progress of revolution.*
*It is governed by its own more or less mysterious laws.*

LENIN

AT THE SAME TIME as Bure was making his climb to the Soviet national team, a mutiny was brewing in the upper ranks. Several of the country's top players had grown dissatisfied with the dictatorial regime of Central Army and national team coach Viktor Tikhonov. Emboldened by the spirit of *glasnost* that was loosening the Communist grip on the Soviet Union, players began speaking out for the first time. In October 1988, the Russian magazine *Ogonyok* published an open letter from Igor Larionov in which he revealed how his travel visa had been withheld, how some players were injected with drugs and how Tikhonov had created an oppressive climate of fear and isolation. Larionov spoke about how the players were separated from their homes and families for 10 months of every year and were forced to undergo endless hours of training. As Alexander Mogilny put it, "They take us out of the cage and let us sing and then they put us back in the cage again."

Shortly after Larionov's criticisms were made public, Viacheslav Fetisov added his voice to the dissent, claiming in an article in the magazine *Moskovsky Komsomolyets* that Tikhonov was intent on turning his players into "ice robots." As Fetisov explained, "With Tikhonov every fault on the ice is a catastrophe. A game lasts 60 minutes, and for Tikhonov it is 60 minutes of catastrophe after catastrophe."

Tikhonov lashed back, accusing Fetisov, the team's captain, of breaking training regimen, of getting drunk and beating up a Second World War veteran, and of abusing heroes of the Chernobyl tragedy. Tikhonov suspended Fetisov from both the Central Army and national teams and had him assigned to desk duty at the Red Army barracks.

As the 1989 World Championships approached and Fetisov's status remained in limbo, the core players on the national team rallied to his cause, appearing on national television and issuing an ultimatum to Tikhonov: "Either Fetisov plays or we don't." Tikhonov ultimately backed down and restored Fetisov to the team. The players then drove their point home by reelecting Fetisov as captain. United by their dislike of Tikhonov, the Soviet team won 10 straight games and captured another world title. Fetisov was voted the tournament's top defenseman. But when the victorious team left Sweden and returned home to Moscow, one seat on the plane was empty. Mogilny had disappeared.

On May 2, the day after the Soviet team won the gold medal, the Buffalo Sabres' director of player development, Don Luce, received a phone call from a Russian named Sergei Fomitov, who told Luce that Mogilny wanted to come to Buffalo. The Sabres, who had selected Mogilny in the fifth round of the 1988 NHL Entry Draft, claimed the call took them by surprise. Luce had last talked to Mogilny in December at the World Junior Championships in Alaska, when he gave him his business card. At Luce's request, Fomitov put Mogilny on the line, and he confirmed he wanted to defect. Luce and Sabres general manager Gerry Meehan flew to Stockholm later that same day. On May 3, they met Mogilny and Fomitov in person. The four men flew to New York City on May 4. As they boarded the plane, Mogilny turned to Meehan, smiled and said, "I am free now."

Upon arrival at Kennedy Airport, Mogilny was interviewed by U.S. immigration officials and the FBI. From there the group flew to Buffalo.

At a news conference, Meehan confirmed that Mogilny had signed a contract with the Sabres. The Russian player had entered the United States on a seven-day visa, but he would later be granted political asylum.

Fomitov, who shared a town house with Mogilny and served as an interpreter for the 20-year-old during his rookie season, reportedly received half of Mogilny's US$150,000 signing bonus from the Sabres for his role in engineering the young forward's defection. He was also put on the Sabres' payroll for a year as Mogilny's personal aide.

The Soviets accused the Sabres of piracy and charged Mogilny with desertion from the Russian army. They labeled him a selfish, money-hungry ingrate. "The player showed by his action that's it's not happenstance that he didn't have friends on the team and that he was a person of secret intentions," Tikhonov said.

Mogilny had indeed kept his intentions secret. He had informed his parents of his decision by telephone in Stockholm, only a few hours before his departure. His mother, Nadezheda, had pleaded with him to change his mind, but to no avail. However, at least one other Soviet player had known about Mogilny's plans. His roommate, Sergei Fedorov, was with him when he packed his bags and slipped away. Before leaving, Mogilny tried to persuade Fedorov to accompany him. "Oh, no!" Fedorov cried. "I couldn't. My father. My mother. My family. What about them? No, you go, Alex. Best of luck to you in your new life."

Mogilny had been considering defection for a year. The incident that had finally spurred him to take action occurred in February 1989. As punishment for getting into a fight during a game with Spartak's Yuri Yashin, he was given a 10-game suspension, was fined a month's pay and was stripped of the prestigious Master of Sport medal he had received after winning his Olympic gold medal in 1988.

Mogilny answered the Soviet accusations of his selfishness by saying, "I've heard that they write I think only of myself. But who is thinking about me when I finish playing hockey in the Soviet Union? They don't think about that. I am doing what I have to do now while I'm still young and strong." Asked for his thoughts about Tikhonov, Mogilny replied, "Only his wife and dog like him and I do not understand how they do."

Some NHL executives were concerned that Mogilny's defection would jeopardize negotiations to acquire Soviet players through official channels, but those fears proved unfounded. A few days after the 1989 Entry Draft, New Jersey Devils general manager Lou Lamoriello traveled to Moscow to meet with Soviet hockey authorities. On June 26, 1989, Lamoriello announced he had signed Viacheslav Fetisov and Sergei Starikov to contracts. On July 1, Pat Quinn inked center Igor Larionov to a multiyear deal. Later in the summer, Quinn would also sign Vladimir Krutov, Larionov's linemate. Early in July, Calgary Flames GM Cliff Fletcher acquired Sergei Makarov, the third member of the KLM line. Before the summer was out, the Quebec Nordiques signed goalie Sergei Mylnikov and the Minnesota North Stars brought over 37-year-old forward Helmut Balderis. All of the deals involved the payment of substantial transfer fees to Soviet hockey officials.

The arrival of the Russian players was the talk of the hockey world prior to the start of the 1989–90 season. In an October 6 *Hockey News* cover story, Bob McKenzie wrote: "The first wave of the Soviet invasion is closer to a flood. The 1989–90 season will be forever remembered as the Year of the Soviet." Everyone had an opinion on what sort of impact the Soviets would have. In New Jersey and Vancouver, there was unbridled optimism. In Fetisov, the Devils had landed a premier defenseman, the captain of the Russian national team. In Larionov and Krutov, the Canucks had acquired two-thirds of the fabled KLM line. The high-scoring duo was expected to solve the Canucks' most glaring shortcoming: a lackluster offense. Vancouver had scored the fewest goals in the NHL in 1988–89, and yet had still come within one overtime goal of upsetting the Calgary Flames, the eventual Stanley Cup winners, in the playoffs. It didn't seem unrealistic to believe the addition of the two gifted Russians might help propel the Canucks into the elite ranks.

But there were many questions yet to be answered. What effect would culture shock have on the Russians? How would they stand up to the NHL's physical and intense play? How easily would they be accepted by their teammates? How motivated would they be? With the exception of Mogilny, all of the Russian imports were in their late twenties or early thirties and had played a lot of hockey. How many miles did they have left on their odometers?

Other European players who had made the transition to the NHL sounded cautionary notes. "To Russian guys, puck is like toy," said

Czechoslovakian center Dusan Pasek of the Minnesota North Stars. "Here, NHL is hard work. Puck is not toy."

In retrospect, the caution was warranted. Most of the Soviet players struggled in their first NHL season. The social adjustments were as difficult as the new brand of hockey. Even North American viruses left their mark. As Larionov remarked early in the season, "In Russia, we have small apartment, small car, no food, but we're healthy all the time. In Canada, we have big house, big car, lots of food and we're sick all the time."

Both Larionov and Krutov received three-year contracts worth $375,000 per year. According to the terms of the deal, Sovintersport, the organization set up by the Soviets to negotiate transfer fees for their athletes who left to play in the West, would also receive the same amount per year. In total, the Canucks were paying a hefty $1.5 million annually for the Soviet duo.

Neither player lived up to his billing. Larionov tallied 17 goals and 27 assists for 44 points in 74 games, whereas Krutov collected 11 goals and 23 assists for 34 points in 61 games. But while Larionov made an effort to fit in with the team and impressed everyone with his friendly manner and classy bearing, the moody and taciturn Krutov became a distraction. He reported to training camp woefully out of shape and did little to remedy the situation as the season progressed. His usual routine before practice was to stop at a 7-Eleven convenience store and order two hot dogs, a bag of potato chips and a soft drink. After practice, he would return for a second order.

Jim Sandlak, the Canucks player who shared a house with Krutov, regaled his teammates with tales of Krutov's slothfulness. The Russian, who was dubbed "Vlad the Inhaler," in recognition of his uncanny ability to empty refrigerators, spent most of his free hours watching TV and eating junk food in his room. His bedroom floor was covered with discarded plastic wrappers, pizza boxes and soft-drink cans. Krutov was so lazy that he used hockey tape to rig a makeshift trip wire to his light switch so that he could simply jerk the tape and turn out the light without having to rise from his bed.

The enigmatic Mogilny proved as puzzling to Buffalo Sabres coach Rick Dudley as he had to Tikhonov. After a fast start, he suddenly tailed off in his play. Midway through the season, he developed a fear of flying and had to undergo therapy. By the time the playoffs rolled round, he was a frequent healthy scratch. At the same time, Fetisov's performance with New Jersey was inconsistent and he wilted in the playoffs.

The one Soviet who excelled was Makarov, who benefited by joining a powerful veteran team that had won the Stanley Cup the previous year. Unlike Larionov and Krutov, Makarov wasn't expected to perform miracles with Calgary. Freed of that pressure, he recorded 24 goals and 62 assists and won the Calder Trophy as the NHL rookie of the year. He was a controversial selection. The idea of a 31-year-old international veteran being voted top rookie offended hockey purists. Less than a month later, the NHL Board of Governors passed what has come to be known as the Makarov Rule, which limits rookie-of-the-year candidates to 26 years of age and under.

The influx of Soviet players into the NHL sparked fresh speculation about when Bure might be able to join the Canucks. In an interview with the *Toronto Star*, Bure said with the aid of an interpreter, "There is a rule in my country that a hockey player does not have the right to go abroad and play until he is 28 years old. But everything is changing at home very quickly these days, so who knows what the future brings? To be in the NHL is not any large goal of mine, but a man wants to know other countries, and to play hockey in a new place would be a way to find out." Asked if he would consider defecting, Bure replied, "I could never do what Alexander [Mogilny] did, no matter what happens. I could never leave my family and friends that way."

The Soviet authorities wouldn't allow the Canucks to contact Bure personally after the 1989 Entry Draft, but the club did manage to send him some souvenirs and golf shirts. The attention from overseas was a novelty to the Bures. As Vladimir recalls, "The NHL was like moon to us. When we heard that Pavel was drafted by Vancouver Canucks, I say, 'Draft? What is draft?'" Vladimir became curious to know more about this faraway team that now owned his son's NHL rights. "Sometimes I look in the paper and see what happens to the Canucks. Lose. Lose. Lose. This is a very bad team."

Bure's promotion to the senior Central Army senior squad and the Soviet national team meant an another upgrade in his lifestyle. His salary was raised to 120 rubles (about $750). Between playing for Central Army and various exhibition and tournament games with both the junior and senior Soviet national teams, he was a very busy player in 1989–90. Central Army would win the league title and Bure would contribute 14 goals and 10 assists for 24 points in 46 games.

Bure suited up with the Soviet national team at the 1990 World Junior Championships in Helsinki, Finland. Once again, the competition for the gold medal was decided between Canada and the Soviet Union on the final day. This year, however, the two teams didn't meet in the decisive game. Earlier in the tournament, Canada had overcome a 3–0 deficit to defeat the Soviets 6–4 in their one head-to-head encounter. That result left the Soviets with a 5–1–0 record entering their final game against Sweden, needing a win to capture the gold medal. Canada was in second place with a 4–1–1 record. In order to take the gold, Canada had to defeat Czechoslovakia in its final game and hope the Swedes could defeat or tie the Soviets. The two games were played simultaneously. The U.S.S.R. led 5–3 in the third period when Sweden rallied to score a pair of goals, netting the tying marker with just one second left on the clock. Canada received word of the 5–5 tie during the third period of its game with the Czechs. Leading 2–1 at the time, Canada hung on to preserve the win and clinch the title.

Bure and his teammates had better luck at the 1990 World Championships in Switzerland in April. Bolstered by the addition of Fetisov and Makarov, who had rejoined the club after their teams had been knocked out of the NHL playoffs, and backed by the solid goaltending of Latvian Arturs Irbe, the high-powered Soviet team racked up a 8–1–1 record and captured the gold medal. Bure, in his first appearance at the world championships, picked up two goals and four assists.

The victory provided a financial windfall for the Soviet players, who were each rewarded with a gift of US$10,000. The money allowed Bure to purchase goods beyond the reach of the average Soviet citizen, but not the item he most desired: a new Lada. "In Russia, you can't just go out and buy a car," he told interviewer Jim Taylor in *Sports Only*. "You have to line up, to get on a list, some people for years. But if you do something special, something big like win a world championship, then you get a favor. You still have to buy the car, but you get to go to the top of the list."

According to Taylor, after the Soviet team won the world title, Bure went to Tikhonov and asked, "Can I get car now? He says, 'No.' I have to do something else. So we go to the Goodwill Games, which is very big, almost like the Olympics for us. We win that, too, and I say, 'Now can I get it?' He says, 'Yes, now you can.' Even then I waited six or seven months, so it was a big deal getting that Lada."

Having his own automobile at age 19 was a rare privilege, and it made Bure stand out. As he recalled in *Sports Only*, "The police used to stop me all the time because they could see me driving this car. In Russia you're not allowed to drive your father's car without special permission. They would stop me and ask for my driver's license, then ask whose car it is. I say, 'Mine.' And they say, 'How come?' Then, 'Oh, you must be hockey player. Is okay then.'"

The 1990 Goodwill Games, held in July in Seattle, was a huge athletic event, similar in scope to the Olympic Games. The hockey tournament, involving eight countries, was won by the Soviets, who defeated the United States in the final. Bure scored four goals and an assist in five games and displayed flashes of dazzling speed, giving Vancouver sportswriters better insight into why other NHL teams had been so irate with Ziegler's ruling regarding Bure's draft eligibility.

But the biggest story of the "friendly" tournament was the defection of the Detroit Red Wings' draft choice, Sergei Fedorov, who disappeared after an exhibition game with the U.S. team in Portland, Oregon, just before the tournament began. Fedorov was next seen a week later in Detroit, where the Red Wings announced that the 20-year-old had signed a five-year contract.

The Red Wings' courtship of Fedorov began shortly after the club drafted him in June 1989. After an exhibition game in Finland that August, the young center was handed a letter, translated into Russian, detailing the Wings' interest in him. The letter offered Fedorov US$250,000 to defect and an extra US$25,000 for his family, who would remain behind in Russia. Later that winter, when Fedorov traveled to North America with the Central Army team to play NHL clubs in the 1989–90 Super Series, Michel Ponomarev, a Montreal-born photographer of Russian parents, arranged a clandestine meeting between Fedorov and Detroit Red Wings vice president Jim Lites, at which Fedorov was offered a contract.

Lites was the Red Wings' point man in recruiting players from behind the Iron Curtain. As Detroit general manager Jim Devellano put it in a *Detroit Free Press* article, "My job was to draft the best players in the world. Lites' job was to go get them." In 1986 Lites had smuggled Czechoslovakian star Peter Klima out of a hotel in Austria under the noses of men with machine guns. Lites intended to have Fedorov leave the Soviet team after the Goodwill Games, but when the Red Wings got word that another player on the team, Dimitri Kristich, was considering defecting to the Washington Capitals, he moved the schedule up.

On Sunday, July 24, as the Soviet players were having a team meal, it became apparent that Fedorov was missing. A team official was sent to look for him. By chance, he met Fedorov in the elevator. The nervous hockey player, who was on his way out of the hotel, reached into his pocket, handed the official some cash and the man let him walk away. Ponomarev was in a car outside. He drove Fedorov to the Portland airport, where Red Wings owner Mike Ilitch's private jet was waiting to fly them to Detroit.

The Soviets protested what they felt was outright thievery by the Red Wings and asked for Fedorov's return, but Detroit refused to comply, insisting that the player wasn't seeking political asylum, but merely pursuing a career in the NHL. "He's asked me to tell everyone that he was very happy playing with the Soviet national teams and would like to continue to play for his country when the NHL schedule permits," Lites said.

The Red Wings' aggressive pursuit of Soviet players didn't stop with Fedorov. The club was also plotting strategy to get another of its 1989 draft picks, defenseman Vladimir Konstantinov, out of Russia. Konstantinov, a lieutenant in the Russian army and the captain of Central Army, had been contacted by an envoy for the Red Wings, Valeri Matveev, a sports journalist from *Pravda*. Konstantinov originally told Matveev that defecting wasn't possible, because as an army officer he would be accused of treason, and felons couldn't get U.S. visas. However, Konstantinov changed his mind after he toured North America with the Central Army team during the 1990–91 Super Series and observed firsthand how Fedorov was living.

Using US$30,000 in bribe money provided by the Red Wings, Matveev had Konstantinov admitted to a Russian medical clinic where he was diagnosed with a rare, fictitious disease. Prior to the 1991–92 season, Konstantinov's wife, Irina, went to Central Army manager Valeri Gushin and coach Viktor Tikhonov and begged them to send Konstantinov to the United States for medical treatment. A skeptical Tikhonov dispatched Konstantinov to Burdenka, an elite Russian military hospital, for tests. Again, using money supplied by the Red Wings, Matveev convinced the Burdenka doctors to go along with the charade. They informed Tikhonov they could neither confirm nor deny the existence of the disease, but agreed that Konstantinov couldn't continue his military or hockey careers.

Having obtained Konstantinov's release from the military, the Red Wings intended to have him fly to the United States, but when Matveev discovered that Gushin had instructed guards at Sheremetyevo Airport to confiscate Konstantinov's passport and detain him if he showed up, he arranged for the defenseman, his wife and his daughter to leave Russia by train with forged documents. Lites and a U.S. immigration lawyer met them in Budapest, where they boarded Ilitch's plane and flew to Detroit.

The Red Wings also employed cloak-and-dagger tactics to acquire Viacheslav Kozlov, the U.S.S.R.'s rookie of the year in 1990. In November 1991, the 19-year-old Kozlov had suffered serious head and facial injuries in a car accident outside Moscow. His passenger, another young Russian hockey player named Taras Kirilov, was killed in the crash. While Kozlov was convalescing, Matveev convinced Russian doctors to determine that Kozlov had suffered brain damage, a diagnosis that cost the Red Wings US$25,000 and a new Chevrolet Caprice. Gushin was aware of what was happening and tried to bribe the doctors with free trips with the Central Army team to European tournaments, but couldn't compete with Detroit's cold, hard U.S. cash. After Kozlov was smuggled out of Russia for "treatment," Gushin tried to sue the Red Wings, but the Russians couldn't afford the legal bills. The suit died, and Kozlov joined Detroit in March 1992.

Bure's rapidly rising profile got more exposure in the West when he traveled to Saskatoon in Canada to compete in the 1991 World Junior Championships in January. The tournament featured several future NHLers. In addition to Bure, the Soviet team had Viacheslav Kozlov and Sandis Ozolinsh; Canada's squad included Eric Lindros, Geoff

Sanderson, Darryl Sydor and goalie Felix Potvin; the United States had Doug Weight and Keith Tkachuk; Sweden had Mikael Renberg; Czechoslovakia had Zigmund Palffy, Martin Rucinsky and Jiri Slegr.

After losing Fedorov, the Soviets were understandably paranoid about bringing their best young players to tournaments in North America, and so prior to the 1991 World Junior Championships, they convinced the NHL Board of Governors to agree to a US$250,000 fine for any representative of an NHL club who tampered with a Soviet player.

Tournament organizers had arranged the schedule so that Canada and the Soviet Union would meet in the final game, a clash they hoped would decide the champion. But Canada stumbled, tying the United States and losing to Czechoslovakia, and carried a 3–1–1 record into the final game. The Soviets won their first four games and needed only to beat Finland in their second-last contest to clinch the title. The game was a wild affair. Finland jumped out to a 4–0 lead, only to have the U.S.S.R. rally to score five straight goals. Bure led the attack, scoring his team's third, fourth and fifth goals of the game. But the Finns got a late chance when the Soviets were penalized for having too many men on the ice and Jarkko Varvio scored the equalizer with just 15 seconds left.

For the second straight year, a Scandinavian team had dashed the Soviets' gold-medal aspirations in the final seconds of a game. This year, however, the Soviets had a second chance. A tie or a win against Canada would give them the gold.

At the morning skate, the Soviets watched the Canadian players going through their paces. Bure and Kozlov, who both stood five foot nine, were amazed at the size of some of their opponents. Seeing the six-foot-four, 230-pound Lindros, Bure gestured to Kozlov, raising one hand high in the air.

When the Soviets took the ice, the Canadian players gathered to watch. "Which one is Bure?" Pat Falloon asked, as reported in the *Toronto Star*. "I'll go out and break his leg."

"Go ahead, Paddy, and we'll arrange for you to take home two gold medals," Mike Craig joked.

Although games between Canada and the Soviet Union were always emotionally charged affairs, the changing political climate had modified perspectives in the Soviet camp. In the past, Soviet coaches could motivate their players by appealing to their nationalism, but as Soviet coach Robert Cherenkov admitted, that wasn't enough any longer. Money was the new stimulant. "Maybe we don't like it and maybe we've avoided it in the past, but it's a fact of life now," Cherenkov said, displaying a frankness that would have earned him a one-way ticket to Siberia a few years earlier. "We told our players before the game that they should do their best, because they'll be seen by everyone in hockey and maybe they'll be offered a professional contract."

The Canadian players, most of whom had already been drafted, were able to draw patriotic inspiration from the noisy, flag-waving Saskatoon crowd. Canadian coach Dick Todd had forward Kris Draper doggedly shadow Bure throughout the game. Draper kept Bure off the scoreboard, and Canada won 3–2 to capture the gold medal.

Afterward, Cherenkov was asked how many Soviets would be coming to the NHL in the near future. He replied: "A few years from now Canada will have so many Soviet players they won't want to see any more."

Cherenkov was asked whether Bure wanted to play in the NHL. "It's not a matter of whether he wants or doesn't want," the Soviet coach said. "It is quite possible after 1994 to see him in the NHL if he decides to choose that route."

Although Lindros was voted the tournament's top forward, Bure led all players with 12 goals. The effort gave him a total of 27 goals in world-junior competition, a record that still stands. Bure's 39 points ranks third in world-championship play, three behind Sweden's Peter Forsberg and one behind the Czech Republic's Robert Reichel.

Late that night, Canadian national-team publicist Mike Murray heard a knock at his door. He opened it and was surprised to see Bure. "Pavel said he was restless and bored with the scene at his hotel and he wanted to talk," Murray recalls. A few minutes later there was another knock at the door. *Toronto Sun* reporter Tim Wharnsby had been alerted to Bure's presence. Wharnsby interviewed Bure, who spoke enough English to make himself understood. Bure told Wharnsby he was unwilling to defect because he feared that Soviet officials would punish his brother, Valeri, a budding hockey star who was about to turn 16. "He is a very good player and I don't want to make things difficult for him," Bure said.

Although he was still a junior-age player, Bure led the Soviet elite league in scoring in 1990–91, with 35 goals in 46 games, 15 goals more than Central Army's number-two scorer, international veteran Valeri Kamensky. But for the second straight year, it was Moscow Dynamo and not Central Army that won the league title.

The 1991 World Championships, held in April in Finland, marked the last time the Soviet players wore the familiar CCCP crest on their chests. The political fragmentation of the Soviet Union meant that the longtime hockey power would compete as Russia after 1991.

The Soviet team, composed of the best players in the country's elite league, along with a few returning veterans from the NHL, made it to the final round, but lost the gold medal to Sweden 2–1. Bure, who scored three goals and eight assists to tie Kamensky as the Soviet's top scorer, was voted to the tournament's second All-Star team on right wing. The 20-year-old speedster was an object of intense curiosity. NHL agents, dollar signs dancing in their heads, were all over the little Soviet, telling him how they could "fix it so he didn't have to play for Vancouver, but could play with Wayne Gretzky in L.A."

After a brief break, Bure began training for the upcoming Canada Cup, which was scheduled to be played in September. Although Mogilny and Fedorov had left, Tikhonov still had the third jewel in the crown. Bure was now regarded as a cornerstone of the country's national squad. Recognizing his value, Central Army hockey officials tried to convince Bure to sign a three-year contract extension that would bind him to the team through the 1992 and 1994 Winter Olympics. But Bure, unwilling to cut off his options, stubbornly refused. As punishment, Tikhonov dropped his young star from the national squad and left him behind in Moscow when the team flew to Canada in late August.

If Tikhonov hoped that iron-fisted discipline would bring Bure to heel, he was sadly mistaken.

CHAPTER FIVE

# From Russia, With Lawyers

*Do not judge a house by its appearance,*
*but rather by the warmth of its welcome.*

RUSSIAN PROVERB

O N SEPTEMBER 6, 1991, Vladimir Bure and his two sons, Pavel and Valeri, boarded a plane at Moscow's Sheremetyevo Airport and flew to Los Angeles. They stated on their visas that they would only be gone a month. In truth, this was intended to be a long-term relocation.

Upon arrival, the Bures headed immediately to the Manhattan Beach residence of player agent Ron Salcer. Salcer contended that the appearance of the Bures on his doorstep caught him off guard. "The boys and the father elected to make a move. The father wanted to give his sons a life he didn't have. I heard they might be coming, but I didn't know they were here until they actually landed in Los Angeles. I was surprised."

Although the Bures' departure from Russia may have been sudden, Salcer would certainly have been aware of what was transpiring. Serge Levin, a business associate of Salcer's, was involved in orchestrating their exit. The 50-year-old Levin, a former Russian sports journalist and TV producer with connections to influential people in Moscow, immigrated to the United States in 1979. After a stint dealing blackjack in Las Vegas, Levin moved to Los Angeles and began producing Russian-language radio and TV programs. An old friend of the Bure family, he knew both Vladimir and Pavel's grandfather, Valeri. "I saw Pavel on the day he was born," says Levin, who would later be instrumental in bringing other Russian players into Salcer's orbit. Asked how difficult it would have been for the Bures to leave Russia at that time, Levin responds cryptically, "It was not easy and it was not difficult."

Salcer, a slight and balding man whom David Cruise and Alison Griffiths describe in their book *Net Worth* as having "the earnest manner of a Methodist preacher," had gotten into the agent game after moving to Los Angeles from New York City in 1975, where he had worked as a financial consultant. His first sports clients were members of the Los Angeles Kings, notably winger Dave Taylor.

Salcer, who worked out of an office in his home, tried to make the Bures feel welcome and give them a taste of the Hollywood scene by taking them to a taping of the TV show *Who's the Boss?*, starring one of Salcer's show-business pals, actor Tony Danza. Salcer also contacted the Canucks to inform them of Bure's arrival. Brian Burke, the Canucks' vice president and director of hockey operations, took the call. He was dumbfounded. "When Salcer told me that Bure was in L.A., I didn't believe him," Burke recalls. "I said, 'Bullshit! Put him on the line.' We had no idea he was coming."

The sudden transition from the shabby grayness of Moscow's streets to the sun-drenched beaches and palm trees of Southern California must have been a severe blast of culture shock for the Bures, but Vladimir wasted no time in reminding his two sons of their mission—they were here to further their hockey careers. With militarylike precision, Pavel and Valeri reported to the beach every morning for a run. The rest of the day consisted of weight training and more running and games of volleyball or basketball. They also began conducting daily hockey drills at the nearby Culver City Ice Arena. Vladimir, who had never learned to skate, would stand on the ice in gum boots and put his sons through the paces, barking out instructions and making notes on a clipboard.

In order to have a live target to shoot at, they hired a goalie. Oddly they picked a woman—a 23-year-old, six-foot-tall netminder named Shawn

Barfield, who had played collegiate hockey at California State North-ridge. The Bure brothers jokingly nicknamed her "Sean Burke," after the NHL netminder whom Pavel had played against at the 1991 World Championships.

Barfield was apprehensive about her assignment. Facing a player of Pavel Bure's caliber was definitely not routine. "I couldn't believe it was happening," she admits. "I was pretty nervous at first. But I don't think he was trying to kill me. The thing is, I was used to players coming in and deking at 10 miles per hour and Pavel was deking at about 100 miles per hour. He used to kid me after he scored. He'd wag his finger and say, 'Don't believe me when I make that move.'"

Initially Barfield wasn't overly impressed with Bure's shot. Then one day he unleashed a slapper that caught her behind the pad on the side of the knee. "I thought my leg was broken. I was lying in pain on the ice, and Pavel's father was yelling at me, 'C'mon, get up, get up, you're okay.' I had a bruise on my leg the size of a grapefruit for a month afterward."

Barfield practiced with the Bures for three weeks. Pavel, she recalls, expressed a keen interest in cars. He wanted to get a Mitsubishi 3000. She found him modest, but also troubled by self-doubt and worried about his uncertain situation. "Some days he'd be really down on his chances of playing in the NHL. He'd say, 'Maybe this is all a dream.'"

Barfield told her friends she was practicing with an NHL prospect. "'Yeah,' they said, 'we've heard that before.' No, I told them, there's something special about him."

Shortly after arriving in California, Bure did something else that aroused considerable curiosity—he got married. According to news reports at the time, he had wed an American fashion model in Los Ange-les. Her first name was variously reported as Jymi or Jamie. No last name was ever provided. The mystery deepened when his wife seemed to van-ish from the face of the earth after the marriage ceremony. When asked about her absence, Pavel explained that she was in Europe on a model-ing assignment.

Bure later claimed he met his bride at a house party during the Goodwill Games in Seattle in July 1990 and that they had continued their relationship through letters. As he told *Vancouver Sun* reporter Iain MacIntyre, "After a couple of months she comes to Moscow for visit. Lot of talk on the phone. Sure, I miss her. But the job, hockey, comes first. We'll be together after the season. We will look for a home."

All of this was fiction. In truth, the event had been hastily arranged. According to a copy of Bure's marriage certificate, he was married in Las Vegas on September 11, 1991, only five days after he touched down in Los Angeles. His bride's name was Jayme Bohn. The marriage had been set up by Salcer and Levin as a legal parachute to ensure that Bure wouldn't risk deportation if contract negotiations with the Canucks and the NHL proved problematic. Bohn, who was 20 at the time, was from Manhattan Beach. The connection with Bure had been made through friends of hers in the Russian community.

In an interview, Bohn, who is stunned at being tracked down, guardedly claims she recalls little about the entire experience or "the paperwork" involved. "We flew to Las Vegas. We got married. We videotaped it. I remember that much. Then we gambled and we flew back to L.A." Bohn admits that she and Bure never lived together and that they were divorced the following spring. She says she hasn't kept in touch with her former husband or followed his hockey career. Aside from a couple of close friends, she admits she has never previously discussed the marriage with anyone.

Today Bohn works as a costume designer in the film-and-television industry. Judging by her credits—*Alien Avenger, Humanoids from the Deep, Black Scorpion*—she appears to specialize in cheesy science fiction films. Bohn recently made her acting debut in *Black Ball*, a film scheduled to be released in 2000. Her role is a small one. She is listed as "Party Girl #1."

The public became aware of Bure's presence in California in mid-September when Vancouver *Province* sports columnist Tony Gallagher interviewed the Russian by telephone. Speaking through an interpreter, Bure confirmed he had left Moscow on September 6 and was now living in Los Angeles. "This is paradise here, but I want to come as soon as possible to Vancouver. I'm skating a little bit now and I have been preparing for the season for three months with the [Soviet] national team. I am anxious to get going."

For a 20-year-old who had yet to play a minute in the NHL, Bure displayed a healthy dose of confidence. "I don't want to make too many predictions, but I will want to score at least 50 goals every season," he told Gallagher. Considering that only two rookies in NHL history—Mike Bossy and Joe Nieuwendyk—had ever scored 50 goals in a season, Bure's expectations were lofty ones. The Russian also indicated he expected to be well paid for his services, estimating that "$1 million may be a fair price." Asked if he knew of anyone in the hockey world who was quicker on skates, Bure paused for several seconds, then replied, "I don't know of anyone. I think I'm the fastest in the world."

Canucks management couldn't have been thrilled to read about Bure's salary expectations, as the club had paid captain Trevor Linden a mere $125,000 for his rookie season, just two years before. Bure's asking price was on par with what such headline players as Paul Coffey and Chris Chelios were earning at the time. Wayne Gretzky, the NHL's top-paid performer, was making $3 million. However, salaries were on the rise and the million-dollar figure wasn't out of line with what at least one other Russian was getting—former Central Army player, 25-year-old Valeri Kamensky, had just signed a four-year-deal worth $3.8 million with the Quebec Nordiques.

On September 15, Brian Burke flew to Los Angeles to meet with Bure and Salcer. They had lunch at a Manhattan Beach restaurant. It was ostensibly a social call, but the always-intense Burke, who had once described himself as "Pat Quinn's pit bull," may not have been the ideal choice as a glad-hander. Although Burke assured Bure he was pleased to see him, Bure later recalled that the Canucks vice president wore a deadly serious expression throughout the encounter. According to Burke, Bure soon lost interest in the meeting. "He wanted to go shopping for clothes, so I went with him to a mall."

The first face-to-face contact with a member of the Canucks' management, brief as it was, was an encouraging sign for Bure, who was growing increasingly uneasy with his nebulous status. He believed he would quickly be able to sign a contract and begin his professional career. But there was a procedure to follow. Before Canucks management could initiate contract talks, it had to receive clearance from the NHL. The clearance depended on a ruling from NHL president John Ziegler on the legality of Bure's contract with the Central Army team. If the Canucks didn't wait, they claimed they could be accused of tampering, which carried a US$250,000 fine. However, this was all hazy legal territory because contracts in Soviet hockey were a new phenomenon, having only been introduced after Fedorov's defection in 1990.

Oddly, no one in the Canucks' front office had contacted Ziegler in an effort to resolve Bure's situation. The NHL president first learned of the Russian's whereabouts on September 17, after the *Vancouver Sun* approached Darcy Rota, Ziegler's special assistant, for a comment on the matter. "He has heard nothing," Rota informed *Sun* reporter Elliott Pap. "He knew nothing about it. I had to tell him everything you told me," Rota said. "He just shook his head."

Three days later, a copy of Bure's Soviet contract reached the Canucks' headquarters. At first glance, Burke said it appeared to be a valid document. "If he's under contract for one more season, then our hands our tied. We're not allowed to interfere, both by law and the NHL rules." Burke went on to say that "Plan A has been to try to sign him if the contract is invalid. I don't know what Plan B is yet. One option would be to approach the Soviets about a transfer fee, but my interest in any type of transfer fee is extremely limited."

Salcer was confident the contract would be declared invalid. "It was signed under duress and it says nothing about his obligations. It says two years and 300, but it doesn't say 300 what. I mean, it could be 300 rocks. It doesn't say how much he gets paid, it doesn't say where he can go, it doesn't say what his obligations are. It doesn't even say what team he plays for."

The optimism displayed by Salcer wasn't shared by the Canucks' management, which had displayed no great sense of urgency about resolving the situation and getting Bure into uniform. If anything, from the curiously tepid nature of the Canucks' public statements, the club appeared to regard the young Russian as an unwelcome houseguest.

The reticence of Vancouver's management may have been influenced by its continuing difficulties with Vladimir Krutov. The Canucks wanted nothing more to do with Krutov after his first season, or with his newly hired agent, an aggressive, muscle-bound Ukrainian émigré named Vitaly Shevchenko, but ridding themselves of the rotund Russian proved problematic. The club balked at buying out the rest of his contract which, according to NHL bylaws, would have cost them two-thirds of Krutov's salary.

When the Canucks finally dropped Krutov from their roster in September 1990, they claimed he had broken his contract by failing to report to camp in good physical condition. Krutov responded by hiring Vancouver lawyer William Faminoff, who sued the Canucks for failing to uphold his contract. The suit, which was still pending when Bure arrived in North America, eventually went to arbitration in a Swedish court in February 1992. The Canucks came out on the short end of the verdict. The arbitrator ruled the Canucks were wrong to discontinue transfer payments, and they were ordered to pay $800,000 to Sovintersport, Central Army Sports Club and the Soviet Ice Hockey Federation. They were also forced to pony up nearly $500,000 in legal costs, making it one of the worst financial boondoggles in club history.

Judging by Quinn's comments about Bure at the time, the Krutov debacle was weighing on his mind. "I saw a fairly negative reaction when Kruts came in late with a big contract, and we can't allow something like this to happen again. Bringing in a player late can be disruptive."

Any hopes Bure and Salcer had of easily resolving the issue were dashed on September 27 when Ziegler informed the Canucks that, in his judgment, Bure had a valid contract with the Central Army club for the 1991–92 season. That same week the *Vancouver Sun* dispatched sports columnist Mike Beamish to Los Angeles to get a firsthand look at Bure. The day after Ziegler's ruling Beamish watched the two brothers practicing drills with their father at the Culver City rink. Mike Ramsey, a veteran NHL defenseman with the Buffalo Sabres, was also working out at the arena, rehabilitating a knee injury. Beamish asked Ramsey if he thought Bure was the genuine article. "Are you kidding?" Ramsey replied. "This kid's going to be awesome."

In the afternoon, Beamish accompanied the Bures to Manhattan Beach for Pavel's first North American photo session. Upper Deck, the California-based sports-card company, had assigned a photographer to get a picture of Bure to be used in an upcoming hockey-card set. He snapped some shots of the Russian clad in a blue T-shirt, blue shorts and Rollerblades. Next, after positioning Bure against the backdrop of the crashing surf, the photographer asked the youngster to slip on a Canucks jersey. Bure refused. To complicate matters, having grown bored with the posing, he now petulantly refused to smile for the photographer.

"At that point," Beamish recalls, "Vladimir walked over and gave Pavel a sharp slap across the face. Pavel began crying and walked away quickly, clearly humiliated by the scene. He had to go off by himself for about 20 minutes to compose himself."

A suddenly embarrassed Vladimir plunged into the sea and began swimming away. The photographer, realizing his work was done, began packing up his equipment. Salcer attempted to explain away the incident. "It hasn't been like this, really," he told Beamish. "Usually they're joking around together, having a good time. But this is kind of like a hump day. I think this waiting is just starting to get to everybody."

"Pavel was in a funk for the rest of the day," says Beamish, who remembers the entire experience as odd. "They refused to allow me to see where he was staying. I don't know why. During the afternoon, we were driving around in a van and I complimented Pavel on his recent marriage. But I also noticed he wasn't wearing a wedding ring, and I asked, 'Where's your ring?' He just gave me this stare and said, 'I don't want to talk about my personal life.' He was very, very wary. There was a Garbo-esque quality to him. I guess you could say he was an international man of mystery right from the start."

In an article that appeared in the *Sun* on September 28, Beamish recounted the photo-shoot fiasco and Salcer's growing disenchantment with the Canucks. Salcer said he couldn't understand why the club hadn't been more aggressive in pressing Ziegler for a decision and why it hadn't taken action to get Bure to Vancouver. The agent also claimed the Canucks had broken a promise to send Bure equipment and had failed to communicate regularly.

"When Brian Burke came down here, he said that it was his number-one priority to get this situation resolved as soon as possible," Salcer said. "But maybe being typical attorneys [both Burke and Quinn have law degrees] they're moving slowly to cover their asses. We're talking about a premier player who could be a star in Vancouver for the next decade. It's not as if the Canucks couldn't use him. For a team with their mediocre record over the years, you'd think the Canucks would be doing everything in their power to get him into the fold."

Quinn had made telephone calls to Salcer and Bure that weekend in an attempt to ease their feelings of rejection, but after reading Salcer's comments, Quinn was in a testy mood. He told reporters, "This has been a circus created by someone who doesn't know what the hell is going on. If people were only aware of different rules and procedures, there might be a different thing reported than what has been reported."

The Canucks insisted they could do nothing until the matter of Bure's contract with Central Army was resolved. However, their position was contradicted by Rota, who claimed the team had permission to discuss contract terms with Salcer as long as no deal was implemented before the dispute with the Soviets was settled.

The case didn't move forward until Bure launched a lawsuit in the United States against the Soviet Ice Hockey Federation in early October. The suit, filed by lawyer David Chardavoyne, alleged that Bure's contract with Central Army was invalid because it was signed under duress. Bure claimed he had been locked in a room by Red Army officers in August 1990 and threatened with a posting in Siberia unless he re-signed for three more years. When he refused, the Soviets wouldn't allow him to practice or play with the team.

The Soviets answered the complaint, which was a welcome development for Bure and the Canucks because at that point they had no legal means of pressuring the Soviets to come forward. It also meant the case would be fought on home territory—in a U.S. court. Behind the scenes, Burke began working toward a legal resolution. He researched the state that would be most likely to give a favorable verdict, and chose Michigan. "We gave Bure's agent US$25,000 for legal fees, we hand-picked the jurisdiction and we recommended the counsel," he says.

At the initial hearing, lawyer Howard Gourwitz, a tax attorney who was representing Central Army, asked for a delay in order to call officials from Russia to rebut Bure's charges. Wayne County Circuit Court Judge Kathleen MacDonald granted his request, adjourning proceedings until October 30. However, because the case was now in litigation, the Canucks were free to offer Bure a conditional contract.

In the meantime, the Bures had vacated Los Angeles and moved to Spokane, Washington, where Valeri was trying to get permission to join the Spokane Chiefs of the Western Hockey League. The connection had been made through Salcer, who was a friend of Bobby Brett, co-owner of the Spokane franchise and the brother of baseball star George Brett.

When the hearing regarding the validity of Bure's Soviet contract reconvened at the end of October, Central Army manager Valeri Gushin was on hand to give the Soviets' side of the story. By a strange coincidence, the Buffalo Sabres were in Detroit for a game with the Red Wings on October 30, and Bure had dinner with Fedorov and Mogilny, his two former linemates.

Although a solution to the dispute was near, the Canucks, who still hadn't agreed to terms with Salcer on a contract for Bure, now had a new concern. If Judge MacDonald ruled that the Russian was free and clear of his Central Army contract, Vancouver would retain Bure's rights for only 15 days. If he didn't agree to terms within that time, Bure would become a Group IV free agent and would be free to entertain offers from other NHL teams. If he accepted any of those offers, the Canucks would have to match the price to retain his rights.

In a bid to protect themselves and halt or delay the possibility of Bure signing with a rival team, the Canucks had hired a second set of lawyers, who were prepared to contest any such ruling by MacDonald and argue on behalf of the Soviets and the validity of their contract with Bure. In this bizarre legal game, the Canucks were paying two sets of legal teams to prepare winning arguments for opposite sides of the issue.

Burke characterizes those days as "probably the most difficult work of my life. I'd begin discussing the case with the two sets of lawyers at 7:00 in the morning and it would continue on until supper time. Then, in the evening, I was on the phone with Salcer, negotiating Bure's contract, sometimes until 2:00 or 3:00 A.M."

Finally, on October 30, Burke told Salcer: "Either we come to an agreement tonight or else we [Canucks management] go in tomorrow on the side of the Russians." Later that night they came to terms.

In court the next day, after hearing the opposing arguments, it was clear to Judge MacDonald that this was essentially a dispute over money. The Russians knew they weren't going to get Bure back and were now more interested in what they could squeeze out of the Canucks in the form of American greenbacks. Rather than deliver a ruling, MacDonald asked the two sides to work out a compromise.

Burke, Bure, six attorneys and three translators spent six hours haggling like carpet merchants in a room on the 11th floor of Detroit's

City-County Building. The initial proposals were miles apart. The Soviets asked for $800,000 in transfer fees; the Canucks offered $25,000. Eventually bartering brought them closer. The Soviets came down to $300,000 and the Canucks went up to $200,000. But when it appeared neither side would budge from its position, an impasse that might have delayed the case indefinitely, Bure stood up in court and said he would make up the $50,000 difference out of his own pocket. As he made his proposal, Burke turned to Bure's lawyer and said, "What the hell is he doing? Tell him to sit down and shut up." Bure's response? "He completely ignored me," Burke recalls.

With Bure's proposal on the table, Judge MacDonald said to the Soviet delegation, "You have an offer of $250,000. I strongly recommend that you accept it." The Soviets, noting the conviction in her voice, agreed.

Salcer, who was in Boston attending an arbitration hearing with another of his clients, defenseman Gary Galley, may not have approved of Bure's move, but Bure's lawyer David Chardavoyne said, "I think this is the best thing for the young man. He was so desperate he was willing to spend some of his own money to play in the NHL."

Burke agrees that it was a noble gesture, but notes, "Pavel never had to pay the $50,000. When [Canucks owner] Frank Griffiths heard about it, he said, 'Pay the money.'"

The Soviets were satisfied with the result, since this was the first time they had received such a large lump-sum payment for a player. As a face-saving measure and as a prerequisite to the deal, they were also able to obtain the acknowledgment that Bure's contract was legitimate.

For Judge MacDonald, who had the task of mediating this peculiar dispute—between a Russian hockey player, a primitive one-page Soviet document and an NHL hockey team—it was a legal first. But MacDonald left no doubt that she was a sports fan. When the case was settled, she approached Bure to shake his hand and wish him well in his career. "I'd like to see you play someday," she said. "But you can't beat the Red Wings, though."

Immediately afterward, Burke called his staff to tell them Bure was coming. Later that day he revealed to reporters that Bure and the team had reached agreement on a four-year contract. Although the Canucks didn't release any figures, the Vancouver media reported that the four-year pact would pay Bure $2.7 million. Including a signing bonus of $800,000 and another $200,000 in legal expenses, the total package was actually worth in excess of $3 million. The deal made the Russian rookie the second-highest-paid player on the team, behind captain Trevor Linden, who had just signed a four-year $3.7 million deal.

Shortly afterward, Quinn was asked to comment on the team's newest recruit. The Canucks' hockey boss expressed caution. "Many people in hockey say he is a world-class player. Now we have to consider how we'll develop his talent. We hope it won't upset the chemistry of our team. Our players are well-paid professionals and their goal is to win hockey games. They can't control who is in the dressing room."

The news of Bure's signing didn't escape CBC-TV commentator Don Cherry, who did his bombastic best to stir the pot on his "Coach's Corner" segment a few days later during the *Hockey Night in Canada* telecast. "He's making $700,000," Cherry barked. "Think of Cliff Ronning getting $160,000 and he's leading the team in scoring, and he's fourth in the league in scoring. Think of Odjick—Gino! Gino! Gino! Everybody yells it out there—good Native kid, making $130,000. All right, think about this. Gino—you're watching this, I know you're watching it out there—if a guy is capable of making $700,000, he's capable of taking care of himself. Right, Gino boy?"

Burke and Bure met the following day at the Canadian immigration offices in Seattle to process Bure's Canadian work permit. Burke had intended that they would fly to Vancouver, but when a Vancouver TV crew showed up in Seattle, he changed his mind. "I figured it would be best to avoid all the media that would be waiting at the airport," he says. "So, I just got a rental car and drove him to Vancouver."

What did the two talk about on the trip? "He spent the entire time working on his English," Burke recalls. The conversation, as he recounts it, went something like this.

"What's that?" Bure asked.

"A river."

"What's that?"

"A truck."

They arrived in time to attend the Canucks' game against the St. Louis Blues that evening. Bure was escorted up to the Canucks' executive suite at the Pacific Coliseum, where he met Quinn and vice chairman Arthur Griffiths. An impromptu news conference was held in the media lounge. Bure was introduced and Griffiths gave him a Canucks sweater to put on. Bure's face lit up in a radiant smile. The vibration was entirely positive, but some observers were still skeptical. For a savior, Bure looked awfully young and small.

*Vancouver Sun* hockey reporter Iain MacIntyre remembers the scene as chaotic: "It was a media scrum more than anything else, with camera lights blazing and everyone trying to ask questions at the same time. A Russian woman was handling the translation. Bure looked like a spooked deer. You got the definite sense that all he wanted to do was to get out of that room."

The clamor worried Canucks management. Expectations were being raised, perhaps to unrealistic heights. Vancouver assistant coach Ron Wilson observed, "It's not fair of the press to say he's a savior at this stage. He's so young and he hasn't played in six months. We have to have patience and his talent will come through. He's got speed and speed kills. You can't have too much of it. He'll be a fun player."

Bure suited up for his practice the next day. The morning skate, which was held at Britannia Ice Rink, a small community arena in Vancouver's east end, attracted a standing-room-only crowd of 2,000 excited spectators. When members of the Canucks' publicity department began handing out some photos of Bure, there was a near-riot to get the souvenirs. "Our people were getting mauled," Burke admits. "We were totally unprepared for it. They mobbed Bure after the practice. We finally had to push him into a car and speed away."

The next day the Canucks took Bure to the University of British Columbia to have him physically evaluated. The five-foot-nine 170-pound Russian astounded them by bench-pressing a 200-pound barbell 14 times, a feat that only the team's biggest and strongest players could match. His anaerobic and aerobic capacities were superb, and his body-fat ratio registered a remarkable 5.8 per cent. "Most males fall in the 15- to 18- per-cent range," explained Ted Rhodes, the UBC sports scientist who did the testing. "We try to get the Canucks players down to about 10 per cent. Bure's numbers were comparable to an Olympic athlete. He's a remarkable physical specimen." But it wasn't simply Bure's test scores that impressed Rhodes. "He has the attitude you want. He came in here in an attack mode."

For his part, Bure, who had last played competitively in August during exhibition games with the Soviet national team, claimed he wasn't near his physical peak. "Of course, I don't have good shape right now. I'm probably 50 per cent." Although Bure was chafing at the bit, Quinn opted to have him practice again with the team before joining the line-up. On November 3, he sat in the press box and watched the Canucks thump the Edmonton Oilers 7–2. Igor Larionov, who had been pointless in nine games at that point, counted a hat trick. The decision to have Bure sit out the game was influenced by the fact the Canucks were retiring Stan Smyl's number 12 that night in a special pregame ceremony, and Quinn didn't want to detract from that event.

After the Edmonton game, as Bure headed downstairs to meet his new teammates, he was surprised when the people lining the corridor not only recognized him, but burst into spontaneous applause. He was even more astonished the next night when, while driving around with Salcer, he stopped to ask a passerby for directions to a restaurant and the man said, "Hey, I know who you are. You're Pavel Bure."

The victory over the Oilers improved Vancouver's record to 6–2–1 and put the club alone in first place in the NHL's Smythe Division. With the team firing on all cylinders, it was decided Bure would get his first taste of NHL action on November 5 versus the Winnipeg Jets.

Asked for his thoughts on his NHL debut, Bure said through translator Serge Levin, "It should be a very difficult game for me. I will try my best, but I can't be sure." Asked if he thought he could score a goal in his first game, Bure replied, "It is my dream to score in every game, not only tomorrow night. I can't promise anything, but I will try."

"He's very nervous," said Larionov, who was putting Bure up with his wife and two daughters at his North Vancouver home. "I've tried to talk to him about the physical play. I think he'll be ready."

The waiting game was over. The big time beckoned.

# CHAPTER SIX

# Rocket Launch

*Hitting Pavel Bure is like trying to hit a ray of sunshine.*
HARRY NEALE, HOCKEY ANALYST AND FORMER NHL COACH

A BONE-CHILLING RAIN pounded down on the people hurrying toward the doors of the Pacific Coliseum. The onset of another long, dark winter is normally cause for depression in Vancouver, but the atmosphere around the Coliseum on the night of November 5, 1991, crackled with excitement. Despite the evil weather, scalpers were out in force, demanding and getting double and triple value for their tickets. By game time, the crowd would number 16,123, a complete sellout. The anticipatory buzz had nothing to do with the visiting team. The Winnipeg Jets were merely background music. Everyone had come to get a look at this mysterious, blue-eyed kid from Moscow.

The long, drawn-out dance that had preceded Bure's arrival had only heightened the sense of curiosity and expectation. For long-suffering Canucks fans, the Russian represented hope. With the exception of Eric Lindros, Bure was reputed to be the best player in the world outside the

NHL. If his press clippings could be believed, Bure had the potential to be the star who might finally lead Vancouver out of the wilds of mediocrity. Spectators came to the Coliseum on this stormy night like pilgrims to Lourdes, looking for a sign from the hockey gods that their prayers would be answered.

Today virtually every Vancouver hockey fan claims to have been at the Coliseum or else to have watched the contest on television. The latter is impossible. The game wasn't televised. Pat Quinn, who many remember standing behind the bench, was in New York City attending a league meeting. Instead, assistant Rick Ley subbed as coach. Bure played without a face shield. He didn't don his familiar visor until several games later. The Russian wore number 10, but it wasn't his first choice. He had requested 96, but Quinn, who had a distaste for high numbers, vetoed it. Bure's jersey appeared to be too big for him, perhaps because it was so often inflated with wind.

Bure lined up for the opening faceoff on the right wing of a line with left winger Greg Adams and center Trevor Linden. It was essentially an excuse to have the rookie introduced and receive a round of welcoming applause. After a 40-second shift, he returned to his assigned spot with Ryan Walter and Gino Odjick on the fourth unit. In truth, it didn't matter who was paired with Bure. After just two practices and with only a faint grasp of English and even less of the NHL game, he was essentially playing solo. Walter's duties as Bure's center were simple: "Give him the puck with speed and then go to the net."

Unlike Mario Lemieux, who scored on his first NHL shift, or Alexander Mogilny, who turned on the red light only 20 seconds into his NHL debut, Bure made no splashy entry into the record books. He didn't score in the game and didn't pick up an assist or a penalty. In fact, there is nothing in the statistical summary to indicate he did anything memorable. But the Russian left an indelible impression. In the words of *Vancouver Sun* columnist Archie McDonald, "Bure raised goose pimples so big you could scrape carrots on them."

Every time Bure touched the puck, a murmur went through the building. Anyone could see this kid was a dangerous entity. But it wasn't only his skill that impressed people; it was his pedal-to-the-metal style of play that got everyone's blood pumping. He attacked the Jets' defense with reckless abandon. There was no hint of intimidation, no sense of being awed by the moment. It was a high-adrenaline symphony.

Bure made three jaw-dropping rushes. The first, which occurred early in the second period, was the most spectacular. After corralling the puck deep in his own end, he headed up ice, weaving past Jets defenders in the neutral zone and hurtling toward the Winnipeg defense. Just before he reached the Jets' blueline, he momentarily lost control of the puck. At that point, Bure did something magical. Without slowing down, he kicked the puck back up to his stick *behind his back*. The move froze the Jets' defense, and Bure burst through, heading toward goalie Rick Tabaracci at warp speed. There was a flurry of close-in dekes, an unsuccessful attempt to stuff the puck between Tabaracci and the post, followed by a tumble into the boards. By the end of the rush, the crowd was on its feet, roaring in unison.

Global TV sports anchor Barry Macdonald, who was then with CBC, was in the studio that night, preparing his script for the late sports report. CBC had an in-house feed from the Coliseum, a single camera following the puck that the network used for highlights. Macdonald had trouble focusing on his work: "I couldn't take my eyes off the screen. In that first rush, he did just about everything a player can do on the ice, except score. He went coast-to-coast in a heartbeat. It was the single most electrifying play I'd ever seen." Watching replays of the rush, Macdonald was struck by the reaction of the crowd. "People had their hands held up to their faces, and they were looking at their neighbors with this expression of stunned disbelief."

Macdonald's impressions were confirmed when veteran cameraman Rick Warren returned to the studio following the game. "You have to understand," Macdonald says, "that cameramen tend to be a pretty jaded lot. They've seen it all and are hard to impress. Well, Rick came in all red in the face and the first thing he says is, 'Jesus Christ! I've never had anyone like that in my viewfinder in my entire life.'"

Tom Larscheid, radio colorman for the Canucks broadcast on CKNW, remembers the roar of the crowd rising in volume as Bure raced down the ice, until it finally reached a frenzied crescendo as he reached the Jets' net. "He literally lifted people out of their seats," Larscheid says. "I had never witnessed anything like that at the Coliseum."

As Iain MacIntyre of the *Vancouver Sun* notes, "Before he played there was still a lot of skepticism about Bure. He'd gotten a huge contract by Canucks' standards, the largest ever offered to a rookie. We were all wondering if he could possibly live up to the hype. He dispelled any such fears in that one rush."

One rush would have been enough, but there were two more sorties from Bure, each effort leaving a trail of Jets flailing in his wake like turnstiles, and each one resulting in a clear chance on the net. Both times, Tabaracci stopped him.

Bure's speed was stunning. Faced with such velocity, the Jets seemed at a loss how to stop him. In a fit of frustration, Winnipeg winger Doug Evans attempted to slow down the Russian by massaging his face with his stick. The blatant foul earned Evans a five-minute major and a game misconduct. The Canucks failed to capitalize on the power play, and despite a wide edge in play, only managed to salvage a 2–2 tie on a rare goal by plodding defenseman Robert Dirk. Coach Ley later blamed the Canucks' ineffectiveness on the dust storm Bure had stirred up. The Vancouver players had been as mesmerized by the rookie as the crowd.

After the game, Dirk, the game's unlikely goal-scoring hero, said, "Man, can that kid skate. I'm just glad he's on our team and I don't have to play against him."

Asked for his thoughts on his NHL debut, Bure said through interpreter Serge Levin, "It was very exciting. I will remember this day all my life. It was beautiful. Beautiful."

The next day's newspaper accounts were glowing. Even Tony Gallagher, the *Province's* resident curmudgeon and most persistent Canucks critic, was moved to exclaim, "Hip hip Bure." Gallagher praised Bure's performance and noted that "win or lose, the prospect of watching this fellow for the next 10 years would have to bring a smile even to the kisser of Don Cherry."

MacIntyre began his game account in the *Sun* by asking, "If Winnipeg are the Jets, then what do you call Pavel Bure? How about the Rocket? It fits Bure perfectly. He is the fastest Soviet creation since Sputnik." MacIntyre hadn't actually put the two R words together, but he had planted the seed. Before long everyone was calling Bure the Russian

Rocket. With its rolling alliteration and dual allusions to Cold War weaponry and supersonic speed, the moniker had an irresistible appeal.

Although he showed flashes of speed in his second game against Wayne Gretzky and the Kings in Los Angeles, Bure did nothing extraordinary as the Canucks won 4–3. He picked up his first NHL point in his third game, assisting on a goal by Cliff Ronning, as the Canucks thumped the New York Islanders 6–0 at the Pacific Coliseum.

Bure notched his first NHL goal in his fourth game when Vancouver hosted Los Angeles on November 12. After intercepting an errant pass by defenseman Brian Benning, he darted in on goalie Daniel Berthiaume and beat the Kings' netminder with a backhander at 7:17 of the second period. The crowd erupted in cheers and Bure, arms raised above his head, jumped for joy. Bure's unassisted tally ignited the Canucks, who rifled in four goals in a span of 98 seconds in an 8–2 mauling of the Kings. He added a second goal at 18:12 of the third period on a setup from Ronning and Sergio Momesso. After the game, the Russian rookie was beaming. "My first NHL goal. I'm so excited. I just hope I can sleep tonight."

The Canucks didn't lose with Bure in the lineup until November 19, when the New York Rangers edged them 4–3 at the Coliseum to snap a seven-game undefeated streak. Despite the loss, a quarter of the way through the season, Vancouver boasted the best record in the NHL. It was a remarkable turnaround for a team that had barely made the playoffs the previous year.

The Canucks' early-season success inspired giddy euphoria in Vancouver, where a winning hockey team was as rare as a sunny day in December. Since its creation in 1970, the franchise had been a study in failure. The team entered the 1991–92 campaign riding a streak of 15 consecutive losing seasons, the longest run of futility in NHL annals and only one year shy of the longest losing streak in the history of North American professional sports—16 consecutive losing seasons—set by baseball's Philadelphia Phillies from 1933 to 1948.

The lone highlight in Canucks history, their miraculous run to the Stanley Cup finals in 1982, had been a mere blip on the landscape. The team quickly reverted to its doormat status. When Pat Quinn took over as Vancouver's general manager in 1987–88, he faced a monumental rebuilding task. "It was harder than I anticipated," he told the *Vancouver*

*Sun.* "I'd always been a person who looked forward to the next day. But when I came in, I saw athletes and an organization that couldn't get its chin off the ground."

In Quinn's first four years at the helm, the Canucks showed only marginal improvement. With time running out on his five-year plan, Quinn added a new title to his portfolio when he fired Bob McCammon on January 31, 1990, and went behind the bench. Although the Canucks' revival coincided with Quinn's first full year as coach, the sudden transformation was really the result of a series of shrewd trades that Quinn had engineered within the span of a year. With the exception of Doug Lidster, the Canucks' entire defense had been revamped with other teams' castoffs: Jyrki Lumme from Montreal in March 1990 for a second-round draft pick; Gerald Diduck from Montreal in January 1991 for a fourth-round draft pick; Dana Murzyn from Calgary in March 1991 for Ron Stern and Kevan Guy; Dave Babych from Minnesota for Tom Kurvers in June 1991. Midway through the 1991–92 season, Quinn added veteran Randy Gregg to the mix, getting the five-time Stanley Cup winner to return from retirement.

But Quinn's greatest coup was the March 1991 fleecing of St. Louis, in which the Canucks acquired forwards Cliff Ronning, Sergio Momesso, Geoff Courtnall and defenseman Robert Dirk in exchange for Garth Butcher and Dan Quinn. That trade supplied much-needed depth to the forward lines. Five other forwards—Trevor Linden, Jim Sandlak, Petr Nedved, Gino Odjick, Gary Valk and Igor Larionov— came via the draft route. Ryan Walter was signed as a free agent in July 1991. Tom Fergus was acquired on waivers from Toronto in December 1992. Those players, along with winger Greg Adams and goalie Kirk McLean, acquired from New Jersey in 1989, made up the team. Bure's arrival in November was the icing on the cake. He gave the club that rare commodity: a game-breaker.

Not only did Bure add a new dimension to the Canucks' offense, his presence helped to rejuvenate the play of Larionov. Prior to Bure's arrival, Larionov was in a fog. He hadn't scored a point in his first nine games of the season and he had been benched several times. As Quinn noted, "He was playing like a man whose career was over." But from November 1 to December 31, the cagey center scored at a clip of a point per game.

Two weeks after Pavel joined the Canucks, his brother, Valeri, made history by becoming the first Soviet player to play in Canada's major-junior-hockey system. Because Valeri was also technically the property of Central Army, the Canadian Amateur Hockey Association initially refused to provide clearance for him to play. But after the Spokane Chiefs prepared to file a court injunction, the CAHA backed down.

With his father and brother in Spokane and his mother still in Moscow, Bure was suddenly on his own, a stranger in a strange land. For his first two weeks in Vancouver, Bure lived with the Larionovs and their two young daughters. "They helped me with everything," Bure told Jim Taylor in *Sports Only*. "I couldn't even call a cab myself because I didn't know the words." Learning English was a struggle. "If I didn't know the word, I would ask. Like, 'What is that? Fork? What is fork?' And they show me and I say, 'Fine, that is fork.' Sometimes I would write them down to remember. I learn sometimes three words a day, sometimes five."

Bure's lack of English created a gulf between him and his teammates. In 1991 Russian players were still a novelty in North America, and NHL dressing rooms weren't the most enlightened sectors of society. It is easy to imagine there was some resentment toward the rookie because of his big contract. One Canucks player who attempted to reach out to Bure was 21-year-old Gino Odjick, a six-foot-three, 215-pound Algonquin from the Kitigan Zibi reserve near Maniwaki, a Quebec lumber town north of Hull. Odjick came from an unusual family. In addition to their own six children, his parents, Joe and Giselle, had raised another 38 foster children on their big, rambling farmhouse at Kitigan Zibi.

Odjick had been drafted 86th overall by the Canucks in 1990 because of his size and toughness. In two years with the Laval Titans of the Quebec Major Junior Hockey League, he had compiled 558 minutes in penalties in 101 games, plus another 129 minutes in 16 playoff games, and had earned the nickname the Algonquin Assassin. In his first game with Vancouver on November 21, 1990, Odjick made a vivid impression on the local citizenry by dropping the Chicago Blackhawks' hulking enforcer, Stu "The Grim Reaper" Grimson, with an overhand right.

Physically Bure and Odjick were an unlikely pairing. The Russian was small and fair with cherubic, teen-idol features. Odjick was large, dark and menacing. He resembled the sort of character loan sharks send around to collect on overdue debts. It was generally assumed their relationship was based on the same dynamic that had once existed between the Edmonton Oilers' Wayne Gretzky and Dave Semenko—the superstar and his bodyguard. But the bond ran much deeper. What they shared in common was their status as cultural outsiders. They both came from places far removed from the Canadian mainstream. As Odjick noted about Bure in Roy MacGregor's *The Home Team,* "He's from another country. He gets lonesome. He had no one at all." Odjick, who is a far more sensitive and softhearted individual than his on-ice demeanor suggests, found Bure's honesty refreshing. "He tells it the way it is, and that's it. There's no pretense. He won't buddy-buddy up to anyone unless it's sincere."

As electrifying as Bure was with the puck, he had trouble scoring in his first month in the NHL. Despite a half-dozen breakaways, he hadn't scored on one yet. He invariably got in too close, attempting to literally stickhandle the puck into the net. But there was a general feeling that the goals would come. In the meantime, goals or not, in virtually every game Bure appeared capable of doing something people hadn't seen before.

"In many ways," the *Vancouver Sun*'s Iain MacIntyre says, "Bure's most special year was his first. He surprised so many other teams. In his first few months in the league, no team was able to cope with his speed. They were totally unprepared. It took teams a while to realize that if they simply stood up at the blueline, they were going to get beaten. They either had to try to slow him down in the neutral zone before he reached top speed or else the defensemen had to drop back and give him the shot."

Like many sportswriters, MacIntyre initially had trouble believing what he was seeing. "It was incredible. This was the NHL, the greatest league in the world, but even at this level, this 20-year-old kid was able to dominate and make veteran defensemen look like juniors."

"We'd seen them bring other guys in," Global TV's Barry Macdonald says. "Trevor Linden busting his ass, Stan Smyl, the Steamer, digging and banging in the corners. But we'd never had what Bure brought to the ice—ever. In 23 years, the Canucks had never had a superstar that could lift you out of your seat, never had a player who you went to see. I was raised in Vancouver and had always been a Canucks fan. We rooted for the home team, but we always went to see the guys on the other team, the [Guy] Lafleurs and the [Bobby] Orrs. This was different. Now we finally had a star of our own."

Bure moved into his own apartment in a downtown high-rise overlooking False Creek. He obtained a driver's license, purchased a car and began taking English lessons. Late in November, his mother arrived from Moscow. She was accompanied by Elena, Bure's Russian girlfriend.

Early in December, Quinn put Bure on a line with two players who could better complement his offensive skills: center Larionov and left winger Greg Adams. Both were strong skaters. Adams possessed the strength and grit needed to battle for the puck in the heavy-traffic areas around the net and in the corners, and Larionov could handle the puck and pass with a jeweler's precision. The line clicked immediately in a 3–0 win over Montreal, as Adams recorded a hat trick.

After their early-season surge, the Canucks hit a lull in December, losing four of five games. But the club pulled out of the dive. By the end of the month, after recording back-to-back wins on the road against San Jose and Los Angeles, Vancouver was alone in first place by 10 points.

The December 31 game with the Kings highlighted the Canucks' newfound mettle. Despite trailing 2–0 after two periods, they refused to wilt and rallied to tie the score. Even after falling behind again 3–2, they retained their focus, eventually rolling to a 5–3 victory. Bure got the game winner, his first goal in eight games, snapping home a wrist shot from 25 feet.

It had been a frustrating month for Bure, who couldn't find the back of the net. He had nine shots against Montreal, eight against San Jose and seven against Philadelphia without earning a single point. After the Flyers game, Quinn noted with some irritation, "Pavel is holding the puck too long. He holds it and holds it and holds it. He's getting in too deep on the attack and by now teams have a book on him." Bure was worried enough to ask Larionov if he thought the team might demote him to the minors. Larionov assured him they wouldn't. He told him to be patient, that the goals would come. "I room with him on the road and he's a good kid, but this is a tough time for him," Larionov said. "He's getting a feel for what the NHL game is like.

Part of the learning process was adjusting to the level of violence and being aware of the opposition teams' loose cannons. Every NHL team had a goon, a player whose primary role was stirring up trouble. Canadian players were indoctrinated into the culture of intimidation in the junior ranks, but Soviet players had to learn on the job. Before a game in San Jose in late December, Bure asked Odjick, "Gino, who is the crazy guy on this team?"

Because he was a scoring threat, and simply because he was a Russian, Bure was a prize target. For years Canadian hockey players had perceived Russians as the enemy. Those attitudes hadn't changed overnight. When asked to comment on Bure's speed, Chicago Blackhawks defenseman Chris Chelios replied, "We'll see how well he skates with a stick up his ass."

In early January, when the *Vancouver Sun* published its midterm report cards on the Canucks' players, there were far more As and Bs than in years past. Bure received a B. "The Russian Rocket gets an A in excitement, skating and ability to create scoring chances. But lack of finish (six goals in 79 shots) and defensive-zone coverage need improvement before he can join Linden and Ronning at the head of the class. Needs to shoot more and stickhandle less."

As well as the Canucks had played, the most crucial stretch of their season still lay ahead. January and its long eastern road swing had always been the Canucks' Waterloo. No Vancouver team had ever played .500 hockey during that dreaded month. This January's schedule was especially daunting. The team would play 11 games in total, seven of them on the road, including five road games in nine days.

But this was a different Canucks team, more talented and resilient than those in the past. The club exceeded all expectations, going 7–3–1 in the month, and concluded the road trip with five straight wins against Winnipeg, Edmonton, Quebec, Detroit and St. Louis. In the 4–2 win over Winnipeg, Bure recorded three assists, setting up the tying goal by Adams and the winner by Larionov. On the tying goal, Bure led the Jets' defenders on a merry chase around the Winnipeg zone before deftly feeding a pass to Adams in the slot. In the Canucks 5–3 victory over the Nordiques, the Larionov line accounted for 10 points, with Bure getting a goal and two assists.

Even though the Canucks lacked an effective power play, their superb performance at even strength carried them through the winter. Cities such as Philadelphia, Montreal and Chicago, graveyards for past Vancouver teams, no longer inspired terror. By March, it was the Canucks and their brilliant rookie winger who were generating fear in other teams.

On March 12, the Canucks downed the New Jersey Devils 2–1 to set a new franchise record for most wins in a season with 38. Bure set up the first goal by Ronning on the power play and then scored a stunning third-period goal to win the game. While cruising across the top of the faceoff circle, he casually tipped Adrien Plavsic's hard pass, directing the puck into the net over the shoulder of startled goalie Chris Terreri. After the game, Devils coach Tom McVie said about Bure: "This kid is frightening. I'm glad he plays in the Smythe Division and we only play them three times a year. I thought Fedorov was fast, but this kid is even quicker. He's one of the best young players I've seen in a long, long time."

McVie's reaction wasn't unique. Bure was a special player. Just how special hit home for *Province* sportswriter Tony Gallagher late that winter. "It was just before the trading deadline and the Coliseum was crawling with scouts and GMs. Bure was putting on a spectacle, making those amazing moves of his, and I looked over and the scouts were eating it up, laughing and smiling and going on. You have to understand that this is never done. Scouts will sit and watch the greatest players and never show a trace of emotion. But they were just awed by this kid."

For long-suffering Canucks fans, everything seemed too good to be true. The team was cruising to a first-place finish. Then, suddenly, a black cloud rolled into view. On April 1, just four months after assuming control of the NHL Players' Association, Bob Goodenow led the first players' strike in NHL history. Despite the timing, this was no joke. Not only were the last few games of the regular season at stake, but the playoffs, as well. The dispute lasted an anxious 10 days before the two sides came to terms. The players won some improved free-agency provisions and also gained greater financial control over the licensing of hockey cards. But the timing of the strike was less about issues than it was about Goodenow's desire to establish the NHLPA as a force to be reckoned with in the future.

Vancouver concluded its best season in franchise history by splitting games with Los Angeles and Calgary. Bure, who had scored 22 goals in his last 23 games, potted one in the last game to tie Ivan Hlinka's club record for most points by a rookie (60 in 1981–82). Despite playing only 65 games, his 34 goals led the team. Had he been in the lineup from the start of the season, he likely would have scored 40. As it was, he ranked second in rookie scoring behind the New York Rangers' Tony Amonte, who notched 69 points on 35 goals and 34 assists in 79 games. Bure won two team awards—the Molson Cup for the most three-star selections and the award as the Canucks' most exciting player. Goalie Kirk McLean was voted team MVP.

The Canucks topped the Smythe Division with 96 points, the second-best total in the conference and fourth best in the NHL. They were the league's most improved team, having bettered its previous year's total by 31 points. The club set franchise records for wins (42) and points (96) and posted a winning road record for the first time. It had been a Cinderella season, but if the Canucks were to avoid turning into pumpkins they had to produce when it counted most—in the playoffs.

The Canucks' first-round opponent was the fourth-place Winnipeg Jets. The Jets had allowed fewer goals than any team in the division during the regular season, and they shut down Vancouver in the opener, winning 3–2. The Canucks' power play went zero for six and the team managed only five shots on net in the third period and just 19 shots overall, the first time since October 26—70 games ago—that it had been held to under 20 shots in a game.

Prior to the game, Vladimir, who had just watched Valeri play in the junior playoffs, warned Pavel that the NHL playoffs were a different type of hockey, but Pavel stubbornly disagreed, telling his father, "No, it's the same." After the first game, Pavel called Vladimir and told him, "You're right. It's different hockey."

After the game, several Vancouver reporters cornered a slight, dark-haired man in the Winnipeg entourage and began asking him questions. It was Igor Kuperman, the Russian journalist who had assisted the Canucks in establishing Bure's draft eligibility in 1989. Kuperman was now employed by the Jets. He had joined them in January to work in the club's media-relations department.

Kuperman, who is now the director of hockey information for the Phoenix Coyotes, says that the Vancouver reporters wanted to know how much the Canucks had paid him for his Moscow research. They didn't believe him when he told them, "Not a cent."

The Canucks played more physically in Game 2, taking the body and employing a dump-and-chase style. Yet despite outshooting the Jets 41–28, Vancouver only scratched out a 3–2 victory when Lumme took a third-period feed from Larionov and wired a shot over goalie Rick Tabaracci's shoulder into the top corner.

Back in Winnipeg in Game 3, it was the Jets who controlled the play in a 3–2 win. Vancouver's sputtering power play failed to convert in seven opportunities, including a five-minute major in the second period. Bure was a virtual nonentity. In the subdued Canucks dressing room after the game, he admitted he had never experienced such tight checking before. "I could not fly tonight. I only play so-so. It's my fault."

On *Hockey Night in Canada*, Don Cherry took another run at Bure, showing a video replay of the Russian kicking Keith Tkachuk's skates out from under him. "There, right there, see that?" Cherry barked. "You would never catch a Canadian kid doing that. Bure, ya little weasel."

Asked to comment on Cherry's broadside, the Russian replied blankly, "What is weasel?" Did Bure even know who Cherry was? "Sure, I watch him on television—Don Cherry, rock 'em, sock 'em hockey," he said, inadvertently giving Cherry's hockey video of the same name a plug. Cherry's comments angered the Canucks' fans, but they created a sudden bonanza for Vancouver entrepreneurs. Weasel Power T-shirts were for sale in the streets the next day.

Quinn juggled his lines in a bid to spark his team's sputtering offense in Game 4. Nedved was inserted into the mix, Courtnall was benched, Momesso replaced Adams on Bure's line, while Adams joined Ronning and Linden. But the changes had no effect as the Canucks went down 3–1. The difference was the performance of the two teams' power plays. The Jets went two for five on theirs, while the Canucks came up empty in three opportunities. Their success rate with the man advantage in the series was now a pitiful one for 23. Bure was held pointless for the third straight game.

The Canucks returned home with their backs to the wall, needing to win three straight games. Desperation proved to be the ideal wake-up call. The Canucks took the game to the Jets from the opening faceoff, storming the Winnipeg net and directing 19 shots at Tabaracci. By the 7:20 mark of the second period, they had scored five times and had driven the Jets' goalie from the nets, en route to an 8–2 triumph.

Vancouver's game plan included finding ways to get Bure the puck with speed. Part of the rookie's problem, Quinn felt, was that he was getting too far ahead of the play and then having to stop and wait for the puck to come to him. In an attempt to change that dynamic, Quinn introduced a new wrinkle. During a Vancouver power play, as the club brought the puck up the ice, Bure headed in the opposite direction, skating back into the Canucks' zone and circling behind the net. Then, like a horse charging through the home stretch, he came ripping down the wing to join the rush in the neutral zone. At that point, the puck carrier had the option of either hitting Bure with a pass in full flight or else using him as a decoy.

The play didn't produce a goal, but Bure, who had more jump in his stride, got things going late in the first period, fighting off Teppo Numminen's check and sliding a backhander under Tabaracci's pads. On the Canucks' second goal, Bure broke his stick on a slap shot, but the puck skittered to Jim Sandlak, who blindly whipped it home. Bure finished with a goal and three assists. Larionov chipped in with three helpers of his own. The snake-bitten Adams, despite 10 shots on net, failed to score.

Bure's improved play in a must-win game was an encouraging sign for the Canucks, but it cut him no slack with Cherry, who again used his platform on "Coach's Corner" to denounce the Russian Rocket. "Bure has one good game in five, so I figure next year he'll have 16 good games," Cherry said caustically. "Give me five Trevor Lindens against five Pavel Bures and we'll see who comes out on top."

Cherry's comments fell on deaf ears in Vancouver, where Bure's youthful good looks and flashy play had elevated him to superheated celebrity status. "Pavelmania," they called it. Just as a rock star drew groupies, Bure invariably attracted shrieking mobs of teenage girls. The attention grew so intense during the playoffs that the Canucks had an usher retrieve the Russian's car from the parking lot and drive it inside the building. Bure would then simply go from the dressing room to the car, and when the big gate had been lifted, run the gauntlet of fans from the safety of his Dodge Stealth in a scene similar to the Batmobile bursting out of the Batcave.

The two teams returned to Winnipeg for Game 6 and a sea of pulsing white pom-poms. The white noise increased when Tkachuk scored at the 5:03 mark of the first period. But Ronning replied with a breakaway goal just 32 seconds later to quell the crowd. Two minutes later Bure tuned down the volume even more, banging home a rebound to make it 2–1. Ronning, Linden and Tom Fergus scored in the second period to put Vancouver up 5–1. The Jets fought back with two goals, but the Canucks responded in kind, as Bure and Fergus both netted their second goals of the game to restore the four-goal bulge. Then, at 11:02 of the third period, Bure administered the coup de grâce. Sent in alone by Larionov, he fired a shot past Tabaracci to complete his first NHL hat trick, as Vancouver won 8–3.

Both clubs looked tight in Game 7. Bure had a chance to get Vancouver on the scoreboard when he went in on a breakaway six minutes into the contest, but he shot wide. The Canucks didn't get their first shots on net until midway through the first period, but they made them count. Dave Babych let fly a drive from the point, and Fergus slammed home the rebound. With McLean calmly manning the cage, Vancouver scored four more unanswered goals, including three from Courtnall, and breezed to a 5–0 victory.

It had been a heartbreaking series for the Jets, and Kuperman couldn't help but feel guilty. The work he had performed two years earlier on behalf of the Canucks had circled around like a cosmic boomerang and helped destroy his team's chances. Bure had been the difference. Today Kuperman still sounds wistful: "We couldn't stop him. Nothing we tried worked."

The Canucks advanced to face the Edmonton Oilers, who had defeated the Los Angeles Kings in the other division playoff. Although Edmonton had lost most of its players from its glory years in the mid-1980s, it still boasted a solid cast, headed by Vincent Damphousse, Bernie Nicholls, Esa Tikkanen, Joe Murphy and Kevin Lowe, and a stellar goalie in Bill Ranford.

Quinn had to make one lineup change for the Oilers series. Greg Adams had sustained a broken wrist when he was slashed by Mike Lalor in Game 6. He would be sidelined for the rest of the playoffs. Quinn moved Momesso into Adams's left-wing spot with Larionov and Bure.

The first game of the series was telling. The Canucks controlled play, firing 40 shots on Ranford, but the Edmonton goalie was at his acrobatic best. In the first period alone, he made several sensational stops, stoning Bure twice from the slot, robbing Sandlak from in close and foiling Adrien Plavsic on a breakaway. "For a period and half, Billy saved our bacon," Oilers coach Ted Green said.

Despite being closely guarded by Tikkanen and Kelly Buchberger, Bure had seven shots on goal, and when he buried Sandlak's pass to put Vancouver up 3–2 at 12:45 of the third period, Vancouver looked to be on its way. But two minutes later Courtnall left Damphousse unattended near McLean and he converted a pass from Murphy to send the game into overtime. Early in the extra frame, Babych tried to make a risky clearing pass up the middle of the ice. The puck ended up on Murphy's stick, and the Edmonton center calmly walked in on McLean and drilled a laser beam to the top corner. The goal completed the hat trick for Murphy and put the Canucks behind the eight ball. They had squandered the first game on two defensive miscues and had lost the home-ice advantage.

The Canucks' spirited play in Game 2 was reminiscent of their performance in the last three games of the Jets series. They dominated action in the first period, outshooting the Oilers 15–1 and scoring three times on Ranford. The Oilers' netminder, who had been injured when he took a slap shot in the shoulder, left the game after the period. Edmonton failed to mount a counterattack and the Canucks won 4–0 to even the series.

Any illusions the Canucks had of steamrollering the Oilers were dispelled in Game 3 in Edmonton. With the advantage of the last change, Oilers coach Ted Green was better able to match lines and shut down Larionov's unit with his checking trio of Tikkanen, Buchberger and Craig MacTavish. Murphy notched another hat trick, and the Oilers skated to a 5–2 win.

The Canucks came out flying in Game 4, firing 19 shots at Ranford in the first period, but couldn't break through. The game settled into a close-checking contest, and the Oilers eventually prevailed 3–2 on goals from Peter Klima, Tikkanen and Scott Mellanby. Ronning, with two, was the only Canuck to beat Ranford.

Returning home, down three games to one, the Canucks found themselves peering out of the same hole they had dug for themselves in the Winnipeg series. Playing inspired hockey in front of the hometown crowd, the Canucks jumped out to a 4–0 lead. But when they adopted a defensive posture in the second period, Edmonton rebounded to score three times. McLean was forced to make several saves in the last few frantic minutes to thwart the Oilers' comeback.

In order to win Game 6, the Canucks would need production from someone other than Ronning, who had scored twice in Game 5 to give him six goals in five games against the Oilers and eight in his last seven games. Larionov and Bure, who were now teamed with Momesso, missed Adams's presence on the wing, and Bure was growing exasperated by Tikkanen's hounding. The Finnish superpest was all over the Russian, hooking him, knocking him down and tugging on his sweater. The fact that Tikkanen, shadow to the stars, had been given the assignment was a supreme compliment to Bure, but it was one he had trouble appreciating.

With only one goal and an assist in the first five games of the series, the Russian Rocket was taking heat for his lack of offensive impact. The criticism, while understandable in light of his inspired performance against the Jets, was patently unfair. Few NHL teams expect a rookie to carry them in the playoffs. CBC-TV analyst Harry Neale tried to paint a bigger picture, noting, "I like the effort Bure gives when he doesn't have the puck. We all know what he can do when he thinks he can score, but he's killing penalties, he's checking, he's doing a lot of things. I don't want to knock Sergio Momesso, but they need a guy on his left side that the other team worries about or they'll just gang up on Pavel. They know Larionov isn't going to shoot, which is fine because he's a good player. But they need a speedster on the left wing—and I guess Greg Adams was the guy before he got hurt."

Determined to end the series on home ice, the Oilers came out with guns blazing in Game 6, outshooting the Canucks 18–3 in the first period and scoring twice. Lumme, who had been the Canucks' best defenseman all year, was the goat on both goals. On the first, he made an ill-timed pass to Larionov on a Canucks power play. MacTavish promptly stole the puck and beat McLean with a weak shot through the pads. On the second Edmonton goal, Lumme let Damphousse slip by him on the rush, then after McLean stopped Damphousse's initial shot, he failed to prevent the Oilers winger from cashing his own rebound.

The Canucks regrouped and pressed forward in the last two periods, but couldn't beat Ranford, who stopped 26 shots to record the goose egg. Tikkanen, Bure's nemesis, finished Vancouver off by sliding the puck into the empty net with 1:03 left in the game to complete a 3–0 win.

The Canucks went home bitterly disappointed. They had held a territorial edge in several games, but had committed costly defensive blunders and the opportunistic Oilers had made them pay. "I think everyone learned something," a distraught Linden said, "but the point wasn't to learn. The point was to win. The time to do it was now. We weren't thinking about next year."

The best season in Canucks history had ended on a sour note, but Bure had one more highlight ahead. At the NHL awards gala in June, he claimed the Calder Trophy as the league's outstanding rookie. It marked the first time that a Vancouver player had ever won an NHL award. As he accepted the Calder, Bure thanked Larionov, saying, "Iggy taught me everything about playing in the NHL. Iggy is awesome."

Quinn, who picked up the Jack Adams Trophy as coach of the year, praised his Russian rookie. "I watch him every day and he's not just a kid with skill, but a kid with determination and a work ethic. The best thing is, I think, is that he's only going to get better."

# CHAPTER SEVEN

# Portrait of Pavel

*Don't become a violin if you don't want to be stroked.*
RUSSIAN PROVERB

THE CALDER TROPHY HAD STAMPED an exclamation mark on Pavel
Bure's rookie year. In hockey terms, he had arrived. Regular readers of
the sports pages knew the basics of his story, they had seen his face,
heard his voice, watched him play, but as for his personality, little was
known. He had yet to consent to an in-depth interview. The Russian's
essence remained as hazy as a desert mirage.

Nature abhors a vacuum, and so does the media. Curious to know
more about Bure, John Keyes, the editor of *Vancouver* magazine, decided
to do a cover story on the Russian, sensing that his youthful good looks
could help sell a lot of copies of the magazine. Keyes asked me to write
the feature. He said he needed 3,000 words. They proved tough to find.

My initial problem was arranging an interview. The Canucks' offices
were closed because it was the off-season. Bure was in town, but no one
would give me his phone number. As it turned out, Bure was scheduled
to make an appearance to sign autographs at a sports-card show. I figured
I would simply approach him and ask him for an interview in person.

The card show was at the Agrodome, on the grounds of the Pacific National Exhibition. The arena, which was used for livestock shows in summer and hockey in winter, was jammed when I arrived. A half hour later, when Bure made his appearance, I realized that approaching him wasn't going to be a simple task. He needed an escort to force his way through the shrieking throng. Fortunately, after signing for an hour, Bure stopped for a lunch break and adjourned to a room beneath the stands. I found him inside, chowing down with his entourage, and explained that I wanted to do an interview. "How much time?" he wanted to know.

"An hour."

"Sure," he said. "Set it up with my dad." And he gave me Vladimir's number.

Vladimir didn't deliver Pavel, but he did agree to be interviewed himself. A stocky, tough-looking character with a bushy mustache, he revealed himself to have a droll, understated sense of humor. Chain-smoking and gesticulating, Vladimir admitted he was still having trouble adjusting to the reality of life in North America. Even simple things that we took for granted were new to him. He had never had an account in a bank, had never signed a check before, had never used a cash machine.

Vladimir had spent a good part of the previous hockey season in his car, driving around the northwest watching his youngest son play. "Kamloops, Victoria, Spokane, Portland. Never sleep. I meet with Valeri 10 minutes, then he's gone."

Vladimir hadn't seen Pavel's first Vancouver game because he hadn't acquired a Canadian visa yet. He saw his second game after driving all the way from Portland to Los Angeles. Watching Pavel play was difficult. "I'm all the time nervous inside," he admitted.

Vladimir was mystified by all the fighting he witnessed in North American hockey. "In boxing and karate, they wear gloves. Only in hockey they don't wear gloves. In the Western Hockey League, there is fight every five minutes. After three seconds in a game—a fight. Unbelievable. Between gooners, is okay, but sometimes you have a guy 200 pounds fight a guy 150 pounds. Who knows? Maybe somebody get killed." It was all quite strange to him. "I watch Canada Cup—no fights, but very strong hockey."

Vladimir was worried about the sudden wealth affecting Pavel. "Now Pavel is a big man, of course. He has his own apartment and his own account. I talk to Pavel all the time about the mental approach. Money is not bad, but the best motivation for a sportsman is to play well for the team. Always dream about winning. After the game, think about money."

Pavel, Valeri and Vladimir had attended the 1992 NHL Entry Draft on June 20 at the Montreal Forum. Valeri, who had distinguished himself during the WHL playoffs with Spokane, scoring 17 points in 10 games, was expected to be a fairly high draft pick. Vladimir hoped Vancouver would draft Valeri, so his sons could play together, but the Canucks took a Czech center named Libor Polasek with their first pick (21st overall). Quinn said the club intended to take Valeri in the second round, but Montreal erased that possibility by picking Valeri 33rd overall, seven picks before the Canucks, who then chose center Mike Peca from the Ottawa 67's. Vladimir told Valeri he shouldn't be disappointed because Montreal had "the best organization in the NHL."

It took a while, but my interview with Pavel was set up, arranged through the assistance of Canucks management. Bure agreed to talk at his apartment. There was a complication, though. He refused to attend a separate photo shoot. If the magazine wanted pictures, it had to take them during the interview session. Robert Karpa, the photographer, was less than pleased. Producing a photograph for a magazine cover was normally done in a studio, where light and background conditions could be easily manipulated. The scenario wasn't ideal—we were going to have to share our time with the star—but Karpa had it worse. He and his assistant had to carry in a stack of lights and equipment.

Bure met us at the door. He looked as if he had just strolled in off the beach. He wore a blue T-shirt, shorts, sandals and the talisman of professional athletes everywhere—a glittering gold chain. The healthy glow emanating from him was almost radioactive. His sinewy body resembled one of those anatomical diagrams one sees posted in a doctor's office. On the ice, surrounded by broad-boned giants, Bure appeared slight. In person, you could sense the power behind his explosive speed.

The vibrancy of his physical presence was totally at odds with the bland furnishings of his condo. The place had the feeling of a still life— anonymous and unlived in. There were no books, no magazines, no clutter. The wall clock was stuck at 11:45. The few personal touches were all hockey-related: a mounted hockey card, the shot of him on Rollerblades taken at Manhattan Beach; a photo taken with Evgeny Davydov of the Winnipeg Jets; and a picture of him posed with two of his hockey idols, Igor Larionov and Gordie Howe.

Bure had spent the off-season, as was his habit, in constant motion. There were two visits to Moscow, another to California, a Club Med holiday in Cancún, Mexico, a trip to Montreal to collect his Calder Trophy and a brief stop in Las Vegas to get a divorce. The divorce was one subject that wasn't up for discussion.

When Bure first arrived in Vancouver, he spoke virtually no English. Although his comprehension had improved, he was still uneasy with his halting command of the language. As a result, he had arranged to use a translator, a woman named Lindsay Novokshonoff. She was dressed in a business suit, sneakers and white sweat socks. Like a doting aunt, Novokshonoff fussed over Bure, calling him Pascha, the diminutive of Pavel. Seen in the light of her affection, he seemed very young.

I posed questions in English. Novokshonoff translated them into Russian. Bure responded in kind, and she supplied the answers in English. It made for a stilted interview, but then Bure didn't have much to say in either language. He proved as forthcoming about himself as Ted Kennedy was about the events at Chappaquiddick. Virtually every answer was shorter than the original question.

"What have you found to be different about the lifestyle in North America?" I asked

"Just about everything."

"What do you like to do in your spare time?"

"Hang out with my friends."

"Among the other NHL teams, which players have most impressed you?"

"All NHL teams have skilled players. There are too many to mention."

"What do you find to be the most surprising thing about the NHL?"

"That I had to wear a suit and tie to every game."

Hoping to draw him out, I asked Bure about Don Cherry, one of his most scathing critics. Bure said he paid no heed to people like Cherry. "They can throw dead wood at me."

"Excuse me," I said. "I'm not familiar with that expression."

"It's a Russian saying," explained Novokshonoff. "It means something like 'sticks and stones may break my bones, but words can never harm them.'"

Sensing my puzzlement, Bure elaborated. Novokshonoff tried again. "Oh, it has something to do with old and young trees. You enjoy the living ones and ignore the dead ones."

Don, the dead Cherry Tree.

In a previous interview, Bure had been quoted as describing the sensation of skating as akin to flying. I asked him what he meant by that.

Bure said he must have been misquoted, that he didn't see it that way. "I don't think about skating in a game. The object is to score goals. I'm totally focused on that. Skating is something that just comes. Some days it's easy and some days it's not. Who can say why?"

There were two cellular phones sitting on the table in front of Bure, and several times during the session he paused to place a call or answer an incoming one.

"Why do you need two phones?" I asked.

"One is car phone. Different numbers."

The cellular conversations were all brief and conducted in Russian. During one, Bure uttered the word *interview,* with the sort of inflection you might use if you found a dead insect in your soup.

The interview chugged on for an hour. I learned that Bure drove a Dodge Stealth that he was given as part of a promotional deal with a local car dealer, that he enjoyed action movies and that his first game with the Canucks was his greatest hockey thrill. Through it all, he remained reserved and enigmatic, regarding me with an insouciant gaze.

The one subject he did warm to was eating. He dearly loved Soviet food—borscht, Russian sausage, shish kebab and the distinctive heavy salads of his homeland. "The salads you eat here," he said, "in Russia, we would throw in the garbage." But despite his fondness for food, Bure admitted he got no thrill from cooking. "You work for two hours to get it ready, and then 10 minutes later it's gone."

Bure's guardedness made it difficult to get a fix on him. I had the sense he was capable of providing more illumination about himself but that it simply didn't interest him. It was a trait that would frustrate interviewers throughout his career. His attitude toward the media was typical of most Soviet players. In the closed society in which they were raised, it wasn't prudent to be candid with strangers.

It was also true that Soviet athletes had little preparation for dealing with the Western media. In Russia the relationship between players and the fans and the press corps was far more distant. As recently as the mid-1980s, loud cheering was forbidden in stadiums. Fans were permitted to clap, but anything more boisterous would earn them ejection from the arena and arrest by the militia that was always on hand to maintain order at games. Between periods the public-address announcer often reminded spectators to remain calm during the action so as not to violate the socialist sense of decorum. Nor was there ever any attempt to sell or package hockey to the masses. Soviet sports reporters customarily had to submit copies of their stories to the athletes they were writing about to get their signatures of approval before anything could be printed.

Bure proved to be equally uncomfortable posing for photos. He was good at conveying impassiveness, but not much else. Karpa's request that he remove his shirt for a shot was rejected, as was a suggestion that he lie on his bed. However, he did display some marketing savvy. As Karpa started clicking, the Russian Rocket suddenly looked down and then excused himself to change shorts. The ones he had been wearing bore an Adidas label. "No endorsement deal," he explained.

Karpa attempted to get Bure to flex his biceps and adopt a strongman pose. One of those shots was eventually chosen for the cover of the magazine. The intent was to convey a lighthearted sense of power, but the photograph revealed something else—a dark, mischievous gleam in Bure's eyes. He looked like Cupid, the beautiful winged boy of Roman mythology whose invisible arrows caused his targets to fall irrevocably in love.

Prior to leaving Russia in September 1991, Bure was regarded as the brightest
young star in the Soviet Union, and a cornerstone of the country's national team.

*Above, top:* Vladimir Bure fled Russia with his two hockey-playing sons, Pavel (right) and Valeri (left), in the fall of 1991 and came to North America in search of fame and fortune. I. UTKIN/ITAR-TAAS

*Above:* Happiness reigned in Vancouver when Bure donned a Canucks jersey at his first North American media conference on November 1, 1991, at the Pacific Coliseum. KEN OAKES/*VANCOUVER SUN*

*Facing page:* Bure earned his nickname, the Russian Rocket, in his first NHL game by bedazzling fans and the Winnipeg Jets alike with an astounding display of speed and daring. PETER BATTISTONI/*VANCOUVER SUN*

*Above:* A stranger in a strange land, Bure moved into a downtown condo shortly after arriving in Vancouver. Because he had few friends and spoke little English, his first NHL season was often a lonely experience. BILL KEAY/*VANCOUVER SUN*

*Facing page, top:* Bure capped his brilliant freshman season by capturing the Calder Trophy as the NHL's rookie of the year. The prestigious award earned him a $100,000 bonus. BILL BECKER/CANADIAN PRESS

*Facing page, bottom:* Even airborne, Bure is a scoring threat. Here he lines up a shot while being upended by an Edmonton Oilers defender. CHRIS RELKE

*Left:* Fending off a check from the New York Rangers' Sergei Zubov, Bure cuts in on goalie Mike Richter during Game 4 of the 1994 Stanley Cup finals. Bure led all players in goals during that year's playoffs. JON MURRAY/*PROVINCE*

*Below:* Throngs of well-wishers and autograph hounds have pursued Bure throughout his NHL career. The crush was especially intense during the 1994 playoffs when Bure's celebrity rose to new heights. JEFF VINNICK/ *VANCOUVER SUN*

*Following page:* During Bure's early career, his celebratory leap became a familiar sight in NHL arenas. The Russian Rocket scored 154 goals in his first three seasons. Only Mike Bossy and Wayne Gretzky have netted more. ARLEN REDEKOP/*VANCOUVER SUN*

CHAPTER EIGHT

# Great Expectations

*Success is not the result of spontaneous combustion.*
*You must set yourself on fire.*
FRED SHERO, FORMER NHL COACH

How many can he score? That was the question on everyone's mind as the Vancouver Canucks assembled for training camp in September 1992. The most common prediction was 50. Some said 60. After all, Bure had scored 34 goals the previous year in only 65 games, 22 of them in his last 23 games. When asked how many goals he thought he could score, Bure told *Vancouver Sun* reporter Iain MacIntyre, "Almost everyone comes up to me and says, 'Next season, 50 goals.' I say, 'I can't promise anything. It's difficult.' They say, 'Don't worry, it's a piece of cake.' But it isn't a piece of cake. Only a few players can score 50 goals. You never know what's going to happen. I feel a little bit of pressure. But these are nice people. They will understand if I do not score 50."

Bure may have overestimated the public's patience, but he was correct about one thing: only a few players can score 50 goals. Although the plateau no longer possessed the prestigious aura it had in the 1960s prior to expansion, scoring 50 goals was still a formidable feat. Only four NHLers had reached the half-century mark in 1991–92: Brett Hull (70), Kevin Stevens (54), Jeremy Roenick (53) and Gary Roberts (53).

Those confidently forecasting a 50-goal campaign for Bure were ignoring a couple of key details—there had been no sophomores in the 50-goal club the previous three years, and high-scoring rookies typically had trouble bettering their performances in their second seasons. The sophomore jinx was no myth. Of the 30 players in NHL history who had notched 34 goals or more in their freshman seasons, only 10 had increased their counts in their second years. Gilbert Perreault, Steve Yzerman and Dale Hawerchuk had failed to do it. Wayne Gretzky had raised his total by a mere four goals, Mario Lemieux by five. The only two rookies to up their totals by more than 10 goals were Mike Bossy and Jimmy Carson. Bossy had vaulted from 53 to 69, a jump of 16. Carson had jumped from 37 to 55, an increase of 18. To reach 50, Bure would have to match Bossy's leap.

In addition to the pressure of public expectations, Bure would also have to contend with some new obstacles. He wasn't going to surprise anyone this year. Other teams were well aware of his talent, and he could expect more of the tenacious checking that Edmonton had used to keep him under wraps during the 1992 playoffs. Bure would also be missing his friend and linemate, Igor Larionov, who had left the Canucks to play in Switzerland.

Larionov had balked at re-signing with the Canucks because it meant the club would have had to continue to pay transfer payments to Russian hockey officials equal to Larionov's salary, something he was adamantly opposed to. The Soviets eventually proposed a $150,000 buyout, but Larionov opposed that, as well. He didn't want them to get a cent.

Canucks management let Larionov depart, believing that at 31 his days as a useful player were numbered. However, Larionov's Swiss contract had a clause that would allow him to return to the NHL at the end of the Swiss season in March, opening up the possibility that if he cleared NHL waivers the Canucks could re-sign him without any entanglements with Russian officials. However, the San Jose Sharks eliminated that prospect by claiming Larionov on waivers in October. The soft-spoken Russian seemed genuinely saddened to leave Vancouver, but Quinn, when asked if he was disappointed that San Jose had claimed Larionov, said, "No. We weren't going to bring him back, anyway."

Yet even without Larionov around to feed him passes, there were two factors that might work to Bure's advantage. Because of the addition of two expansion teams, the Ottawa Senators and the Tampa Bay Lightning, the schedule had been extended by four games from 80 to 84 games. As well, the NHL had introduced some rule changes designed to boost offense. In the aftermath of the 1992 playoffs, during which TV viewership had fallen to an all-time low and several marquee players had been struck down by injury, the NHL finally took steps to address the problem of lax officiating. Instead of turning a blind eye to hooking, holding and interference fouls, referees were instructed to call games by the book. High sticking would now be called from the waist up instead of from the shoulder up, holding an opponent's stick would also be a penalty and new penalties were introduced for players who instigated fights. It was hoped that the rigorous officiating would create more room for the stars to shine and result in more scoring.

At training camp, the Canucks were pleased to discover that Bure had added nine pounds of muscle to his chiseled physique, most of it in his upper body. Sports scientist Ted Rhodes observed, "Bure is setting the curve for everyone else. He has probably the greatest athletic ability of anyone in the group. He's really worked on his strength. He's just solid."

The Canucks opened the 1992–93 campaign with two games against their 1992 playoff nemesis, the Edmonton Oilers. Vancouver took the first game in Edmonton 5–4. Bure, skating on a line with Adams at center and rookie Dixon Ward on the left side, broke the tie late in the third period when he pounced on a loose puck that had caromed weirdly off the back boards and drilled it past a startled Bill Ranford.

Afterward, Quinn remarked, "The winning goal was an alert play on Pavel's part. He was positioned well, and when he saw that wicked bounce, he turned it into a goal. He's a cut above in those situations. We have 10 other guys who would have probably missed the net."

The Canucks also won the return match with the Oilers 5–2 back in Vancouver. Bure was in a touchy mood. Irritated by the Oilers' close checking, he picked up six minutes in penalties, two minors for high sticking and one for elbowing. Two nights later against Winnipeg, Bure put his energy to more constructive use, scoring four goals and an assist in an 8–1 rout of the Jets. The second period was the Russian's own personal highlight reel as he scored three times and added an assist in a 12-minute span.

He notched the first goal while the Canucks were short-handed, gathering in a loose puck and breaking in one-on-one against defenseman Phil Housley. In what had become his patented move, Bure dropped the puck from his stick back to his skates, then kicked it ahead. Housley managed to get a piece of the puck, but Bure regained control and whipped a shot past goalie Bob Essensa. The Russian's second goal was even more remarkable. Pursued by a swarm of defenders, he eventually circled behind the Winnipeg net, towing Thomas Steen behind him. With Steen literally climbing his back, Bure came out front and then, while falling backward, somehow flicked a wrist shot high into the top corner.

He scored his third goal on a nifty backhand and added his fourth marker, another short-handed effort, late in the third period, stealing the puck at his own blueline, then scooting down the wing and blowing a 40-footer past Essensa. In all, Bure equaled five franchise records in the game: most goals in a period, most points in a period, most assists in a period, most short-handed goals in a game and most goals in a game.

After the game, Greg Adams spoke for many when he said, "Pavel is so exciting every time he touches the puck, you expect something to happen and he never seems to disappoint." The only people he disappointed that night were reporters.

Bure offered no insight into his on-ice magic. "It just happened. I just play like normal," he said nonchalantly. His four-goal performance was certainly not normal, and although Bure may have been trying to deflect attention away from himself, his response could just as easily be construed as arrogance.

On November 3, the Canucks acquired 30-year-old Russian center Anatoli Semenov from the Tampa Bay Lightning in exchange for minor-leaguer Dave Capuano and a fourth-round draft pick. Semenov, who had played 11 seasons with Moscow Dynamo and 116 games with the Edmonton Oilers before being picked up by Tampa Bay in the Expansion Draft, was viewed as a potential replacement for Larionov on Bure's line.

"I think he'll be able to help us out and perhaps help Pavel out," Quinn said. "We were looking around for a centerman who has some playmaking skills. What I like about Russian centers is they're trained very well on the defensive part of the game, and that's an area that has been hurting us here."

Semenov debuted with the Canucks on November 6 against the visiting Ottawa Senators and set up Bure for the Canucks' first goal. Bure scored again during the second period and delighted the crowd with a couple of whirlwind rushes as Vancouver won 4–1. He also made a vivid impression on Ottawa rookie goaltender Darrin Madeley, who was starting only his second NHL game. In Roy MacGregor's book *Road Games*, Madeley described the sensation of playing against the Russian Rocket as "hypnotic."

On Bure's second goal, MacGregor noted, "the 21-year-old Russian had flown up the right side of the ice and fired the puck so lightning-quick past the skate of a retreating Senators defenseman that Madeley did not even realize he had been scored upon until the crowd roared and the linesman arrived in a spray of ice to fish out the puck." It was an unsettling experience and one the Ottawa goalie didn't look forward to repeating. Bure could give a netminder the cold sweats. As Madeley told MacGregor, "They should get rid of him. Kick him out of hockey—make him illegal."

Semenov offered his own assessment of his new linemate to reporters after the game. "Nobody plays like Pavel. Nobody. In Russia you say the name alone—Bure!"

The addition of Semenov was a tonic for Bure and Adams. In their first three games together, they notched 18 points and sparked the Canucks to three easy victories. In addition to his scoring prowess, Bure has begun displaying traits not usually associated with European players. In a 6–2 win over the San Jose Sharks on November 10, as he carried the puck through the circle to the left of the Sharks' net, Bure was clobbered by San Jose's Brian Lawton, who knocked Bure to his knees. Undaunted, Bure retained control of the puck, regained his feet, made a beeline to the crease and jammed the puck past goalie Brian Hayward.

"A lot of guys would have quit on that play," Quinn noted. "We've had a lot of great—well, great's not the word—highly talented Europeans come to our game. A lot of them don't have the grit to fight through the hooking and bumping and holding and battle for the puck. Well, this kid's got grit."

After 20 games, Bure had 20 goals, two behind league-leading Mario Lemieux, and his line with Adams and Semenov had posted 27 points in their first five games together. Still, there was cause for concern in the Canucks' camp. Many of the club's other core players were struggling. Linden, for one, was mired in a dreadful slump. At the 20-game mark in 1991–92, he had led the team with 27 points. At the same point in 1992–93, he had just 13 points and wasn't playing with the intensity expected of the team's captain and highest-paid player. Was his lucrative long-term contract dampening his desire, or was the problem—as some fans and members of the media had suggested—that he was in a funk because he had been unseated by Bure as the team's most popular player?

Linden angrily refuted the notion that there was friction between him and Bure. "That's a ridiculous comment. He's great for our organization and great for our city. I played some of my best hockey last year when Pavel arrived." Linden's stature had changed, however. Before 1992–93, he was the only Canucks player who needed an assistant to handle his fan mail. Now he had company.

Bure was receiving an average of a thousand pieces of fan mail a week. When he returned from a road trip in January, there were 26 pounds of paper waiting for him. The volume was so heavy that Bure had to hire a Russian-speaking Canadian, Nick Shevchenko, an employee with Canadian Airlines, to help him cope with the tidal wave. The letters came from all over the world—the United States, Europe, Asia, Australia and from as far north as the Arctic Circle. Parents wrote, praising Bure as a role model. Teenage girls gushed endearments. "If you don't have a girlfriend, I'm available," one wrote. Most everyone wanted an autograph and a photo.

For others, though, Bure was regarded as some sort of Soviet Santa Claus. "You're rich. Send me the following items," demanded one pushy adolescent, enclosing a page-long list. A boy in Sweden asked for a helmet. Others voiced complaints. One woman chastised Bure for chewing gum. "I see you have descended to the level of your boss, Pat Quinn," she huffed.

The letters were just one manifestation of Pavelmania. Everywhere he went, Bure was accosted by admirers—at airports, in restaurants and on the street. At the Canucks' training camp, one fan had vaulted over the boards and walked out on the ice in the middle of a practice to ask for a signature. He hadn't thought to bring a pen and was miffed when Bure didn't have one concealed in his equipment. Bure's mother, Tatiana, complained that the crush of autograph hounds and their ubiquitous Sharpie pens were ruining her son's expensive suits.

At the Canucks' Winning Spirit sports-apparel outlet at the Pacific Coliseum, Bure's merchandise was outselling all the other players' by a three-to-one margin. The store stocked Bure T-shirts, posters, photos, silver medallions, hats, school binders and even kids' pajamas. By the end of the season, the store had sold 70 authentic Bure jerseys at $230 a pop.

In November, Shevchenko founded the Pavel Bure Fan Club. Ninety people attended the inaugural meeting. The club began holding monthly get-togethers and published a newsletter featuring Bure-related gossip, trivia and candid photos. Shevchenko also booked guest speakers, preferably someone who could offer a juicy Bure anecdote or two. Larionov and broadcaster Jim Robson stopped by. Both of Bure's parents were guests. But Bure himself, the object of everyone's desire, never made an appearance.

Other Bure admirers were more troublesome. Groupies began following his car home after games. He eventually vacated his downtown condo after packs of teenage girls began gathering below his window and calling out his name. He rented a home in North Vancouver, but left after two burglaries. Because of security concerns, he finally moved into a private apartment complex where guests had to be escorted onto the premises.

Living in the glare of the media spotlight and carrying the hopes of an entire franchise was a heavy burden for a 21-year-old, and Quinn, for one, had concerns about how it might affect Bure. "I hope he doesn't become a recluse out of this. It happened to Bobby Orr. He started to disappear and hide from people and it was just because he was smothered."

Confirmation of Bure's fame arrived in November when *Sports Illustrated* sent writer Austin Murphy to Vancouver to write a profile of Bure, chronicling the Russian Rocket's popularity. Although Murphy interviewed Bure, he got little in the way of useful quotes. He had better luck with Valeri, whom he found much more outgoing. The younger Bure greeted Murphy by saying. "*Sports Illustrate*, huh? Those swim-ming-suit ladies damn great chicks! They look that great in real person?"

The Canucks rang in the new year by downing Los Angeles 4–0 to move past the Kings into second place, five points back of Calgary. Vancouver finished December with a 9–1–1 record, the club's most suc-cessful month in franchise history. They had trampled the opposition, outscoring them 57–27. Quinn, who had seen his team compile an amazing .833 winning percentage since late November, said he was now shooting for first overall: "I'd like to see the President's Trophy sitting in Vancouver."

On January 12, the hockey world received some sobering news. It was revealed that Mario Lemieux, who was already out of Pittsburgh's lineup with back problems, had Hodgkin's disease, a type of cancer marked by an enlargement of the lymph nodes. He would have to undergo radia-tion treatments. It hadn't been a good year for the NHL's two biggest superstars. Wayne Gretzky missed the first 39 games of the season with a herniated disk in his back. The struggle of Lemieux and Gretzky to over-come adversity was one of the major stories of the 1992–93 season. The other was the sudden emergence of the Europeans.

All of the NHL's brightest young talents had foreign passports. Alex-ander Mogilny of the Buffalo Sabres, now in his fourth season, had over-come his fear of flying with the aid of a hypnotist and had raised his game to a new level. Jaromir Jagr of the Pittsburgh Penguins had emerged from Lemieux's shadow to stake his claim to being the NHL's most dynamic forward. Mats Sundin, the Quebec Nordiques' gifted Swede, had begun the year by scoring points in his first 30 games. Only Gretzky and Lemieux had ever scored points in more consecutive games. The stylish Sergei Fedorov had combined with Steve Yzerman to give the Detroit Red Wings the strongest one-two center punch in the league. But the European who was making the biggest impact was the Winnipeg Jets' Finnish freshman, Teemu Selanne.

Philadelphia's Eric Lindros was supposed to be the year's most domi-nant rookie, but Selanne with his turbo-charged speed and ebullient personality had proved more impressive. The Finnish Flash had single-handedly raised the nearly invisible profile of Winnipeg's small-market team, earning more votes than any other right winger in the midseason fan balloting for the All-Star team.

Jets coach John Paddock compared Selanne's impact to the excitement generated by Bure the previous year. "He has the charisma to attract people. He has a chance to be a star who people will flock to see." When the Jets held a charity carnival that winter, fans waited in line for four hours to have their photo taken with the affable Finn. Selanne signed 3,000 autographs that night.

The Europeans had raised the skill level of play in the NHL, but not everyone welcomed the change. The league's less-talented teams could only compete by slowing the game down with grinding hockey. They also bitterly complained about the new style of officiating, or the "European rules," as they mockingly called them. Some observers, including Don Cherry, claimed that the greater number of penalties were ruining hockey by slowing down the games and making the results too dependent on the whims of referees and the play of special teams. It was true the games were longer and penalties did disrupt the flow, but it was felt that the players would eventually adjust to the stricter officiating. The thesis was never proven. Although the NHL didn't officially rescind its policy, as the season wore on, the referees reverted to their old habits and the pendulum swung back toward the clutch-and-grab game.

On January 15, the Buffalo Sabres visited Vancouver. Sportswriters billed the game as a personal showdown between Bure and Mogilny, the two former linemates who, in Lemieux's absence, were now vying for the NHL goal-scoring lead. On this night, the duel went to Bure. The Russian Rocket scored twice, and his line with Adams and Courtnall accounted for all of Vancouver's goals in a 4–1 win. Mogilny, despite seven shots on net, was held off the scoresheet.

On January 19, the defending Stanley Cup champion Penguins beat Vancouver 5–2. The loss snapped the Canucks' 18-game unbeaten streak on home ice. They had gone 16–0–2 in that span. Despite playing with an assortment of linemates, Bure continued to fly, putting together a 13-game scoring streak. Following a 3–3 tie with Minnesota, a game in which the Russian scored once and fired a dozen shots on net, the suitably impressed North Stars general manager Bob Gainey said, "I don't know if you can get any quicker and stay inside the boards. If he is having a big night, then we're not going to."

By the All-Star break, Bure had racked up 77 points on 44 goals and 33 assists in 53 games. He was the lone Canuck picked for the Campbell Conference squad. The All-Star Game was a blowout. The Wales beat the Campbells by a score of 16–6. Bure scored the last two meaningless goals for his side.

Just after the All-Star break, a list of NHL salaries was released by the NHL Players' Association. Bure, at $600,000, didn't even make the top 100. The figure wasn't entirely accurate because his contract included incentive bonuses that, according to his agent Ron Salcer, boosted his total earnings to almost $1 million. Even so, there were 45 players making more than Bure.

On February 9, in a 5–1 triumph over Quebec, Bure scored his 45th goal to break Tony Tanti's single-season team record. On February 12, the Canucks and the Sabres met again, and once more all the pregame hype was about the Mogilny-Bure matchup. Neither player scored, but Bure picked up three assists to Mogilny's one as the Canucks prevailed 3–1 in a bruising, physical game. The turning point came in the first period. With the Sabres leading 1–0 and pressing for a second goal on the power play, Bure took the puck and headed up the ice. He froze defenseman Ken Sutton and goalie Grant Fuhr with a fake shot and then slipped the puck over to Semenov, who tapped it into the yawning cage.

Bure got his 49th of the season on February 24 in a 5–4 win over the New York Rangers. Two nights later he scored number 50 versus the Jets in Winnipeg, only to have the goal called back. On the play, Winnipeg's Phil Housley clanged a shot off the crossbar behind McLean. The foghorn sounded in celebration, and Housley raised his arms in the air, but referee Ron Hoggarth didn't blow his whistle and allowed the action to continue. Bure alertly scooped up the puck, raced down to the Jets' end and beat goalie Rick Tabarraci. Now it was Bure's turn to celebrate. The Jets protested and Hoggarth consulted the video replay, which revealed that Housley's shot had actually entered the net. He waved off Bure's goal, counted Housley's and had the timekeeper put 11 seconds back on the clock.

Bure finally potted number 50 when the Canucks met the Sabres in a neutral-site encounter in Hamilton, Ontario, on March 1. The goal came at 18:06 of the first period when Dixon Ward hit Bure with a pass just outside the Buffalo blueline. The Russian moved in and released a 35-foot wrist shot that slipped through goalie Grant Fuhr's pads. The goal seemed to inspire Bure. He played his best game in weeks and netted a second goal on a rink-length rush.

The game marked the third and last head-to-head encounter of the season between Bure and Mogilny. The Buffalo sniper had reached the 50-goal plateau a month earlier than Bure, scoring his 50th in his 46th game on February 2, but for the third time he came up empty against the Canucks. The final tally? Bure: four goals and five assists; Mogilny: no goals and one assist.

The day after Bure hit 50, Selanne, who had reached the milestone on February 28, thrilled Winnipeg fans by registering a hat trick against the Quebec Nordiques to break Mike Bossy's rookie record of 53 goals in a season.

Vancouver returned home to meet the New Jersey Devils on March 9. Contrary to expectations, there was no special ceremony for the first player in Canucks history to score 50 goals. Instead, during a break in play in the first period, the public-address announcer plugged special commemorative T-shirts the team had made up for the occasion. Almost as an afterthought, just before play resumed, Bure's name was flashed on the scoreboard and the fans were asked to applaud his achievement.

That night Bure picked up two assists in a 7–2 Canucks win to set another franchise milestone. The pair of assists gave him 92 points for the season, breaking Patrick Sundstrom's team record of 91. But it wasn't this milestone that the media focused on, but rather the team's failure to pay homage to Bure for his 50th goal. Nine days later, before a game with Winnipeg, Bure was belatedly honored for his 50th goal in a pregame ceremony at which he received a plaque, a special-edition art print and airline tickets.

Getting his 50th was supposed to take pressure off Bure's shoulders, but instead he simply stopped scoring. When St. Louis beat Vancouver 3–1 on March 22, it marked the eighth straight game he failed to put one in, the longest drought of his brief NHL career. Still, it wasn't as if he didn't have his chances. In the Blues game, goalie Curtis Joseph stopped Bure twice on breakaways on the same shift during the third period. Bure's struggles mirrored the team's, which posted a 5–8–1 record during March. The Canucks were playing without precision or passion, and Quinn was finding it hard to motivate his players. Even the threat of the second-place Calgary Flames snapping at their heels inspired no great urgency.

Just before the NHL trade deadline, Quinn acquired forward Murray Craven from the Hartford Whalers in exchange for little-used forward Robert Kron and future considerations. Craven was a versatile sort who could play center or wing, fill in on the power play, kill penalties and take faceoff draws. Quinn slotted Craven at left wing in Adams's place on the Bure-Semenov line. The trio clicked immediately as Bure broke his slump, scoring twice in a 6–2 win against Los Angeles. Two nights later Calgary came to town and dumped the Canucks 3–1 to close within three points of first. On April 1, the day after his birthday, Bure scored a short-handed goal, his seventh of the season, the most ever by a Canucks player. The goal gave him 100 points for the year.

On April 7, the Canucks returned home from a four-game road trip to face Edmonton. The Canucks came out flat and trailed the Oilers 4–1 after two periods. Bure turned the game around in the third, strafing goalie Bill Ranford with eight shots, scoring twice and getting an assist. He ignited the comeback at the 8:16 mark, one-timing Craven's soft pass behind Bill Ranford. A few minutes later Bure scored again, flipping Nedved's feed into the net. Then he set up Adams to even the score at 4–4. Geoff Courtnall eventually won the game in overtime. In all, Bure collected 13 shots on net in the game, establishing a new club record.

The elation of the victory was swept away two nights later when Calgary thumped Vancouver 8–1 at the Saddledome. The two teams had now met six times, and the Canucks had lost five and tied one. Even so, Vancouver still led Calgary by four points and could wrap up first place by defeating the Flames in their last head-to-head encounter on April 11. The importance of the contest sharpened Vancouver's focus. The team played a disciplined game and prevailed 6–3 to clinch first. Bure potted his 60th goal of the season at 12:13 of the third period to ice the game. He picked up one more assist in the Canucks' second-last game, a 7–4 win over Los Angeles, to finish the year with 110 points on 60 goals and 50 assists.

Quinn left Bure, Semenov, Lumme and Lidster behind in Vancouver to rest when the team flew to Los Angeles for its final game. The Canucks won 8–6, as Ronning led the charge with three goals and three assists. The victory gave Vancouver 101 points, the highest total in franchise history. Although they had captured the division, their total was the seventh-best in the NHL and a long way short of the Pittsburgh Penguins' league-high 119 points. Still, it was a successful campaign. They had improved upon their 1991–92 record by five points and had scored 346 goals, a franchise record. For the first time in team history, the Canucks boasted four players with 30 or more goals: Bure (60), Nedved (38), Linden (33) and Courtnall (31).

Bure had lived up to all the preseason hype, improving his rookie goal total by 26, far exceeding the leaps of Mike Bossy and Jimmy Carson. Yet, as good as his season had been, it was overshadowed by some other incredible performances. After returning from cancer treatments on March 2, Mario Lemieux scored 30 goals and 26 assists in his last 20 games to finish with 69 goals and 91 assists for 160 points in only 60 games. Gretzky overcame career-threatening back miseries to post 65 points in 45 games. A record 20 players notched 100 points, and an unprecedented 14 players topped the 50-goal plateau. Mogilny and Selanne tied for the league lead with 76 goals, the fifth-highest total in NHL annals. Offense, thanks largely to the influence of the Europeans, had returned with a bang. Three of the NHL's top five goal scorers — Mogilny, Selanne and Bure — were from overseas. So, too, were three of the top five rookie scorers: Selanne, Winnipeg's Alexei Zhamnov and Quebec's Andrei Kovalenko.

No team had jumped so heavily onto the European bandwagon as the Winnipeg Jets who, for the second year in a row, supplied the Canucks' opposition in the first round of the playoffs. The Jets had eight Europeans in uniform, including two Finns, two Swedes and four Russians. But their most dangerous threat was Selanne, and the series was billed as High Noon on Ice: the Finnish Flash Versus the Russian Rocket.

Most observers expected to see Bure's unit matched against the Selanne–Zhamnov–Tkachuk line, but Quinn chose to play a defensive combo composed of Semenov, Gary Valk and Tim Hunter against the

Jets' high-powered trio. The strategy worked perfectly. Selanne's line was limited to three shots and failed to score as the Canucks took the opener 4–2.

Vancouver shut down the Jets' top guns again in Game 2 and eked out a 3–2 victory. Linden was the Canucks' most impressive performer, tossing his weight around and earning plaudits from Jets coach John Paddock: "Trevor's been the best player in the series. He's been a force every time he's been on the ice. He's done everything, he's hit, he's taken faceoffs. There's not much he can't do."

While Linden led by example, Bure supplied the killing blow with four minutes left, taking a pass from Adams, then deking goalie Bob Essensa and acrobatically roofing a backhand over him as he fell to the ice. The Russian Rocket's sensational goal dominated conversation after the game. "We got a great athlete making a good play on something that wasn't there really," Quinn said. "What are there, 500 guys in the game? And there are only three or four who are able to score that goal."

Prior to Game 3, Bure's name surfaced in the media in a very different context. The *Province*'s Tony Gallagher reported that Bure had been asked to "disassociate" himself from an unsavory individual who was known to latch on to Russian players. "The last time I saw him was in Montreal [at the All-Star Game]," Bure said. "They asked me not to see him anymore and I haven't and he understands. I don't know he's a bad guy. He's a Canadian. I met him through the other guys [teammates]. They seem to know him better than me."

"A person like Pavel is subject to meeting all sorts of people," Bure's agent, Ron Salcer, said. "Guys in his situation have to be very careful who they associate with and he understands that now. He is new to all this business."

Winnipeg rebounded to win Game 3 back on home ice, thanks to a pair of glaring Canucks turnovers by defensemen Doug Lidster and Jiri Slegr that resulted in breakaway goals by Luciano Borsato and Selanne. Selanne's goal was his third of the game. In the dressing room afterward, the grinning Finn wore a ball cap with the slogan Alien with an Attitude.

The Canucks played with more discipline in Game 4 and got goals from Adams, Dana Murzyn and Sergio Momesso in a 3–1 win. Back at home for Game 5, Vancouver came out strong and took a 3–1 lead into the dressing room after the first period. But the Canucks were unable to finish off the Jets, who rallied to tie on goals by Darrin Shannon and Tkachuk. The Jets completed the comeback in overtime on a fluke goal when Selanne's one-handed centering pass ricocheted off Hunter's skate and into the net.

Game 6 was a seesaw struggle. Winnipeg scored three times, but each goal was answered by the Canucks. Video-replay technology played a big part in the game. Vancouver had two goals disallowed, both of them by Momesso. The second came in the final second of regulation time. Off a faceoff scramble with two seconds left, Nedved took a shot that bounced to Momesso, who put the puck in, causing a wild celebration by the Canucks. But the green light signaling the end of the period came on and not the red light indicating a goal. The referees called for a video review. When the replay officials couldn't determine conclusively whether the puck had actually crossed the line before the final horn, they ruled no goal.

Had the Jets gone on to win, the ruling would have been a source of major controversy, but Adams put the issue to rest, scoring the series clincher at 4:30 of overtime when he broke past defenseman Tom Lalor, flipped a backhand toward Essensa, then crashed into the crease, knocking the Jets' goalie and the puck into the net.

Vancouver advanced to meet the Los Angeles Kings, who had upset the Flames in six games in the other divisional series. On paper the matchup favored the Canucks. Vancouver had dominated Los Angeles during the regular season, winning seven of nine meetings and outscoring them 46–31, and Vancouver had a decided edge in goaltending. McLean was one of the league's best, while the Kings were still trying to choose between struggling veteran Kelly Hrudey and unproven rookie Robb Stauber. The only area the Kings could match the Canucks was up front, where Gretzky, Jari Kurri, Luc Robitaille and Tomas Sandstrom supplied plenty of firepower.

The question of how to stop Bure was a hot topic on press row. Before the first game, Hrudey was asked by a Los Angeles reporter, "Is there one move you've picked up that he does?"

"Yeah, the one where he raises his hands in the air. That's the one I don't like," Hrudey joked. "Anything else I'll try to contend with."

The first game was played at noon Vancouver time in order to comply with the demands of U.S. television. The crowd, which was several thousand short of a sellout, was curiously subdued, and the players seemed infected with the same sort of lethargy. The Canucks won the sluggish affair 5–2. Kings head coach Barry Melrose promised a better showing in Game 2: "You'll see us play better. We weren't as intense as we have to be."

True to his word, the Kings jumped on top after only 19 seconds on a goal by defenseman Mark Hardy. Vancouver replied 33 seconds later on a goal by Adams, who had now scored a point in eight straight games to set a new club playoff record. The two quick goals set the tone for the game, which was played at a high tempo. Despite having to kill off five minor penalties, the Kings led 3–2 after the first period. Each of their goals had come as result of pressuring the Canucks into making turnovers.

The Kings went up 4–2 in the second period when Tony Granato intercepted a clearing attempt by Gerald Diduck and rocketed a shot past McLean. Bure got the Canucks back within a goal when he spun away from a hook by Mark Hardy and scored on a backhand, but the comeback stalled and the Kings went on to win 6–3. As Quinn remarked, "We could have played anyone and lost the game. We couldn't hold the puck and make simple plays. We got very dangerous and the danger was all against us."

Game 3 featured a tighter brand of play, and the teams went into the third period locked in a 2–2 tie. But Los Angeles broke the game open midway through the third when Robitaille, Kurri and Gretzky scored goals in a five-minute span. The Kings capitalized on virtually every scoring opportunity they had in the period, netting five goals on just six shots, and waltzed to a 7–4 triumph.

Game 4 was a mirror reversal of Game 3. Trailing 2–1 after the first period, the Canucks assumed control and cuffed the Kings around, scoring six unanswered goals to win 7–2. Adams tallied another point to run his streak to 10 straight playoff games. Nedved, who was invisible earlier in the series, turned in a solid effort, but Bure's lone contribution to the offense was an assist on Dana Murzyn's first–period marker.

Prior to Game 5, Quinn voiced his displeasure with the officiating in the series, saying the referees had been ignoring blatant fouls on Bure and Ronning but were calling every infraction against Gretzky, including imaginary penalties the Great One had drawn by taking dives. "If you're going to protect people, the rules have to be the same for both teams," said Quinn, who noted that the Kings' strategy was to intimidate Bure and make him gun-shy about handling the puck. "You do that through a lot of different tactics. One of them is punching him when he goes by. This kid got cut the other night in view of the referee and no penalty was called. It's a joke what's happening."

With the series knotted at two games each, Game 5 in Vancouver shaped up as the pivotal contest of the series. Craven opened the scoring, backhanding in a rebound, but the lead was short-lived. Just 32 seconds later, Sandstrom stole the puck from Semenov behind the Vancouver net and tried to jam it in on a wraparound. McLean made the save, but the puck skittered to Gretzky, who whacked it home. The Kings went up 2–1 when Kurri was left alone in front and cashed in a feed from Robitaille. Nedved tied the game just 47 seconds into the second period, converting a pass from Sandlak.

The game then tightened up. It was still deadlocked midway through the second when Bure bailed out to avoid a hit by Granato and left the puck behind. Granato passed to Robitaille, who fanned on his one-timer, only to have the puck deflect off Lidster's skate and into the net. It was a deflating goal, but Vancouver recovered to tie the game on the power play, as Linden, parked at the top of the crease, fought off a defender and stuffed in his own rebound at 13:40.

There was no scoring in the third period and the game went into overtime. The winning goal resulted from a meltdown by the Canucks' defense. Lumme and Murzyn both got caught out of position, allowing Robitaille to slide a pass to Gary Shuchuk, who beat McLean on the short side. Shuchuk was a most unlikely hero. He was an obscure rookie who had scored only two goals during the regular season and was seeing ice for the first time in the series. Melrose had inserted the feisty little winger into the lineup on a hunch, and it had paid off handsomely.

Flush with confidence, Los Angeles came out determined to finish the Canucks off in Game 6, outshooting Vancouver 21–8 in the opening period, but McLean stopped everything but a point-blank blast from Rob Blake, and the Kings had to settle for a 1–0 lead. Against the flow of the play, the Canucks took the lead in the second period on goals by Diduck and Sandlak. With McLean performing miracles, it looked as if Vancouver might steal the game and prolong the series. But at the 14:07 mark of the second, it all fell apart.

Murzyn was called for a retaliatory boarding penalty on Shuchuk, then compounded the mistake by stupidly cross-checking Mike Donnelly after the whistle to take a second penalty. The Canucks killed off the first minor, but then botched a line change and got caught with too many men on the ice, giving the Kings a two-man advantage for 1:58 seconds. This time there was no reprieve. Kurri wired home a shot from the slot, and Sandstrom snapped in a rebound 17 seconds later. At the 17:44 mark, Gretzky gift-wrapped a perfect pass to Warren Rychel, who scored to put the Kings up 4–2. Linden answered back with one, but it was too little, too late. The Kings won 5–3.

In a game in which they faced elimination, the Canucks had been outshot 50–23. If not for McLean's brilliance, the game would have been a rout. Disbelief was the reaction of the Vancouver media and Canucks players alike. Despite an edge in depth and size, the Canucks had been unable to cope with the Kings' fast-paced transition game and had failed to contain Gretzky, who scored six goals and seven assists to pace the L.A. attack. Critical defensive lapses had led to key goals.

Among the Canucks' forwards, only Linden and Adams had stepped up their games. Bure scored just once in the series and faded badly in the last two matches, prompting speculation that he was secretly nursing a leg injury. Nedved, with two goals in 12 playoff games, was another disappointment. In the handshake ceremony at the end of Game 6, the young Czech asked Gretzky for his stick as a souvenir, and after getting it, skated off the ice with a smile on his face. To many, that act symbolized what was wrong with Nedved and the Canucks—they had too much respect for their opponents, they accepted defeat too easily. This was the playoffs, life-and-death stuff. You didn't ask the victor for his sword after he chopped off your head.

Los Angeles went on to defeat Toronto in the conference finals before succumbing to Patrick Roy and the Canadiens in the finals. It would be Gretzky's last serious shot at the Stanley Cup, and in the disappointment of defeat he openly hinted at retirement.

For the second straight year, Vancouver had topped its division during the regular season but had failed to reach the conference finals. It was small consolation, but this year they had company; the other three division winners—Pittsburgh, Boston and Chicago—had all fallen by the wayside.

The search was soon on for scapegoats. The media fingered Pat Quinn. The consensus was that he had stuck with underachieving players too long and had been outcoached by Barry Melrose, the rookie upstart with the cocky grin and moussed hair. Several sportswriters suggested that it was time for Quinn to relinquish the coaching reins to assistant Rick Ley and concentrate on his GM duties.

George McPhee, who had replaced Brian Burke as the team's assistant general manager, placed the blame on the players. He didn't mention names, but it was clear who he meant: "In the playoffs, the big players have to come through and the only players that you could say had big performances for us were Trevor [Linden] and Mac [Kirk McLean]." Looking ahead, McPhee said, "I think it was painfully obvious that we have to inject more speed into the lineup and maybe go with some young people who are hungry."

Everyone expected changes. Lots of them.

# CHAPTER NINE

# Russian Roulette

*A stranger's soul is a dark forest.*

RUSSIAN PROVERB

PAVEL BURE SPENT the summer of 1993 in the City of Angels. He and his father and brother rented a house near the beach in Malibu. Los Angeles appealed to Bure in ways Vancouver could not. Unrecognized, he could lead a far more normal existence there. He wasn't asked for his autograph and adolescent girls didn't pursue his car through the streets. As well, there was a large Russian immigrant community, with Russian shops and restaurants. But the city also possessed that familiar surging urban pulse he craved. The hot California nights offered a more intoxicating brew of possibilities than sedate, laid-back Vancouver, a place Bure described in one Russian interview as being "a long way from civilization."

As Bure explained, "I love New York and L.A. because I'm from Moscow and it's a pretty big city, too. There is something different about big cities. When I first came to North America and went to New York, I would step off the bus and walk around and think, 'Whew, I'm home.' It feels like the same energy."

During the summer, Ron Salcer attempted to open discussions with the Canucks on a new contract for Bure. Although the Russian Rocket's existing deal, which was now paying him $930,000 a year (including scoring bonuses), still had two more seasons to run, the rapidly escalating marketplace made him feel he was underpaid. When Bure joined the NHL in 1991, only a few superstars were earning seven figures. Now even untested rookies were joining the millionaires' club. The Ottawa Senators had just rewarded Alexandre Daigle, the first-overall pick in the 1993 NHL Entry Draft, with a five-year $12.5-million contract.

Daigle's signing wasn't warmly received by other NHL executives. Edmonton Oilers general manager Glen Sather was indignant. "The rationalization for the salaries that are being paid has gone so far in one direction that many NHL clubs will be forced out of business. This is absurd. There is absolutely no sanity to it. Is this kid good enough to command the types of salaries that Wayne Gretzky, Mario Lemieux and Brett Hull have earned over a number of years in the league? It's sick. The guy who offered the deal should be thrown out of hockey."

According to news reports, Bure was seeking a three-year contract extension that would pay him US$3 million a year, plus a US$1.5-million signing bonus. Keeping Bure happy was going to be an expensive proposition, but from the perspective of Canucks owner Arthur Griffiths, it was a necessary one. Griffiths, who had begun construction on a new $160-million sports arena in downtown Vancouver, had already sold all of the stadium's 88 luxury boxes at annual leasing prices ranging from $70,000 to $135,000, based in no small part on Bure's marquee allure. The term *franchise player*, previously unknown in the Canucks' lexicon, was rapidly becoming synonymous with number 10.

Fortunately contract talks with Salcer hadn't reached the level of rancor that they had with restricted free agent Petr Nedved and his agent, Tony Kondel. Nedved had returned home to the Czech Republic, unwilling to re-sign for the amount of money the Canucks were offering. The Czech had earned $225,000 in 1992–93. Based on his 38-goal performance, he was seeking a pay hike to more than $1 million a year. The Canucks were holding the line at $600,000.

Nedved's disappearing act was the only serious upheaval in the team's ranks. The personnel changes promised after the Canucks' early playoff exit hadn't materialized. The lone new faces in the lineup for the 1993–94 season were free-agent winger Jose Charbonneau, who had most recently been playing in a roller-hockey league, and lumbering center John McIntyre, claimed on waivers from the New York Rangers.

More significant were the players who were missing. Tom Fergus and Ryan Walter had retired; Jim Sandlak had been sent to Hartford to complete the deal for Murray Craven; Doug Lidster had been traded to the Rangers; Gary Valk had been lost to the Mighty Ducks of Anaheim (one of two new franchises) in the Waiver Draft; and Anatoli Semenov had been claimed by the Ducks in the Expansion Draft. Assistant coach Ron Wilson had also left to assume the head coaching job at Anaheim. Wilson had been replaced by former Rangers assistant coach Ron Smith, whose primary responsibility was to improve Vancouver's feeble power play, which ranked third worst in the league in 1992–93. Smith had been an assistant coach with the Canucks in the early 1980s.

Without Nedved and Semenov, Vancouver was wafer-thin at center ice. Quinn attempted to remedy the situation by shifting Adams and Craven into the middle. Bure was paired with Adams and Odjick. Ronning centered a line with Linden and Courtnall, while Craven was flanked by Momesso and Charbonneau. McIntyre, Hunter, Ward and a six-foot-four, 235-pound newcomer named Shawn Antoski were the fourth-line foot soldiers.

The Canucks would compete in the Pacific Division in 1993–94. The league had replaced the Smythe, Norris, Adams and Patrick names with geographical designations. It was a cosmetic change, but one that was in keeping with the strategy of a league intent on selling the game to nonhockey fans. There was no point in confusing Americans with historical hockey figures.

Gary Bettman, a former top executive in the National Basketball Association, had been hired as the NHL's first commissioner and had been given a mandate to expand the league's horizons into untapped American markets. As part of that push, the NHL had added the Mighty Ducks, a team named after a Disney movie, and the Florida Panthers, a club named after an endangered wildcat, while the Minnesota North Stars franchise had been relocated to Dallas, Texas. The migration into the American sunbelt was said to have helped the NHL sign a contract with the Fox network, its first major U.S. television deal in 20 years.

What would prove to be the most exciting season in Canucks history began with a 5–2 victory over Los Angeles and a 5–1 loss at home to Calgary. In the third game against Edmonton, Odjick scored twice on Bure setups to spark the team to a 4–1 win. The line was prominent again on October 19, in a 5–4 triumph over Boston. Bure scored the first two goals, the second on a breathtaking rush. After snaring a pass from Odjick in the neutral zone, the Russian engaged the boosters and burst between the defensive pairing of Ray Bourque and Paul Stanton to beat goalie Jon Casey with a forehand deke.

Two nights later Bure scored two more, as the Canucks dumped Calgary 6–3. His second goal into an empty net was the 100th of his career. He had reached the century mark in his 154th game. Only four other NHLers had hit the milestone quicker: Mike Bossy, Maurice Richard, Joe Nieuwendyk and Wayne Gretzky.

Bure bulged the twine again in a 6–4 victory over San Jose on October 23 to give him five goals in his last three games and seven goals and six assists for 13 points in seven games. Vancouver had a 6–1–0 record, its best start in franchise history. The Canucks' power play was the third best in the NHL, and the team's perceived weakness at center hadn't manifested itself. All signs pointed to another successful campaign.

But discord was brewing behind the scenes. Contract talks between the Canucks and Bure's agent, Ron Salcer, had hit a snag. The two sides couldn't agree about the amount of money or the number of years involved, or even on the type of currency. Bure wanted to be paid in American dollars, but the Canucks, who were worried about the exchange rate, wanted to pay in Canadian funds or, as a compromise, in "Canuck bucks"—a pegged American-dollar rate of $1.15 Canadian. On October 24, Salcer announced that because they hadn't reached an agreement Bure would play out the third year of his contract.

Bure's contract was a major issue for the Canucks, not only because of the Russian's importance to the franchise, but because the dollar value of the deal would set a new benchmark for the rest of the players on the team. Delaying negotiations allowed the club to save money by paying Bure at the lower rate; the tactic also helped avoid the pressure of renegotiating the contracts of other key players, notably Linden. But there was an element of Russian roulette involved in stalling: it meant the team would likely have to pay considerably more when it finally confronted the issue, especially if Bure had another stellar season. As well, the Canucks ran the risk of alienating Bure. Salcer tried to put a positive spin on events, saying, "I had breakfast this morning with Pavel and he's fine with it. He's just 22 and all he wants to do is have fun playing hockey."

Salcer was sugarcoating the truth for public consumption. Bure was upset by the team's reluctance to commit to a new deal. In his mind, it indicated a lack of appreciation for his worth, a sore spot with him ever since the lengthy negotiations and court proceedings that had led to his original signing in 1991. The Canucks had assured him they would take care of him, but now he was having doubts.

Personalities also played a part in the dispute. Bure's sensitive temperament wasn't well suited to the adversarial style of contract negotiations practiced by George McPhee, the Canucks' assistant GM and vice president of hockey operations. Like his predecessor, Brian Burke, McPhee was a belligerent, hard-nosed individual. He had been picked for the job precisely because he possessed those qualities. Quinn needed someone like McPhee to wear the black hat for him because, as coach, he had to maintain a rapport with his players, something that was difficult to do if he was ridiculing their abilities at the negotiating table.

Bure's impatience with management would increase in December when his two former Central Army teammates, Alexander Mogilny and Sergei Fedorov, players whose abilities he judged to be on a par with his own, renegotiated new contracts with their respective teams worth about US$3 million per year.

The contractual impasse coincided with Bure's first NHL injury. He left the San Jose game on October 23 in the third period with a tender groin. The club's training staff left the decision of whether he was fit enough to play in the next night's return match with the Sharks in Bure's hands. It wasn't the wisest decision. On his first shift, Bure crumpled when he was checked, and had to be helped off the ice. He didn't return, but the Canucks eked out a 3–2 overtime victory for their sixth straight win.

The diagnosis was a pulled groin, a common ailment among players with overdeveloped thigh muscles. Bure's loss was felt immediately as the Canucks lost 4–2 to the Washington Capitals. The contest attracted 12,479 fans, the smallest home crowd since October 29, 1991, one week before Bure's first game with the team. The injury kept Bure on the shelf for eight games, and during his absence the team slumped, going 3–5–0. Bure returned to the lineup on November 14 against Anaheim. Although his skating looked tentative, his scoring touch was intact. He tied the game 2–2, with 3:29 left in the third period, popping home a rebound while killing a penalty. Two shifts later the Canucks stole the win when Odjick deflected a shot past goalie Mikhail Shtalenkov.

The Canucks defeated St. Louis two nights later 3–0, led by Odjick, who scored twice and was voted the first star for the second straight game. The Algonquin had already recorded five goals, one more than he had scored the previous season, and was playing with new confidence, an improvement he credited to Bure's influence. Odjick, who wasn't known for his diligent approach to physical conditioning, had spent time working out with Bure and his father during the summer and was in the best shape of his life. "Man, those Russians. It was a tough workout, let me tell you," Odjick told me at the time. "It's not what any North American player is used to."

He wasn't exaggerating. Vladimir's exercise routines could have been designed by the Marquis de Sade. He frequently had Pavel bang out 250 push-ups in a single session. Geoff Courtnall once watched Bure run through a series of 100-meter dashes, 20 at a time, with only a 10-second break between each sprint. "It almost made me puke just watching him," Courtnall said. Bure had two daily regimens. The first consisted of an hour of running, followed by an hour of soccer or tennis. Then, in the early evening, after lunch and a nap, there would be an hour of weight lifting, basketball for an hour, and a half hour of swimming. This was the Russian Rocket's summer routine, six days a week.

The lift provided by Bure's return was short-lived. The Canucks dropped three straight home games to Anaheim, Toronto and Detroit, establishing a pattern of inconsistency that would plague them all season. As the team struggled, the media resumed its criticism of Quinn, whom they had dubbed Three-Hat Pat. He was accused of being too patient, too resistant to shuffling the lineup and benching underachieving veteran players.

On the contract front, the Canucks were no closer to solving the Nedved stalemate. A frustrated McPhee had sent a letter to the young Czech, telling him he was being poorly represented and suggesting he replace Kondel with a new agent. Nedved responded with anger, saying he would never play for the Canucks again.

On December 7, Quinn left assistant Rick Ley in charge while he attended a league meeting, and the Canucks came out of their coma to win back-to-back road games against Hartford and Boston. But when Quinn rejoined the team for the final two games of the road trip, the Canucks promptly went back to sleep, losing 8–4 to Calgary and 7–2 to Edmonton. The two thumpings prompted renewed speculation about Quinn's coaching future. After fielding yet another query about his status, an exasperated Quinn told reporters, "You guys are getting excited about something that's not going to go anywhere. I'm the head coach right now and those are the facts."

Quinn's difficulties weren't entirely of his own making. In addition to Nedved, five other regulars—Adams, Momesso, Babych, Charbonneau and Antoski—were out with injuries. Bure was having trouble regaining his form, and he and several other players were suffering from the flu. With Adams out, there was also the problem of finding Bure a complementary center. He had been skating on a line with Ronning, but their styles didn't mesh. Both players liked to carry the puck and set up from the outside, and Ronning was having trouble adjusting to the added defensive duties required of any center paired with Bure.

It was suggested that Bure needed a Russian center. At one time, such a species would have been hard to find, but not any longer. Since the breakup of the Soviet Union in 1991, NHL teams had been raiding the top Russian clubs with impunity, and there were now 50 Soviet-born players in North America's premier hockey league. But while the globalization of the NHL had expanded its talent base, the phenomenon had also introduced a new and unforeseen problem.

After the collapse of the Communist power structure, Russian society drifted into a state of lawlessness. What the West called democracy, the Russians termed *bespredel,* or disorder. The Russian criminal underground, a subculture known as *vorovskoi mir*—thieves' world—had survived communism by becoming essential to the system, supplying everything that scientific socialism could not: prostitutes, tomatoes, stereos. Armed and organized, these criminal syndicates now had their hooks in virtually every segment of the economy. An estimated 4,000 gangs were operating in the country. Corruption, robbery and random violence were on the rise. People in Moscow had been murdered for their apartments, bankers had been gunned down by racketeers, and even street-kiosk owners were forced to choose between paying protection money or suffering fire bombs.

The Russian word for protection money is *krysha,* which literally means "roof." During the Cold War, the Soviet intelligent services had used the term to refer to a cover set up for their agents working abroad. But in the new Russia, *krysha* described an umbrella of protection, or "bandit roof." In order to survive and prosper, every individual had to have a roof for protection from trouble when doing business.

By the fall of 1993, there were signs that *krysha* had infected the NHL. Rejean Tremblay, a hockey columnist with the Montreal newspaper *La Presse,* was the first to tackle the issue. In a piece published on December 23, Tremblay claimed that several Soviet NHLers had been forced to pay protection to gangsters to ensure the safety of their families back home. He also stated that some NHL-bound Russians had been pressured to sign contracts with mob-controlled Russians living in North America to act as their official agents. Tremblay quoted an unidentified Russian player, who said, "Russian players aren't safe anywhere in the world. The Russian mafiya leaders are in league with the former dictators of the Communist Party. They have all the contacts and they control all the channels."

Tremblay named Viacheslav Fetisov of the New Jersey Devils as one of the Russian players who had to pay *krysha.* Fear of extortion was also said to be the reason why Sergei Fedorov brought his parents and younger brother from Moscow to Detroit just prior to the announcement that he had signed a new four-year US$12-million contract with the Red Wings on December 23.

Tremblay's allegations spread quickly across the news wires, prompting several follow-up articles. Fetisov's agent, Vladimir Zlobinsky, told the *New York Times*, "I'm not aware of any specific incident with Fetisov, but I know it's a general problem." Mark Gandler, a New Jersey–based agent who immigrated to the United States from the Soviet Union in the late 1970s, and who represented about 20 Soviet NHLers, told the *Times* he didn't believe the extortion stories and that reporting them would only give people ideas. "This is a very dangerous topic," Gandler said. "It's very irresponsible. It will make families worry."

Gandler's remarks contrasted sharply with those made by Sergei Lyakhov, one of Russia's top discus throwers, who told *Sports Illustrated* in January 1994: "If you make lots of money, you have to pay a per cent—this is life." The year before, Lyakhov had earned US$15,000 in hard currency. "But this is nothing," he said, "so I'm not in trouble. Now, if you take Fedorov and his $3 million, that's another story."

Several NHL general managers confirmed Tremblay's allegations. Winnipeg Jets GM Mike Smith, whose team had four Russian players, admitted, "It's a huge problem. It affects any Russian citizen who has hard currency. That's how hockey players get tied in. There have been players who have been roughed up. We've had a junior player who was roughed up." The player Smith was referring to was Alexander Alexeev, a 1992 Jets draft pick from Sokol Kiev in the Russian elite league, who was now playing for the Tacoma Rockets of the Western Hockey League. Alexeev had been assaulted in Kiev in the summer of 1993. "It was not too bad," he told the *Tacoma News Tribune*. "They could have killed me. A lot of people are killed these days. They just wanted to scare me."

Don Maloney, general manager of the New York Islanders, echoed Smith's remarks: "It's a widespread problem and most everyone is aware of it. People try to extort money and threaten family members. People have been harassed and bothered. There have been threats and demands for payment. They've had problems with players in L.A., Boston and Vancouver."

Maloney's reference to Vancouver was intriguing. Was he referring to Bure? On December 24, the *Province* published an article that included an allegation from an anonymous police source that Bure "had made two payments, believed to be in the tens of thousands" to a criminal figure.

Bure and his father flatly denied the story. So did Salcer, who said, "As far as I know, it's all unsubstantiated. Pavel has had no occurrences. It's irresponsible reporting." Salcer also played down reports that Alexei Zhitnik, a defenseman with the Los Angeles Kings, whom he and Serge Levin represented, had been threatened and beaten up by Russian crime figures. "It was a minor problem and it's over," Salcer insisted.

In an interview with the *Los Angeles Times*, Zhitnik, a Ukrainian with family in Kiev, was more forthcoming, acknowledging he had been threatened the previous summer. "I have a little problem with the Russian mafiya. They say things like, 'Blow your car up.' If you pay them the first time, the next time you pay much more. But my friends helped me. The cops can't do nothing. No rules. No laws."

According to testimony given at a 1996 U.S. congressional investigation into the spread of Russian organized crime in North America, by "friends," Zhitnik wasn't referring to his neighborhood buddies, but rather to a more powerful crime group.

Although Zhitnik never identified who had threatened him, there was suspicion that his problems were connected with his decision to end his business agreement with Vitaly Shevchenko, the Vancouver-based agent who had represented Vladimir Krutov in 1990. Although there are no qualifications for being a player agent, other than having someone to represent, most agents are lawyers or have a background in financial management. Shevchenko's unconventional dossier listed a stint in the Red Army and employment with a telephone company in Kiev.

Shevchenko had immigrated to Vancouver from Kiev in the mid-1980s, after marrying a Canadian girl, a Russian-language honors student who had been studying abroad. He claimed to have worked as a carpet cleaner upon his arrival in Vancouver, then later as a car salesman and on a fishing boat. His entry into the NHL came in May 1990 when he befriended Krutov, who had become disenchanted with his East Coast agent, Mark Malkovich. Shevchenko convinced Krutov to hire him, obtained his certificate from the NHL Players' Association and became a sports agent at age 24.

After Krutov left the Canucks in the fall of 1990, Shevchenko signed Ukrainian defenseman Alexander Godynyuk, a draft pick of the Toronto Maple Leafs. Shevchenko helped engineer Godynyuk's defection from the Soviet Union to Canada in the winter of 1990 and negotiated a two-year contract for his client with Toronto for $250,000. In 1991 Shevchenko added to his stable two more promising young Ukrainian players who had been drafted by NHL teams: Andrei Kovalenko, who joined the Quebec Nordiques in 1992, and Zhitnik, who joined the Los Angeles Kings in 1992.

According to British Columbia court documents, all three players signed six-year agreements with Shevchenko that gave him 10 per cent of their salaries, double the customary five per cent earned by most sports agents. The contract also entitled Shevchenko to a 25-per-cent share of any income they earned from personal appearances, endorsements or investments.

The three players severed ties with Shevchenko in the summer of 1993. In response, Shevchenko sued them for breach of contract in the B.C. Supreme Court in December 1993, claiming they had been stolen from him by agents who had offered cars and other inducements.

Normally one would expect such a dispute to receive media coverage, especially since the extortion issue and the possible involvement of Russian player agents had just surfaced in the news. But this story was curiously ignored, although all the details were a matter of public record. It wasn't until six years later, in April 1999, when Elliot Almond, a reporter with the *San Jose Mercury News*, began delving into Shevchenko's past after a controversial incident involving another of his clients, Andrei Zyuzin of the San Jose Sharks, that the facts came to light.

The court dismissed Shevchenko's cases against Zhitnik and Kovalenko, who said they had signed their contracts in English, a language they couldn't read. The case against Godynyuk was more complicated, since he had filed a counterclaim accusing Shevchenko of financial impropriety, including taking $25,000 meant to be invested in trust and transferring it into his own personal account. Godynyuk also claimed Shevchenko owed him another $66,000 he had paid the agent. Shevchenko denied both charges. Their dispute was eventually settled out of court in 1997.

Shevchenko, interestingly, was also the representative of Alexander Alexeev, the Jets draft pick who had been roughed up shortly after he, too, decided to end his relationship with the agent.

After leaving Shevchenko, Zhitnik and Kovalenko both signed with Serge Levin, Salcer's partner. Shevchenko was understandably upset by the loss of two of his top clients. Levin says that Shevchenko demanded money as compensation for the breakup. When Levin refused to pay, he alleges that Shevchenko threatened him over the phone, prompting Levin to call the FBI.

The fact that Shevchenko and Levin were at odds and that Shevchenko lived only six blocks from Bure, Levin and Salcer's star client, gives rise to some interesting speculation. There is no doubt that Bure knew Shevchenko. The two had met in Vancouver when Bure first toured Canada as a midget player in 1986. It is also possible that Shevchenko was the "unsavory" individual the Canucks asked Bure to disassociate himself from in the spring of 1993. Was Shevchenko applying pressure on Bure? Had Bure, like Zhitnik, sought out some helpful friends of his own? The people who know aren't saying.

Silence was also the reaction in the aftermath of Tremblay's allegations. Zhitnik was the only Soviet-born NHLer to speak on the record about the issue. The NHL offered no official reaction other than to say it was looking into the matter, and several general managers, Pat Quinn included, claimed they were unaware of any threats against Russian players.

The extortion controversy soon melted away, but not the problem. It would resurface again.

At the same time as the extortion stories were circulating, investigative reporters at the *Province* were looking into a troubling rumor about Bure and his association with some Russian crime figures in Vancouver. The story never made it into print, however, because the reporters were discouraged from pursuing it by management at the newspaper, who feared possible legal repercussions.

Bure had been seen in the company of Eugene and Alexander Alekseev, two Ukrainian émigrés in their mid-twenties. The precise nature of Bure's relationship with the Alekseev brothers is unclear, but if you were to propose 10 reasons for knowing the Alekseevs, nine of them would be bad.

The Alekseevs and another brother duo, Sergei and Taras Filonov, were the ringleaders of a group of cocaine traffickers known as "the

Russians," who had emerged in the Vancouver drug world in the late 1980s. Like stereotypical gangsters, they dressed well, drove sleek luxury cars, consorted with beautiful women and were regulars on the nightclub scene. They were also all bodybuilders and steroid users and, according to the police, ruthless and completely unpredictable.

The Filonovs and the Alekseevs were originally from Kiev. They had immigrated to Vancouver via Los Angeles with their families in the 1980s. Los Angeles was where they bought their cocaine, importing it into British Columbia in the innards of rental cars driven by young women.

In 1989 Vancouver police raided homes belonging to the Russians and seized $9 million worth of cocaine, $150,000 in cash, numerous cars and handguns, and a submachine gun. The Filonovs, the Alekseevs and their parents, and two others were arrested and charged with conspiracy to traffic in cocaine. While out on bail, the Russians, who, between their extravagant lifestyle and mounting legal bills, were believed to be running short of cash, ripped off members of both the Hells Angels and Asian gangs in several drug deals, sparking a vicious feud that resulted in a string of murders.

On May 15, 1990, Sergei Filonov was gunned down in broad daylight by members of the Hells Angels outside a motorcycle shop on Kingsway. His brother, Taras, was beaten with a crowbar, but he and the Alekseevs escaped. Taras eventually met his grisly end in August 1992. His body was found in the woods at the south end of the University of British Columbia campus; he had been tortured and his face had been blown away by a shotgun blast.

The outstanding charges against the Alekseevs and their parents were eventually stayed in November 1992. The prosecution's case had been hampered by attrition. In addition to the Filonovs, the two other accused had disappeared and were presumed dead. In the aftermath, the Alekseevs continued to deal drugs, pump iron and live the high life, tooling around Vancouver in luxury automobiles.

The police, who were keeping close tabs on the Alekseevs, were surprised to observe Bure dining with the two brothers at Vancouver's El Patio Mediterranean Restaurant on Cambie Street on October 30, 1993, when the Russian Rocket was recuperating from his groin injury. The date was the second anniversary of Bure's signing with the Canucks. The group later moved on to Earl's Restaurant at Broadway and Laurel where Eugene Alekseev's stripper girlfriend, Tracey Hill, worked as a manager. Bure evidently left the party and took a taxi home. It was lucky he did, because when the group went down to the parking lot and piled into Alexander Alekseev's Ford Explorer, a bomb went off. The explosion tore apart the dashboard, damaged the underside of the car and rattled store windows along the block. Amazingly no one was seriously injured. Eugene suffered second-degree burns but refused treatment. Police theorized the bomb had been improperly set, or it would have caused greater damage.

Thirteen days later a Chevy Blazer belonging to Alexander was blown sky-high outside the Citygate apartment complex on Quebec Street. Again, miraculously, no one was injured. The bomb had been detonated when Alexander approached the car and turned on the ignition with a remote-control device he had installed after the first bombing. The explosive was intended to kill; the force of the blast blew the hood of the truck a block away.

Associating with the Alekseevs was clearly a dangerous proposition. The Vancouver police briefed Pat Quinn on the situation, who in turn ordered Bure to end his association with the two brothers.

The Alekseevs next appeared in the news on April 26, 1995, when Eugene was found dead in a luxury hotel room in Mexico City. He had been killed by a single shot to the temple from a .38-caliber semiautomatic handgun. The wound, police said, was self-inflicted. At the time of Eugene's death, both Alekseev brothers were about to be charged with conspiring to distribute cocaine. A few months before, Tracey Hill had been arrested in California after she allegedly tossed a suitcase containing 18 kilos of cocaine off a moving train. In Hill's purse was found a prescription-pill bottle bearing the name of Al Cowlings, O. J. Simpson's buddy and Bronco driver. Cowlings later confirmed he knew Hill, providing another tantalizing connection in the case. Alexander Alekseev was never found. According to one report, he was last seen in South America. But some believe his body now lies at the bottom of Vancouver's harbor.

In early January, Bure finally snapped out of his funk, scoring five times in a three-game road trip. After 34 games, he had 20 goals and 22 assists for 42 points. Wayne Gretzky was leading the NHL with 80 points. The Great One's only serious rival in the scoring race was Sergei Fedorov, who was having a banner year with a league-high 32 goals.

Gretzky and Fedorov were among the few players who hadn't succumbed to a league-wide scoring malaise. Offensive production was down all around the NHL. The trend was attributed to better defensive systems, the abandonment of the tighter officiating of the previous year and a rash of injuries to top players. Back miseries would limit Mario Lemieux to just 22 games; Pat LaFontaine would miss 68 games with a knee injury; a ruptured Achilles tendon ended Teemu Selanne's season after 51 games; Steve Yzerman was sidelined for 26 games with a herniated disk in his neck; Eric Lindros missed 19 games with various ailments; and Alexander Mogilny, slow to recover from a broken ankle he suffered in the 1993 playoffs, would score only 32 goals, 44 fewer than in 1992–93.

In mid-January, after Cliff Ronning suffered a dislocated shoulder, Quinn made two deals to bolster Vancouver's depleted offense, acquiring center Jimmy Carson from Los Angeles for winger Dixon Ward and picking up winger Martin Gelinas on waivers from Quebec. The two former first-round draft picks, who had both been involved in the infamous Gretzky trade to Los Angeles in 1988, had fallen on hard times. The scoring touch that had enabled Carson to notch 55 goals at age 19 in 1987–88 had mysteriously deserted him, and Gelinas had never lived up to his early promise. Quinn put the pair on a line with Bure, and they responded by scoring several goals in their first few games together. But the trio proved to be a defensive liability, and within a couple of weeks both newcomers were shifted to other lines.

For the second straight year, Bure was the Canucks' lone representative at the NHL All-Star Game. Although the 1994 match was closer than the 1993 blowout, with the East defeating the West 9–8, it was strictly a no-hitting affair. Bure played alongside Fedorov, and the two Russian speedsters put on a high-velocity show, providing a glimpse of what Bure might be able to accomplish with a center of complementary skills. Bure had two pure breakaways, two partial breakaways and several other scoring opportunities, but was unable to beat Rangers goalie Mike Richter, who won the game's MVP Award for his efforts. Bure noted with frustration: "I had two great chances every shift. I couldn't score. I gave the guy [Richter] the truck. I missed so many chances it was like I put it in his driveway. The guys were telling me that I should be in the front seat beside him."

On March 3, Bure netted goals number 37 and 38 and added an assist as Vancouver blanked St. Louis 4–0. The salvo extended his points streak to 11 consecutive games, two short of his personal best. Behind the scenes, Quinn was close to finalizing a deal for Nedved that would have sent him and Gerald Diduck to Hartford in return for center Michael Nylander and defensemen Zarley Zalapski and James Patrick. But the trade was never finalized. On March 4, the Blues secretly signed Nedved to a US$4.05-million contract over three seasons, including the current one. He also received a signing bonus of US$850,000. Quinn was furious. Not only had the Blues torpedoed his trade with Hartford, the money they were giving Nedved made a mockery of the Canucks' offer. The lucrative deal meant Nedved would earn twice as much as Bure during the 1993–94 season, despite playing only 19 games.

Because Nedved was a restricted free agent, the Blues owed the Canucks player compensation for the signing. Quinn and St. Louis general manager Ron Caron tried to work out a deal. When they failed to come to an agreement, the issue went to arbitration. After bad-mouthing Nedved all season, Canucks management was now put in the position of having to praise his talents in order to get the most value in compensation. The Canucks asked for power forward Brendan Shanahan; the Blues offered center Craig Janney and a second-round draft choice. After weighing the arguments, arbitrator George Nicolau sided with the Blues.

But Janney promptly threw a wrench into the works by refusing to report to Vancouver. Adding to the Canucks' embarrassment, Nedved suddenly went on a scoring tear with the Blues. Meanwhile, the Calgary Flames, the team the Canucks were chasing for first place in the division, completed a deal with Hartford, acquiring Nylander, Zalapski and Patrick, the three players Quinn had wanted in return for Nedved.

Finally, on March 21, just before the NHL trade deadline, the Canucks and Blues worked out an alternative arrangement. The Canucks traded Janney back to the Blues in exchange for defensemen Jeff Brown and Bret Hedican and rookie center Nathan Lafayette. The Nedved affair had finally been settled after seven months. Most Vancouver fans were happy to see Nedved go, but Canucks management, which had taken a pounding over its handling of the affair, still had to absorb one more blow.

Brown, who was considered the key figure in the deal, had been one of the players St. Louis had originally offered the Canucks as compensation for Nedved. *Province* columnist Tony Gallagher obtained a copy of the document the Canucks filed in the compensation discussions and published the club's comments: "Mr. Brown is not considered a top defenseman or a core player. He has weak defensive skills. This is evident by his plus-minus. Further, he is not a character player. This is evident from his lack of scoring on the road and lack of penalty minutes. There is no place for him on the Vancouver roster."

The Canucks' lone bright light in March was Bure. His early-season scoring slump was a fast-fading memory. "He's really flying right now," noted Murray Craven, Bure latest center. "I think he realized halfway through the season that he might not make it to 50. He's been on a mission ever since. I think without a doubt the contract was bothering him. But he's put it out of his mind now."

On March 23, in a game in which Gretzky beat Kirk McLean to score the 802nd goal of his career, surpassing Gordie Howe's all-time NHL record, Bure quietly put his 50th of the season into an empty Kings net to cap a 6–3 Canucks win. It marked the eighth straight game in which he had scored, breaking Tony Tanti's franchise record of seven. With 36 goals in his last 35 games, Bure was the NHL's hottest scorer.

On March 27, Bure notched his third hat trick of the season in a 4–3 win over the Kings. Two of his goals came on power plays, giving him 22 in man-advantage situations, eclipsing Tanti's single-season club record of 20. The next night, in a 3–2 win over Toronto, Bure scored his 54th goal of the season, then hit the 100-point mark when he set up Craven for the winner in overtime.

All told, Bure tallied 19 goals and 11 assists for 30 points in 16 games in March and was voted the NHL player of the month. Yet, despite his torrid surge, the Canucks were still plodding along at the .500 level, securely ensconced in second place in the division, eight points behind the Flames. No one else on the team was scoring anywhere close to expectations. By the season's end, only Odjick improved upon his pace of the previous year, jumping from four to 16 goals. Linden, one of the team's top performers in the first half, went into hibernation following the All-Star break. After scoring 27 goals in his first 52 games, he netted only five goals in his last 32.

Meanwhile, in Buffalo, another Russian extortion incident made headlines. On March 25, two men were arrested outside the Buffalo Sabres' dressing room at Memorial Auditorium. Initially apprehended for trespassing, they were later charged with attempted grand larceny. The pair had threatened to shoot Alexander Mogilny if he didn't pay them US$150,000. One of the men was identified as Sergei Fomitov, the same individual who helped Mogilny defect in 1989, and who had lived with him during his first NHL season. According to Mogilny, Fomitov threatened him after practice. Mogilny said he agreed to give Fomitov $2,000. Claiming he was going to a bank, he drove away and called his girlfriend on his cell phone, asking her to alert the police. Fomitov later pleaded guilty to a lesser charge of menacing and was deported, as was his partner, Viacheslav Petechel.

At the Canucks' last home game of the season, Bure picked up four individual awards: most exciting player, leading scorer, the fans' MVP and the Molson Cup for most three-star selections. In a 2–1 road win over Anaheim in the season finale, he roofed a backhand on a breakaway for his 60th goal to become just the eighth player in NHL annals to record back-to-back 60-goal campaigns. His 60 goals were the most in the NHL, three more than runner-up Brett Hull. Bure now had 154 career goals in 224 games. Only two other players—Mike Bossy and Wayne Gretzky—had ever scored more goals in their first three NHL seasons.

The Canucks limped to the finish line, going 3–4–0 in April to finish with 85 points, good enough for second in the division, but seventh in the conference. The Calgary Flames, seeded second in the conference by virtue of winning the Pacific Division, would supply Vancouver's opposition in the first playoff round. Although Calgary had finished 12 points ahead of Vancouver, the two teams weren't far apart in ability. Still, few observers thought the Canucks possessed the necessary discipline or focus to prevail. They hadn't been able to put together four straight wins since the first two weeks of the season.

Before flying to Calgary, the Canucks' coaching staff tried to shore up the team's confidence. Quinn, who had been remarkably patient with his Jekyll-and-Hyde team, still believed his players had the experience and talent to make a serious run at the Cup. "You're ready to take the next step up," he told them. But there was an unspoken threat behind the challenge. After two straight playoff failures, the players realized that if they came up short a third time, many of them wouldn't be around to try again.

# CHAPTER TEN

# Sudden Death

*Once Pavel sees the blueline he smells blood.*
*When the cameras zero in on him, you can see the determination in*
*his face. He never lets up around the net.*

STAN SMYL, FORMER VANCOUVER CANUCK

**B**LOOD OFTEN HAD to be scraped off the ice when the Vancouver Canucks and the Calgary Flames met. *Hate* wasn't too strong a word to describe the rivalry between the two teams. Even before the series started, the war of words had begun. Discussing Flames enforcer Sandy McCarthy, Gino Odjick said, "A lot of their guys depend on Sandy. I'm sure it helps a guy like [Gary] Roberts, who is chippy and plays dirty, but he'll never fight anymore. If Sandy wasn't there for him, he wouldn't score 40 goals. He would spend a lot of time getting pounded in the head."

Odjick and company would need to do more than pound a few heads to defeat Calgary, a team deepest at the position Vancouver was thinnest: center ice. The Flames had six players who could play in the middle — Joe Nieuwendyk, Robert Reichel, German Titov, Joel Otto, Kelly Kisio and Wes Walz, plus two outstanding wingers in Theoren Fleury and Gary

Roberts. Their defense was anchored by master blaster Al MacInnis. Veteran goalie Mike Vernon was their main man between the pipes.

In addition to being a litmus test for the Canucks' playoff aspirations, the series offered a unique opportunity to evaluate the Nedved deal, as it would pit Zarley Zalapski, James Patrick and Michael Nylander, the three players Quinn had originally tried to acquire for Nedved, against Jeff Brown, Bret Hedican and Nathan Lafayette, the trio he ultimately picked up from the St. Louis Blues.

Prior to Game 1, Bure was asked if he was concerned about the intense checking he was bound to face. "I don't care [about] physical. We've had so many games that were real tough, against Chicago, against Calgary. I think I'm all right. If someone is going to shadow me, it means other guys from the line have more room."

Displaying a focus of purpose that was absent during most of the regular season, the Canucks stunned the Flames 5–0 in the series opener at the Saddledome. McLean stopped 31 shots and Vancouver withstood early power-play pressure before breaking the game open in the second with three straight goals.

Calgary rebounded to take Game 2 by a score of 7–5 in a violent, penalty-filled contest. Turnovers and defensive blunders haunted the Canucks as they lost the battle of the power play. Calgary scored four times in 10 chances, while Vancouver converted one of nine. Bure had an awful game. In the first period, he coughed up the puck in his own end while trying to avoid a bodycheck by Otto, resulting in a short-handed goal by Mike Sullivan. Making matters worse, he was cooling his heels in the penalty box for two of the Flames' other goals. "I didn't feel very well and I don't know why," he admitted after the game. "Sometimes you're flying, but today I was really far from flying. Everything went wrong."

The checking was far more intense in Game 3. The contest remained scoreless until 3:33 of the third period when Walz scored on a give-and-go with Gary Roberts. A few minutes later, the Coliseum crowd got a chance to cheer when Momesso deflected Gerald Diduck's point shot under the crossbar. Later in the period Courtnall missed a glorious chance to put the Canucks ahead, and Fleury scored on the counter rush, blowing a 30-footer past McLean. The Canucks pressed for the equalizer, but Roberts ended their hopes by scoring at 18:23. "It was an excellent hockey game, but unfortunately we weren't good enough to get through it, Quinn said afterward. "When the game was on the line, we didn't have the discipline to win."

Vancouver outplayed Calgary by a wide margin in Game 4, but Vernon was rock-solid, turning aside shot after shot. The Canucks had enough scoring opportunities in the second period to win two games, but were only up 2–1 entering the third. During the second period, Calgary lost both Nieuwendyk and Otto to knee injuries. When they failed to return in the third, the Canucks' odds of evening the series looked much improved. But as was so often the case during the regular season, Vancouver self-destructed. Sloppy coverage on a defensive-zone faceoff resulted in a goal by Walz just 44 seconds into the third period. A few minutes later McLean flubbed a clearing attempt. The puck went directly to Mike Sullivan, who passed to Reichel, who fed Fleury in the slot, and he buried it.

Down three games to one, the Canucks were in dire shape heading back to Alberta. At the start of the series, McLean, Bure and Linden were cited as the three key players for Vancouver, but only Linden had answered the bell. McLean had been outplayed by Vernon, and Bure was stuck on the launch pad. He had only three assists in the series, all of them on the power play. Including the previous year, he was now scoreless in eight straight playoff games. Calgary's strategy of shadowing him with forward Mike Sullivan and defenseman Zarley Zalapski had proved extremely effective, and Bure had reacted to the suffocating coverage with frustration, drawing seven minor penalties and a major.

Commenting on his club's success against Bure, Calgary head coach Dave King told reporters, "I think you feel good that so far your plan has worked. But you're always thinking: Is this the game he'll find a way?"

If Bure didn't find a way, he wouldn't be able to shake the perception that he was a "soft player." No matter how many goals a player scores during the regular season, the ultimate test is producing in the heightened intensity of the playoffs. In hockey vernacular, Bure had yet to prove he could "play though the crap."

An injury to Craven forced Quinn to juggle his lines for Game 5. He put Linden at center between Bure and Adams, but resisted the impulse to replace McLean with backup goalie Kay Whitmore, as the pundits had been calling for. Both decisions paid off. Bure broke his scoring drought at 4:48 of the first period, one-timing Adams's feed to put Vancouver ahead 1–0. Calgary answered 65 seconds later when Murzyn got caught deep in the Flames' zone and Titov scored on a three-on-one break. But after that brief flurry neither team could break through. In a display of steely resolve, McLean kept Calgary at bay, making tremendous third-period stops on Roberts, Reichel and Yawney. Early in overtime, the Canucks' netminder rose to the occasion once more, denying Ron Stern.

The break the Canucks had been waiting for finally came eight minutes in when Flames defenseman Kevin Dahl allowed Diduck's dump-out pass to skip through his skates. The puck was gobbled up by Courtnall, who had just come over the boards on a line change. He broke down the wing and wired a shot from the right faceoff circle that beat Vernon high on the glove side. The Canucks were still alive.

Game 6 offered another dose of drama. After falling behind 2–1 midway through the second period, the Flames took control. Early in the third, Walz tied it up, tipping home Zalapski's point shot. But despite outshooting Vancouver 10–2 in the period, Calgary couldn't get the winner. The Flames buzzed around the Canucks' net like angry hornets in overtime, and McLean was forced to make sensational stops on Reichel and Fleury from in close.

There were four minutes left in the first overtime when Calgary was penalized for too many men on the ice. Incredibly it was Calgary's fourth bench minor of the series and its third for too many men on the ice. Quinn called a timeout and held a conference at the bench. "Don't worry about picking a corner, just get the shot on net," he told his players. Linden won the draw and the puck came back to Bure at the point, who unleashed a low drive. The disk bounced off a body in front directly to Linden's stick and he put it away for the 3–2 win.

Considering the Canucks' precarious situation a week before, a seventh game looked like a gift. The prospect wasn't so eagerly anticipated in Calgary. Collars had begun tightening in Cowtown, and the word *choke* was now bandied about in the newspapers. But if the Flames' players were feeling the pressure, they didn't show it. Calgary started strongly and took the lead on a goal by Fleury at 5:04 of the first period. The Canucks replied on the power play when Bure scooped in a rebound from the edge of the crease. Two minutes later a routine shot by Craven hit the skates of two Flames defenders and deflected to Courtnall in the slot. His quick shot beat Vernon. Outshot 16–6, Vancouver headed to the dressing room up 2–1. But the Flames renewed their assault in the second period, firing 16 shots on McLean, and forged ahead 3–2 on goals by Stern and Fleury.

Fleury's goal loomed huge as the third period progressed. Although their season was on the line, the Canucks were unable to mount any pressure on Vernon. Bottled up by Calgary's persistent checking, they directed only three shots at the Flames' netminder through the first 16 minutes. The reporters in press row were already writing Vancouver's obituary when Bure found Adams with a pass down low behind the Calgary defense. Adams bulled his way into the goalmouth and lifted a backhand at the net. The puck hit Vernon's pads and trickled down the other side and over the goal line. The two teams were headed to sudden death again.

Overtime proved to be a test of nerves and stamina. Both teams had good chances to finish the series in the first overtime, but the best opportunity came midway through the extra frame. The Canucks swarmed the Calgary end when suddenly the play turned in the other direction. A shot by Craven rebounded directly to Roberts, who chipped the puck up the boards past a trapped Dana Murzyn and into the neutral zone, where Fleury hopped on the disk in full flight. Joining him on the rush was a streaking Robert Reichel. Roberts, trailing the play, turned it into a three-on-one. Lumme, the lone Canuck back, positioned himself between the two lead Flames. Fleury, cruising in on the right wing, held the puck, freezing McLean, then feathered a pass across to Reichel, who smoothly one-timed his shot. Half the net was open. A goal seemed inevitable. The red light even went on. But McLean, anticipating the pass, desperately threw himself feetfirst across the crease. The puck hit his toe and rebounded out past the onrushing Roberts before he could react.

Replayed in slow motion and analyzed from various angles, McLean's amazing stop on Reichel would later become known simply as the Save. At the time, though, it merely prolonged the drama. The game remained tied through the first overtime. Weariness was now becoming a factor. The two teams had battled through 24 periods of hard-hitting hockey in 13 days. The pace was slowing. If a goal was to be scored, it would likely come early in the next overtime period before legs turned leaden. Three shifts in, the moment arrived.

Adams dumped the puck into the Calgary end along the left boards. The puck came around to Paul Kruse, who chipped it hard out of the zone. It slid down the ice to Dave Babych, who swept the puck along the blueline to his defensive partner, Jeff Brown. Head up, Brown made eye contact with Bure as he broke out of a cluster of players at the Calgary blueline. The Vancouver rearguard snapped a long pass through the middle that hit Bure's stick right on the tape. The two had hooked up on a similar play in the first period, but Bure had lost the handle on the puck as he had burst free. This time he maintained control, accelerating toward the Flames' net. Zalapski, caught flat-footed, turned and hooked frantically at Bure, once, twice, but the Russian pulled away. "Anyone other than Pavel," Brown said later, "might have been caught." Bure faked to his backhand, went to his forehand, then, with the patience of a practiced assassin, waited for Vernon to extend himself before finally tucking the puck between the goalie's right pad and the post.

Bure began celebrating with an impromptu striptease, tossing away his stick, then his gloves, until he was finally swept up in the joyful embrace of his teammates. The Saddledome crowd was stunned. The series was over.

Assistant coach Ron Smith, who was with the Canucks when they made their surprising run to the Cup finals in 1982, felt he was experiencing déjà vu: "Even when we were down, I felt something was going to happen. It's almost metaphysical, something cosmic. It reminded me of '82 when we had the patched-up defense and everything still fell into place. You have to work hard, but at some point something else takes over."

The Canucks advanced to face the well-rested Dallas Stars, who had swept the St. Louis Blues in four straight games. In a bid to reduce travel, the series featured a new format. Instead of playing the usual two at home, two on the road, and then alternating back and forth between cities for Games 5 through 7, the series followed a 2–3–2 pattern. Because of their higher placing during the regular season, the Stars had a choice between opening at home or on the road. They chose to start the series in Dallas.

The Stars were renowned for their conservative, defensive style, and the series was expected to be a low-scoring, grinding affair, but Dallas, hoping to catch Vancouver in an emotional letdown, dispensed with its typical game plan and opened things up in Game 1. The strategy backfired as the Canucks surged out to a 4–1 lead, aided by some shaky goaltending by Darcy Wakaluk. But Dallas kept plugging and Vancouver began to unravel, allowing three straight goals. Then, just as it appeared the game was slipping away, Nathan Lafayette won a faceoff draw in the Stars' zone and Martin Gelinas snapped off a shot that squeezed through Wakaluk's pads. Linden added an empty-netter and Vancouver had a 6–4 win.

The Canucks stymied the Stars in Game 2 with airtight defense, sublime goaltending from McLean and a scintillating performance from Bure to win 3–0. Linden called it the best game Bure had ever played. The Russian scored twice; his second goal, created seemingly out of thin air, with 21 seconds left in the second period, was the backbreaker. After pouncing on a loose puck in the neutral zone, Bure instantly went on the attack. Zooming around defenseman Derian Hatcher and holding his edge the way a downhill skier would, he cut toward the net and snapped the puck over goalie Andy Moog.

Discussing the goal after the game, Ronning said, "He [Bure] is like a rattlesnake around the goal. You give him a second and it's in. He amazes me, he's so quick." It wasn't Bure's quickness that most people were talking about afterward, however, but rather the vicious hit he had delivered to hardrock Shane Churla in the first period. The incident started when Bure, who had been the target of several unpenalized cheap shots, was cross-checked by Craig Ludwig and then pounded in the back of the head by Churla while down on his knees. When referee Andy Van Hellemond failed to detect either infraction, Bure went looking for revenge, leveling Churla with a flying elbow to the jaw that knocked the Dallas enforcer senseless. Van Hellemond, displaying a remarkably consistent blindness, missed this blatant foul, as well.

According to Stars coach Bob Gainey, Bure should have received a five-minute major and been ejected for a deliberate attempt to injure. Churla felt he had been victimized by a double standard: "If it was the other way around, if it was me who turned out his lights, I'd be gone for about 15 games at least. I'd be splashed all over the community and people would be calling me the biggest goon in hockey."

Bure, finding himself in the rare position of defending thuggery, pleaded self-defense. "It's not my style, but I had no choice. They're trying to kill me. I'm lucky I didn't get hurt."

Quinn blamed the incident on the referees: "As far as throwing stones, it's crap. Any human in the world would take a swing back at someone who was trying to hurt him. This kid has taken a pounding from Calgary and now these guys. It's almost like the referees want to see the Russian get beat up. Let's put the focus where it belongs. Why isn't the focus on the guys beating the crap out of him?"

NHL vice president Brian Burke fined Bure $500 for his act of vigilante justice, but levied no suspension. As the series headed back to Vancouver, the media predicted an explosion of retaliatory violence. The mayhem never occurred. Instead, Dallas stuck to hockey, and after falling behind 2–0, rallied to score four straight goals. Upon taking the lead, the Stars were able to employ their patented defensive game, limiting the Canucks to just two shots on net in the third period and posting a 4–3 win.

Game 4 was a tight-checking nail-biter. Linden opened the scoring from Bure and Adams, but Brent Gilchrist replied for the Stars in the second. Both goaltenders were unbeatable in the third. McLean stoned Paul Broten twice; Moog denied Gelinas on a backhander and then stopped a howitzer from Bure with his mask. Bure appeared to net the winner at 18:47, but the goal was disallowed after the video replay revealed that Bure's arm knocked the net off its moorings just before the puck crossed the line. A Dallas victory in sudden death would turn the series around, but once again destiny smiled on the Canucks. Momesso, who had been buried deep in Quinn's doghouse, emerged to score the game winner, blindly whacking the puck in from the slot to give the Canucks a 3–1 lead in the series.

Two nights later the Canucks avoided a return trip to Dallas, wrapping up the series with a 4–2 victory on home ice. Bure drove the final stake through the heart of Texas, scoring on a breakaway with 3:26 left in the third period.

Instead of faltering as they had in the past two years, Vancouver was gathering momentum as the playoffs progressed. McLean's inspired goaltending and Bure's brilliance were major factors, but the team had also benefited from the Nedved trade. The speedy Lafayette was playing with surprising poise, and Brown and Hedican had given the club a mobility on defense that it had previously lacked. With three solid defense pairs, Vancouver now had the rare luxury of depth on the back line.

To reach the Cup finals, the Canucks had to beat the Toronto Maple Leafs. The geographical absurdity of having Toronto in the Western Conference was never more evident. Whereas Vancouver and Toronto would have to fly nearly 3,000 miles between cities to contest their series, the Eastern Conference finalists, the New Jersey Devils and the New York Rangers, would be able to make the 30-minute commute to each other's arena by bus.

Having played 14 playoff games in 27 days, Toronto copied Dallas's strategy and opted to open the series at home. In order to have any chance of winning, the Leafs had to find a way to throttle the Linden–Bure–Adams line, which had ventilated Dallas's defense for 10 goals and eight assists in five games. Coach Pat Burns decided to counter the Canucks' high-scoring trio with a checking unit composed of Peter Zezel, Bill Berg and Mark Osborne and his top defensive pairing of Sylvain Lefebvre and Jamie Macoun. The Leafs' defensive specialists did their job in Game 1. Leading 2–1 late in the third period, Toronto was on the verge of taking the series opener when Mike Gartner was penalized for holding at 18:18. The Canucks pulled McLean and got the equalizer with 30 seconds left as Linden bolted through the Leafs' defense and beat Felix Potvin with a backhand.

The Canucks had played four overtime games in the playoffs and had won them all. Bure almost made it five when he was sent in alone midway through the extra frame, but he put his shot into Potvin's midriff. Eight minutes later McLean skated into the corner to play Osborne's shoot-in, but failed to clear the zone. Zezel corralled the puck near the boards and flipped a shot toward the net before McLean could get set. The puck floated into the goal. The Leafs had taken the first game.

Historically speaking, there was little sense of a hockey rivalry between Vancouver and Toronto. The last time the two cities had met in the playoffs was back in 1922 when the NHL's Toronto St. Pats defeated the Vancouver Millionaires of the Pacific Coast Hockey Association. But the matchup tapped into the simmering East-West antagonism, and with Canadian bragging rights on the line, a feud quickly built. Columnists Rosie DiManno of the *Toronto Star* and Denny Boyd of the *Vancouver Sun* duked it out in print, and hoary stereotypes began to fly. DiManno described Vancouver as a "blonde bimbo" of a town. Both papers ran a Why I Hate Vancouver/Toronto contest, with the winner receiving a free trip to the city of their loathing.

There was a widespread perception in Vancouver that not only the CBC, with an eye fixed firmly on the ratings, but also the executives in the NHL's head office, wanted the Leafs to win. After referee Dan Marouelli waved off a Vancouver goal in the first game, despite contradictory evidence from the NetCam's fish-eye lens, the paranoia level rose. The Vancouver media, ever-sensitive about eastern slights, became as objective as a convention of Grassy Knoll conspiracy buffs. When a foul by the Leafs' Macoun went unpunished in Game 1, CKNW radio broadcaster Tom Larscheid blurted "Bullshit" into his microphone.

The sheer oddity of a Vancouver-Toronto matchup was evident from the coverage on CBC-TV. Announcer Bob Cole, who usually handled the Leafs' national broadcasts, was clearly unfamiliar with Vancouver's players. He repeatedly confused McIntyre and Lafayette, and he referred to Bure as if he were an exotic species, which for many Ontario viewers he probably was. The Canucks' games were rarely seen by a national audience, and the lack of familiarity with Bure was evident in the stories written about him by Toronto sportswriters, who felt compelled to phonetically spell his name for their readers.

In Game 2, Bure gave them a glimpse of what they had been missing. Despite the Leafs' harassment, he was a constant force, firing seven shots on Potvin and displaying an array of dizzying moves. At one point in the first period, he stunned the Gardens crowd with a boldly imaginative play. While standing behind the Leafs' net, he suddenly flipped the puck forward, high in the air over Potvin's head, then darted around to the front of the net and attempted to bat in the fluttering puck as it hit the ice — in essence, converting his own pass. It was the sort of maneuver most players wouldn't attempt in a summer league, never mind the Stanley Cup playoffs. Asked about the move after the game, Bure admitted it was something he had worked on in practice: "It's my kind of style to play like this. If I get the chance to do something fancy, I do it."

"Fancy" was a fitting description for a goal Bure did score at 18:43 of the first period. After snaring Dmitri Mironov's clearing attempt on the right boards with his glove, Bure faked defenseman Dave Ellett to his knees, danced around him into the slot and whipped a shot past Potvin into the top corner.

The Leafs replied with two power-play goals by Mironov, but Jeff Brown tied it with a low point shot on the power play, and then Craven put the Canucks up 3–2. The Leafs knotted the score in the third period on a power-play goal by Ellett, their third with a man advantage and their third by a defenseman. The game appeared to be headed to overtime until Macoun hauled down Ronning and drew a penalty. On the ensuing power play, Jyrki Lumme took Linden's pass from the side boards, cruised into the slot and snapped home a shot that stood up as the game winner.

Game 3 was decided early. The turning point came midway in the first period just after the Leafs failed to score on a five-on-three power play for one minute and 29 seconds. Linden checked Gartner at the Canucks' blueline and the puck squirted free. Leafs defenseman Bob Rouse tried to poke the puck to his partner, Todd Gill, but Bure intercepted. Kicking into warp drive, he cut strongly across Gill's check, skated in on a partial breakaway and fired the puck over Potvin's glove. The goal keyed a huge momentum shift.

Adams scored a power-play marker at 4:56 of the second period to make the score 2–0, and the Canucks, exhibiting a newfound defensive discipline, threw a checking blanket over the Leafs. With five minutes left and Toronto pressing to get back into the game, Craven blocked Ellett's slap shot and chipped the puck forward directly into Bure's flight path. On a clear-cut breakaway from center ice, the Russian Rocket steamed toward the Toronto net with the Coliseum crowd in full bay. The result was never in doubt. Bure buried the puck between the pads of the retreating Leafs goalie, who tumbled back into the net as if driven there by the Russian's backwash. Gelinas added a late power-play tally to make the final score 4–0.

"We had our scoring chances and we got beat by Bure's speed," Burns said. "He is a quick guy, and when he gets it in that second or third gear, he is a hard guy to catch. He's a helluva player on a helluva roll."

Knowing they needed to win at least once in Vancouver to send the series back home, the Leafs turned in a gutsy effort in Game 4. Yet, despite holding a territorial edge in play and outshooting the Canucks 20–11 during the first two periods, they couldn't beat the coolly efficient McLean.

Doug Gilmour, Toronto's most dangerous offensive threat, was clearly laboring. The combined pounding and wear of the regular season and two hard-fought playoff series had taken a toll. *Vancouver Sun* columnist Denny Boyd described him as looking "ground and chewed down as a sparerib bone. He has the face of a refugee in a warzone newsreel, gaunt, wounded, shot at and totally miserable."

The tense struggle remained scoreless for 58 minutes until Ronning broke away from his check and pulled the trigger on a two-on-one break with Momesso. Bure clinched it with an empty-netter at 19:27. The Canucks were now one win away from the finals.

The Leafs, who had been unable to solve McLean since the series had shifted to Vancouver, finally found a chink in his armor in Game 5 when Mike Eastwood banked a puck in off the goalie's shoulder at 7:54 of the first period. The marker ended McLean's shutout streak at 143 minutes and 17 seconds. Suddenly energized, Toronto added a pair from Gilmour and Wendel Clark before the period was done for a 3–0 lead, but Vancouver regrouped in the second and battled back behind goals by Craven, Lafayette and Adams to tie it 3–3. With both goalies performing acrobatics, neither team could score in the third period or in the first overtime.

The end came suddenly in the second overtime. Only 14 seconds had elapsed when Linden dropped the puck to Babych, who snapped off a quick shot. Potvin stretched and caught it, but it fell out of his glove and Adams, perched on the doorstep, shoveled the puck into the net to send the Canucks to the finals. The goal was sweet vindication for Adams, who had scored just 13 times during the regular season, the lowest total of his career. "That's the biggest goal I've ever scored in my career," he said later in the Canucks' dressing room. "The playoffs have been a whole new season. It's a brand-new start, a chance to redeem yourself."

# CHAPTER ELEVEN

# Enter the Dragon

*Some men can tell eight lies in seven words.*
RUSSIAN PROVERB

THE THEME OF REDEMPTION not only applied to the Canucks, but also to their opponent in the Stanley Cup finals. After missing the playoffs in 1992–93, the New York Rangers had rebounded under new coach Mike Keenan to win a franchise-record 52 games and claim first overall in the NHL. Yet, despite their success, the Rangers were no model of harmony. Keenan's persistent baiting of his players had prompted captain Mark Messier to confront his coach in midseason and demand he ease up. Keenan and general manager Neil Smith, united only by their mutual loathing, had barely spoken to each other in four months. Discord, Keenan's volatile creative medium, swirled around the team like a rumbling storm.

Both teams had survived a seventh-game overtime to reach the finals, but if Vancouver's path was guided by an invisible hand, as Canucks assistant coach Ron Smith had suggested, New York's was powered by a flesh-and-blood force—the steely will of Messier. The Rangers' captain had become a Manhattan folk hero by guaranteeing a victory over the New Jersey Devils in Game 6 of the Eastern Conference finals, then delivering on the promise in dramatic Joe Namath–style. With the Rangers trailing 2–0 and teetering on the brink of elimination, Messier set up New York's first goal late in the second period, then scored a hat trick in the third to carry his club to a 4–2 win.

Having defeated New Jersey in a tension-racked seven games, the Rangers could be forgiven for thinking the hardest part of their journey was behind them. Based on their play during the regular season, the Canucks had no business being on the same ice. The 27-point gap between the two teams was the largest among Cup finalists since 1958. Only two teams—the 1949 Toronto Maple Leafs and the 1938 Chicago Blackhawks—had claimed the Cup with a poorer record than the Canucks. But if Vancouver was bucking the tide of history, so, too, was New York, which hadn't won the Cup in 54 years, a drought attributed to the dreaded "Rangers curse."

The curse was said to date back to the 1940–41 season, the last time New York had the Cup in its possession. In January 1941, the Madison Square Garden Corporation paid off the US$3 million mortgage on its arena. To celebrate the occasion, team president John Kilpatrick put the mortgage certificate into the Cup and, with the other corporate directors looking on, set it afire. Rangers general manager Lester Patrick was appalled. You could do a lot of things to the Cup—drink champagne out of it, kiss it, embrace it, even sleep with it, as the Islanders' Bryan Trottier once did—but you didn't desecrate the Holy Grail by using it as a furnace. Patrick was convinced no good would come of Kilpatrick's rash act. As decades passed without the Rangers winning the trophy again, the hex became part of NHL legend. Superstitious Rangers fans had added a Gothic twist to the tale in recent years, suggesting the curse was protected by a dragon, a sentinel of ill will that lived beneath the Garden's ice.

But Keenan's veteran squad had no reason to believe in curses. Six of his players—Mark Messier, Glenn Anderson, Esa Tikkanen, Kevin Lowe, Craig MacTavish and Adam Graves—had won the Cup with the Edmonton Oilers during the 1980s. Between them, they owned 22 Cup rings. The infusion of big-ticket talent from Edmonton hadn't escaped the notice of Oilers GM Glen Sather, who dryly remarked, "If the Rangers win the Stanley Cup, Neil Smith should kiss my ass."

In contrast, only four Canucks players had ever caressed the silverware in victory: Geoff Courtnall, Tim Hunter, Martin Gelinas and Sergio Momesso, who had all won it once. If past familiarity with Lord Stanley's chalice was any predictor of success, there was no doubt which team had the upper hand.

The Rangers also had another edge. Since the start of the playoffs, they had traveled only 500 miles. New York hadn't played a game outside its own time zone since March 27, and with the exception of one round-trip flight to Washington, hadn't even boarded an airplane during the playoffs. In contrast, the Canucks had already logged 12,000 miles. Still, Vancouver's players could see something positive in the situation. They believed they were tougher and more accustomed to transcontinental travel. The longer the series lasted, the better off they would be.

In the view of New York reporters, the Rangers' only serious worry would be keeping Bure off the scoreboard. The Russian Rocket had notched points in 15 straight playoff games, three shy of Trottier's NHL record, and led all players with 13 goals. Bure's play was dispelling the notion that Europeans lacked the grit and mental toughness to excel in the playoffs because they didn't grow up with the dream of winning the Stanley Cup. As Bure noted, "Once I had a dream of winning an Olympic gold meal, but times change, dreams change. The Stanley Cup is better than a gold medal."

One thing was certain: a Russian would soon see his name engraved on the Cup. New York had four Russians in its lineup: Alexei Kovalev, Sergei Zubov, Sergei Nemchinov and Alexander Karpovtsev. Although none of them would be able to claim the distinction of being the first Russian-born player to hoist the Cup in triumph—an honor that belonged to Johnny Gottselig, captain of the 1938 champion Chicago Blackhawks—1994 would be the first year a Soviet-trained player would capture hockey's greatest prize.

How did Keenan intend to stop Bure? The Rangers coach tap-danced around the question: "Bure's an electrifying player and a great goal scorer and he's very dangerous on the rush. He makes it challenging for every-body. We can try to shadow him, or we can play a certain line against him, or a certain defensive pairing."

Although Bure was the topic on most people's minds, Messier cited a different concern: "I've been watching Vancouver on our off days, and Kirk McLean has been unbelievable."

Messier's observation proved prescient. It wasn't how to stop Bure, but rather how to beat McLean that became the $64,000 question in Game 1. The hard-charging Rangers forwards were on the Canucks' defense like hungry sharks from the opening faceoff. New York's full-court press had the Canucks reeling, and when forward Steve Larmer scored from defenseman Brian Leetch and Kovalev at 3:32 of the first, it seemed as if the floodgates were about to open. But McLean held firm under tremendous pressure.

The score was still 1–0, five minutes into the third period, when Canucks defenseman Bret Hedican beat goalie Mike Richter from the slot. The goal gave anxious Rangers fans pause. It was the first time Hedican had beaten an NHL netminder in 147 regular-season and playoff games. His only other goal had been scored into an empty net on April 14, 1992.

But three minutes later Kovalev, the Rangers' resident Russian artiste, put New York back on top, converting a sweet setup by Leetch. Kovalev was something of an enigma. Blessed with extraordinary talent but prone to mental lapses, he had so frustrated Keenan with his reluctance to make quick line changes that the Rangers' coach had left him on the ice without a change for half a period in a game against Boston earlier in the year. But Kovalev had brought his A game to the finals, and on this night he was the dominant Russian on the ice.

With Vancouver's offense stuck in neutral, the Rangers' lead looked secure. Then, with one minute left, the dragon awoke from its slumber. Ronning wristed a bad-angle shot toward New York's net, and Gelinas, standing at the edge of the crease, tipped it as it flew past. Somehow the puck slipped under Richter's arm and dribbled across the goal line.

The late-minute goal was a heartbreaker for the Rangers, but they refused to wilt and came out skating hard in overtime, attacking the Canucks' goal in waves. McLean was forced to make eye-popping saves on Graves, Leetch, Tikkanen and Stephane Matteau. With Vancouver reeling like a punch-drunk fighter, a Rangers victory seemed imminent. Finally, in the last minute of the period, Leetch beat McLean with a rising shot. But instead of finding twine, the puck clanged off the crossbar and rebounded all the way out to Bure near the Canucks' blueline. He quickly flipped the disk past a pinching Jeff Beukeboom to Ronning, who had just hit the ice on a line change. With Leetch trapped out of position, Ronning broke away on a two-on-one with Adams. Twenty feet inside the Rangers' blueline he calmly laid a pass over to Adams, who one-timed a shot over Richter's shoulder for the game winner.

McLean, the man of the hour or, more precisely, of 79 minutes and 26 seconds, had stopped 52 of 54 shots, including 17 in overtime. Only one other goalie had ever turned aside more rubber in a Cup finals game: Montreal's Ken Dryden, who stopped 56 shots in 1971 against Chicago. Amazingly it was the first time McLean had beaten the Rangers in his NHL career.

Before Game 2, Quinn warned his players to prepare themselves for an early "New York blitz." Whether it was awe at the situation or simply Cup jitters, his words had no effect. The Canucks did nothing early on to indicate they were going to make things easier for their beleaguered goalie. They trailed 1–0 and had been outshot 12–2 by the Rangers when Momesso, on Vancouver's first decent shift, scored at 14:04. The goal injected some life into the Canucks, and they outshot the Rangers 8–2 over the last six minutes of the period.

But the Rangers dominated play again in the second, despite being forced to kill off three penalties. With Graves in the box for tripping, New York netted the game's decisive goal. Linden attempted a risky pass to Brown that was picked off by Messier. The Rangers' captain broke away with Brown in pursuit. Harassed from behind, Messier momentarily lost control of the puck and McLean was able to pokecheck him. Instead of rolling clear, though, the puck hit Messier. The ex-Oiler flipped a pass over to Anderson, the trailer on the play, who eluded Lumme and scored. The Canucks had several chances to tie it in the third period, but the puck had suddenly become magnetized—Bure, Ronning and Adams all rang shots off the iron behind Richter. After Quinn pulled McLean in the final minute for an extra attacker, the Canucks bombarded Richter with shots, but he withstood the barrage. Leetch finally ended the suspense by sliding the puck into the empty net with five seconds left.

The Canucks were fortunate to return home with a split. They had been unable to generate any sustained offense or forechecking pressure in the first two games, and the Linden–Adams–Bure line had been completely neutralized by Messier, Graves and Tikkanen. As Linden noted, "We've got to get over our awe of the New York Rangers. We have to generate more offense. I enjoy playing against Messier, but maybe I've been trying to do too much to stop him instead of doing my own thing."

Quinn was upset with referee Bill McCreary for not penalizing the Rangers for crashing into McLean, a tactic that led to the first goal by Doug Lidster. The Rangers had announced they would try to get more traffic in front of McLean after Game 1, and led by Graves, who bowled over the Canucks' goalie several times, they had followed through on the promise. "When I played, if someone ran your goalie, you just beat the shit out of them," Quinn said. "Now, that's a no-no because of all the antifighting pukes out there. I don't know if beating the shit out of Graves is going to stop him from running the goalie because of the type of player he is, but you should at least be able to find out."

Slowed by a combination of the flu and the soft, slushy New York ice, Bure had been nearly invisible in the first two games. Off the ice, however, he had become the center of an emerging controversy sparked by an article that appeared in the *Toronto Star* on May 31, the eve of the initial game of the series.

The story, by Damien Cox, read:

> News that the 23-year-old Bure has apparently signed a monstrous contract rumored to be worth US$30 million over five years retroactive to this season, stunned the hockey world on the eve of the Stanley Cup final. Now there is rampant speculation that Bure's California-based agent, Ron Salcer, threatened to have Bure sit out playoff games, including last week's Game 5 against the Leafs, if the contract wasn't finalized.
>
> "No, it's just not true," George McPhee, the Canucks' director of hockey operations, told the *Star* yesterday. "I would know if it was, and it's not. Pavel would never do that. He's too competitive."

Contrary to Cox's reference to "rampant speculation" about a threatened boycott, the news caught the Vancouver media by surprise. Jim Jamieson, the Canucks beat reporter with the *Province*, hadn't heard anything about it, nor had the *Sun*'s two hockey writers, Elliott Pap and Iain MacIntyre. Oddly, for such a potentially explosive story, Cox's scoop was given minor play, buried in a sidebar entitled "Hockey Notes." One would expect it to have received much larger exposure. After all, no NHL player had ever been publicly accused of trying to blackmail his team during the playoffs, and Bure was certainly no ordinary player. Even odder, when asked about the article today, Cox, suffering from an apparent attack of amnesia, denies he ever wrote it, claiming, "I don't know any more about it than you do."

The next day Al Strachan, hockey columnist with the *Toronto Sun*, published a more detailed account of the blackmail tale, entitled "Bure Held the Cards":

> Prior to either Game 6 or Game 7 of the Canucks' opening playoff round against the Calgary Flames (definitely not Game 5 of the Conference finals as has been reported elsewhere), Bure's agent Ron Salcer presented Canucks coach and GM Pat Quinn with a demand. Either Quinn would sign Bure's new contract, or else the Russian Rocket would not be playing that night. Quinn went wild, as might be expected, and said that he would not give in to extortion. He told assistant GM George McPhee to call team owner Arthur Griffiths and explain why Bure would not be in the lineup that night. McPhee returned with a message from Griffiths. "Sign it."
>
> Extortion, of course, is a serious charge, but this much is known. The deal was done more than a month ago. Griffiths made the deal, not Quinn. It's a five-year deal, not four years as is being widely reported, and it's worth US$22.5 million, not $30 million.

On June 2, as the Canucks and Rangers met in Game 2, Tony Gallagher of the *Province* checked in with his version of the blackmail story in a column entitled "Bure Threat a Mutual Affair":

> Despite public denials from both club sources and Bure's agent Ron Salcer, it seems the player and his L.A.-based agent threatened to pull

out of the playoffs if their contract demands were not met. And it happened twice. Canucks officials told at least two general managers at the GMs meeting here [in New York] Wednesday that Bure, through his agent, threatened to withdraw from the playoffs if a contract could not be agreed upon.

Gallagher went on to add: "According to one general manager who insisted on anonymity, the threat was made during the Calgary series and repeated just before Game 5 in the Toronto series. The spark was a dispute over when the US$2.5-million signing bonus would be paid and whether or not the team retained total control of the player's marketing rights."

Strachan and Gallagher are good friends and are known to share information and sources, so it is reasonable to assume they collaborated on this story. But was it true? The explicit details in Strachan's account were convincing—it sounded as if he was in the room with Quinn and Griffiths—yet neither columnist offered a source for the allegations.

Gallagher's claim that the tale originated with Vancouver officials confounded all logic. Why would anyone from the Canucks leak a story like this, whether it were true or not, when the team was in the Cup finals? It could only have a destructive impact on team morale and on Bure. On the other hand, if the story was a fabrication, it would mean someone in the organization was trying to sabotage the team from within, suggesting a level of malevolence difficult to comprehend. Gallagher's assertion that Bure had twice threatened a boycott also made little sense. After all, how effective is an ultimatum if you have to repeat it? Even so, other sources also claimed the rumor had come from the Canucks' camp. As Austin Murphy noted in *Sports Illustrated*, the boycott story was "supported by one NHL executive who told *SI* he got the information from a member of Vancouver's front office."

But if the story hadn't originated with the Canucks, then where had it come from? The only people with something to gain by inventing a fallacious blackmail rumor would be the New York Rangers, or perhaps a rival agent seeking to undermine Salcer's relationship with Bure.

Salcer denied that any threat had been made. "I fight hard for my clients, but I would never resort to that," he insisted. "There is absolutely no truth that we would withhold Pavel's services from a game, and I have never had any discussion with Pat Quinn about that in any way, shape or form. None of that happened. It's unfortunate that a person or persons are fabricating such information. Someone with ill will is creating this fiction."

As for the talk about Bure signing a new contract, Salcer admitted he and the Canucks had agreed in principle to a deal before the playoffs. "The next piece of the process is just getting everything on paper, finalizing it and getting it signed." Salcer maintained the controversy hadn't put Bure off his game. "He's an intense guy. He focuses on his hockey, which is the number-one priority for him. That's all he wants to do— win the next game."

It is now known that Bure actually signed the contract in Vancouver prior to the third game of the Canucks-Rangers series, a detail that contradicts Strachan's account, which indicated the deal was consummated during the Calgary series.

Despite denials from all the principals, the story became widely accepted as fact, stigmatizing Bure as a selfish egomaniac. The ease with which the public accepted the story was undoubtedly influenced by the popular perception of Bure and other European players, the one Don Cherry was constantly harping on: they are only here for the money, they have no heartfelt commitment to the game, they aren't team players.

If the rumor had a distracting effect on the Canucks, it wasn't evident in the early moments of Game 3. Backed by a wildly enthusiastic crowd, the Lotus Landers came out flying. Only a minute had elapsed when Linden hit Bure with a terrific lead pass. Streaking into the clear, he fired a 15-footer between Richter's pads, igniting an explosion of fireworks and a massive whirling of white towels. Unlike the first two games, Bure's high-octane fuel was flowing freely. Twice in the first period, Ranger players had to haul down the speedy Russian and take a penalty to prevent him from breaking free.

With the advantage of the last change, Quinn was able to get the line matchups he wanted and he chose to play a muscular unit composed of McIntyre, Hunter and Antoski (combined weight of 625 pounds) against Messier's line. Quinn had asked his troops to take a more physical approach in the game, and McIntyre's line set the tone, thumping Messier and Graves at every opportunity. But the most rousing collision of the period was a bone-jarring bodycheck that Bure delivered to Leetch behind the Rangers' net.

New York tied the score at 13:39 when Leetch flipped the puck into the Canucks' zone and McLean inadvertently deflected the bounding disk into the net. It was a weak goal, but McLean could be excused a mistake. Undaunted, the Canucks continued to press, and when Leetch was penalized for tripping at 17:56, they looked primed to restore their lead. It didn't work out that way.

Midway through the power play, as Bure battled for the puck with defenseman Jay Wells, he took a backward swipe with his stick. The lumber came up high on the follow-through and clipped Wells in the face, knocking him to the ice. When Wells got up, blood was trickling from beneath his eye. Referee Andy Van Hellemond had several penalty options on the play, including the most common in this situation, a double minor, but remembering the abuse heaped on him in the Dallas series when he failed to penalize Bure for cold-cocking Shane Churla, he chose the most severe response, nailing Bure with a five-minute major for high-sticking and a game misconduct for deliberately causing injury.

Although Van Hellemond was within his rights to give Bure the thumb, it illustrated the capricious nature of NHL officiating. Many could recall a virtually identical play in overtime of Game 6 of the 1993 Western Conference finals between the Kings and Leafs when Wayne Gretzky clipped Doug Gilmour with a high stick, cutting him for eight stitches, during a Kings power play. Despite Toronto's protests, referee Kerry Fraser called no penalty on the play. Less than a minute later Gretzky scored the game winner to even the series at three games each, and Los Angeles went on to take the series in seven.

Van Hellemond's call was equally decisive in this game. Bure's expulsion stilled the crowd and deflated the Canucks. Only a minute later Glenn Anderson scored on the power play to put the Rangers ahead 2–1. Although the Canucks continued to throw their weight around, their confidence had been shaken, and when Leetch scored at 18:32 of the second period, the writing was on the wall. During the third period, as New York coasted to a 5–1 win, disgruntled Canucks fans, who had begun the game chanting, "The Rangers suck, the Rangers suck," switched to a new taunt: "The Oilers suck, the Oilers suck."

After the game, Bure offered an unconvincing explanation for the high-sticking incident: "I tried to hit him with my shoulder, and I think my stick just slid on his shoulder and hit him in the face. I tried to use my body. I missed." To most people, though, it appeared that Bure's stick had been propelled upward with considerable vigor.

Game 4 featured stirring hockey: jarring hits, furious skating and numerous scoring chances. As they had in Game 3, the Canucks came out strong and led 2–0 after the first period on goals by Linden and Ronning. Linden's tally, scored with Graves off for holding, was the Canucks' first power-play goal in 20 chances. Leetch, displaying his characteristic fearlessness on the rush, got New York back into the game at 4:03 of the second period with a short-handed marker, his 10th goal of the playoffs. Two minutes later Bure took a pass and began to accelerate into the clear, only to have Leetch trip him from behind. Referee Terry Gregson immediately signaled for a penalty shot.

Often described as hockey's most exciting play, the penalty shot should more correctly be called hockey's rarest play. Only six have been awarded in Cup finals history, primarily because referees are loath to give the offensive team what is perceived as a gilt-edged scoring opportunity. But even that is a misconception. The advantage in such confrontations goes to the goalie. All six previous attempts had ended in failure.

As Bure collected the puck at center ice, Richter rushed out to meet him, then began slowly retreating. As Bure closed in, he feinted to his backhand, then shifted the puck to his forehand and tried to tuck it under Richter on his stick side, a nearly identical move to the one he had used to beat Mike Vernon in overtime in the Calgary series. But Richter, displaying the flexibility of a gymnast, thrust out his right pad and made the save.

Richter later denied he had been anticipating Bure's deke: "He's too good a player to think he can do only one move. I wanted to come out as far as I could to take most of his options away. I knew he would come in with speed. He's a fast, fast player."

Asked if he had considered shooting, Bure said, "He came out from his net. That's why I couldn't shoot. He backed up. Right away I tried to deke him. He didn't give me any room."

Keenan called the save the biggest of Richter's career. It was definitely a major morale boost. Instead of being down 3–1, the Rangers were still very much in the game. At 18:55, Adams was sent off for boarding and New York capitalized, as Zubov blasted home a drive from the point with 16 seconds left in the period.

The Canucks had several good scoring chances in the third, but Richter wasn't letting anything through. The contest was inching toward overtime when, at 14:31, Gelinas took a foolish roughing penalty, tossing Kevin Lowe into the boards directly in front of Gregson. Only 36 seconds later Leetch artfully sifted through the Canucks' defense and teed the puck up for Kovalev, who fired it into the top corner. The Rangers cemented the win at 17:56 when Larmer's 80-foot drifter deflected off Babych's leg and bounced past an off-balance McLean.

As crucial as Richter's save had been on the penalty shot, the architect of the Rangers' comeback was Leetch, who had a hand in all four goals. The smooth-skating Texan had either scored or set up nine of the 14 goals New York had scored in the first four games of the series, and he led all players with 32 playoff points. As Quinn noted, "Leetch is making big play after big play, and we haven't been able to keep him off the board. He's been their best player by a wide margin."

In the Rangers' dressing room, Keenan was asked for his thoughts on the scene that would await the team when it returned to Madison Square Garden for Game 5. "It's certainly going to be in a state of frenzy," Keenan said. "We'll enjoy it. We'll feed off it. The place is going to be a madhouse."

All thoughts of the curse had been banished by the Rangers' two victories in Vancouver. Virtually everyone in Manhattan was planning Cup celebrations. David Letterman had booked the entire Rangers team for his talk show, and Mayor Rudolph Giuliani had invited the team to his mansion for a victory barbecue. "Tonight's the Night!" blared the front page of the New York Post.

The low thunder of a squad of Harley-Davidson motorcycles accompanied the Canucks' bus down Sixth Avenue to Madison Square Garden for Game 5. The police escort forded through the hostile crowd gathered outside the arena and headed underground. "Shoot 'em," squawked one heckler. "Put 'em out of their misery." Through the bus windows, the Canucks could see helmeted riot police already arranged in formation in the street.

Quinn shuffled his lines for the game, moving Craven back between Bure and Adams and shifting Linden to a line with Courtnall and Lafayette. The Canucks expected the Rangers to come out hard, but instead the Blueshirts appeared tentative and jittery in the early going, their focus distracted by the clamor and the fans' incessant chanting of "We Want the Cup."

The Rangers needed a spark. Midway through the first, they got one when Tikkanen wound up and cranked a long slap shot past McLean. As the crowd erupted and the red light flashed, Momesso cross-checked Leetch to the ice. Beukeboom quickly rushed to his defense partner's aid, jumping Momesso, and a wild melee ensued. When it was finally sorted out, the Rangers received two pieces of bad news. Beukeboom had been ejected from the game and Tikkanen's goal has been waved off by linesman Randy Mitton, who ruled that Stephane Matteau was offside on the play. Mitton, however, was mistaken, as proved by the giant video screen, which obligingly reviewed the play in super slow motion to outraged howls from the Garden mob.

The first 40 minutes of play produced only one goal, a scorching drive off the stick of Vancouver's Jeff Brown at 8:10 of the second. During the intermission between the second and third periods, the Canucks talked about playing smart, defensively sound hockey to protect their one-goal lead. Instead, the third period was a crazy free-for-all. Only 26 seconds into the frame, Courtnall scored to snap a 13-game drought. Two minutes later Bure put the Canucks up 3–0, converting a rebound off a shot by Craven. Immediately the Rangers answered back. Lidster beat McLean with a floater through traffic at 3:27, Larmer chipped in a rebound at 6:20 and Messier banked in a tight-angle shot off Babych's skate at 9:02.

With three goals in less than six minutes, the Rangers had reversed the tables. The Cup was now in sight. But with the Garden crowd still on its feet celebrating Messier's goal, the dragon stirred again. Thirty seconds later Babych made amends for his miscue by beating Richter with a low wrist shot from a bad angle. Three minutes after that, Courtnall scored on a rebound. On the Canucks' next rush, Richter kicked out Ronning's shot. It bounced directly to Bure, who put the puck in the back of the net. Eight goals had been scored in a span of 12 minutes and 38 seconds and the Canucks had emerged with a 6–3 win. The champagne celebration was on hold.

At the postgame press conference, an agitated Keenan blamed the media for his team's downfall, saying that the euphoric predictions of victory had "rubbed off on the club." Referring to the *Post*'s front-page prophecy, he said, "Headlines like that are like putting gasoline on a fire. As soon as I saw that headline, I knew we were in deep trouble." Keenan made no reference to another distracting rumor circulating in the media, the one that stated he was going to leave the Rangers to take over as general manager and coach of the Detroit Red Wings.

Linden said that rather than be intimidated, the Canucks had drawn inspiration from the hostile New York crowd and all the talk of a Cup parade through the streets of Manhattan. "The party doesn't start until we've had our say," he said defiantly. The only revelry that occurred after Game 5 took place in Vancouver, where jubilant Canucks supporters partied on Robson Street in the city's downtown core.

Rather than practice before the sixth game, the Canucks took the day off, although several players, Bure included, would report for treatment in the "space shuttle," a hyperbaric oxygen chamber the players had been using to revive their battered bodies. Although the chamber's benefits in treating decompression problems in deep-sea divers and victims of burns, carbon-monoxide poisoning and smoke inhalation were well documented, its effectiveness in treating sports injuries was still largely anecdotal. But the Canucks' players and team doctors believed in its healing powers.

The atmosphere at the Pacific Coliseum for Game 6 bordered on hysteria. "I've never heard the place so loud," Canucks statistician Evan Morgan recalls. "You could feel the sound vibrating in your chest." Unlike the Rangers in Game 5, the Canucks seemed to draw strength from the hometown crowd. Tonight it was Richter who was under siege. Only his acrobatic heroics prevented the Canucks from blowing the

Rangers out of the rink in the first period. The two teams headed to the dressing rooms with the Canucks leading 1–0 on a power-play goal by Brown.

The Canucks were hitting Leetch whenever they had a chance, and the body blows were having an effect. For the first time in the series, the Rangers star seemed less than lethal. In fact, the entire New York team was displaying signs of weariness. At 12:29, Courtnall gave the Canucks a two-goal bulge, finishing off a three-way passing play with Bure and Lumme, but the Rangers closed the gap when Kovalev's centering pass deflected in off Craven's shin guards.

It was still 2–1 with 12 minutes left in the third when Leetch attempted a long clearing pass from deep in his zone. Brown intercepted and drilled home a cannonading drive through a maze of players. It was his sixth goal of the playoffs, and it looked like a coffin closer. As the clock ticked down, CBC commentator Harry Neale remarked, "The Stanley Cup is a slippery trophy, isn't it? And it may be slipping through the hands of the New York Rangers."

There were two minutes left when Lafayette hooked the puck past Beukeboom to Courtnall, who was cutting hard across the slot. Richter, who had shifted to his right with the pass, was caught out of position as the Vancouver winger backhanded the puck just inside the crossbar. The crowd erupted, thinking Courtnall had scored, but play continued. Bure blasted another shot wide, and Leetch gathered up the puck and started down the ice. He hit Anderson with a pass at the blueline, and the speedy winger attempted to dash around the Canucks' defense. Denied access, he tossed the puck across the goalmouth where Messier tapped it into the corner of the net.

The Canucks protested, claming Courtnall had scored before Messier and referee Bill McCreary asked for input from the video-replay officials. It was a tense moment. If the film revealed that Courtnall had scored, then the Canucks had the game in the bag. If it showed that he didn't, then Messier's goal would count and the score would be 3–2 with just over a minute remaining—time enough for the Rangers to tie it. Having received the verdict from upstairs, McCreary removed his headphones and pointed to center ice. A big number four registered on the Canucks' side of the scoreboard. The resulting roar vibrated the walls of the building. The roller-coaster swing of emotions proved too much for overwrought Rangers GM Neil Smith, who fainted and had to receive medical attention.

The two teams were awarded an extra day's rest prior to Game 7. Rather than fly directly to New York in order to give the players two days to adjust to jet lag, the Canucks remained in Vancouver and used the time to book passage in the "space shuttle." Buoyed by back-to-back wins and confident the long series and air travel were having a deleterious effect on the older Rangers players, the Canucks were optimistic about the final road trip of the season. "This is something you dream about as a kid," McLean said. "It's a one-game situation. You couldn't ask for anything more."

Game 7 didn't disappoint. It was a spine-tingler from start to finish. The Rangers drew first blood at 11:02 of the opening period when Messier bulled his way into the Canucks' zone and dished off to Zubov, who found Leetch alone on the rim of the left faceoff circle. McLean, tangled up with Graves in the crease, couldn't get across to cover, and Leetch buried it from a sharp angle. Less than four minutes later, with Lumme doing time for cross-checking, Graves connected from the slot to put the Rangers ahead 2–0.

Play opened up in the second period and Linden got the Canucks on the scoreboard with his first of the series, a short-handed breakaway goal at 5:21. But Messier restored the two-goal margin with another power-play marker at 13:29, New York's second in three opportunities. The Rangers had the NHL's most effective power play during the regular season, and it was producing when they needed it most. The period ended with the Blueshirts up 3–1.

The Canucks needed an early goal in the third to revive their hopes, and Linden, playing like a man possessed, delivered. At the 4:50 mark he sent a shiver through the crowd, whipping home a sharp pass from Courtnall on a Vancouver power play to narrow the Rangers' lead to one goal. Four minutes later the Canucks' captain nearly completed the hat trick, but Richter stretched to get a skate blade on Linden's low backhand.

The boys in black kept coming. Ronning had a terrific chance to score from the slot, but he was secretly playing with a broken hand and couldn't get any zip on his shot. There were six minutes left when Courtnall found an uncovered Lafayette with a perfect pass. The rookie beat Richter with his one-timer, but the puck hit the goalpost with a loud clang. It was the Canucks' death knell. They continued to press but couldn't get the equalizer. With McLean on the bench for an extra attacker, the Rangers repeatedly iced the puck.

The last faceoff took place in the circle to Richter's right with three seconds left. Keenan called on veteran Craig MacTavish to take the draw against Craven. MacTavish won it, and the puck slid harmlessly into the corner. The 1993–94 season was done. The curse had been broken. Bedlam. One Ranger fan held up a sign that read: Now I Can Die in Peace.

The dramatic series capped one of the most entertaining postseasons in NHL history. Seven of the 15 series went the full seven games, and there were an incredible 18 overtime tilts. The largest American TV hockey audience ever and the biggest audience in Canada since the 1972 Summit Series tuned in for Game 7 of the finals. But all this was no consolation for the Canucks, who came up one goalpost short in the final dance.

Sporting blackened eyes and a gash over his nose, a somber Linden mused: "Maybe in a month I'll be able to look back and think what we've accomplished, but right now it hurts too much."

Bure looked equally solemn. His offensive pyrotechnics had been instrumental in the Canucks' march to the finals, and he had led all playoff marksmen with 16 goals, but he had been blanked by the Rangers in the all-important seventh game. "This was the chance of a lifetime," Bure said, "and you never know if you'll have another one."

Down the corridor the mood was joyous. "They talk about the ghosts and dragons," Messier said. "You can't be afraid to slay the dragon. We're going to celebrate like we've never celebrated anything in our lives."

While New York partied enthusiastically, but peacefully, events took an ugly turn in Vancouver. A riot erupted in the city's downtown core when police tried to disperse an unruly gathering of 70,000 people with volleys of tear gas. Rocks and bottles rained through the air, cars were overturned, store windows were shattered, attack dogs were unleashed and angry cops began clubbing bodies with their batons. By the time it was over, some 200 people had been injured and a 19-year-old boy was on life support, his skull punctured by a rubber bullet fired from a police antiriot weapon.

A far different crowd gathered two days later on June 16 at BC Place Stadium to greet the Canucks. To wild cheering, the players stepped up to the microphone and expressed their thanks for the fans' support. When it was Bure's turn to speak, he had to wait nearly five minutes before the ovation subsided.

That same day the Canucks formally announced they had signed Bure to a five-year contract worth US$25 million. The complicated 25-page document included Bure's marketing rights and provided a job for his father as a "fitness and marketing consultant."

"I know it's huge money," Bure said. "I never dreamed about something like this. I worked hard for 16 years to get to this point, and I think I did something unbelievable for myself. I'm really excited that I will be spending lots of years here in Vancouver."

The feeling was entirely mutual.

CHAPTER TWELVE

# The Reluctant Superstar

*A celebrity is a person who works hard all his life to become known,*
*then wears dark glasses to avoid being recognized.*
FRED ALLEN, COMEDIAN

WHEN READERS OF THE *Vancouver Sun* picked up their papers on
September 6, 1994, they came face-to-face with a front-page photo of
Pavel Bure naked to the waist. The picture had been strategically positioned above the fold so that until you opened the paper, it was
impossible to tell how far south his nakedness extended. The shot had
been taken by photographer Ralph Bower as Bure was undergoing a
"pinch test"—sports scientist Ted Rhodes was applying calipers to Bure's
waistline to estimate his body fat. Judging by his densely muscled torso,
there didn't appear to be any.

Canucks management was upset by the beefcake. The *Sun*, it said,
had broken the rules. No players were to be photographed during
physical-fitness testing. The Canucks' sensitivity was the result of an
incident that had occurred a couple of years before when a wire-service
photographer had snapped a picture of a naked Wayne Gretzky as he

emerged from the shower. The Gretzky shot had been cropped at his waist when it was published, but the photographer sent a copy of the full-frontal version to a friend and the photo eventually made its way into the public domain. After that, the NHL banned still photographers from its dressing rooms.

According to Bower, the photo came about completely by chance. He was standing outside an empty theater complex at the Coliseum used for aftergame functions when the Russian was brought in for his physical. Since it was a public setting, Bure was wearing sweatpants. "I looked over and the doc winked at me and I stepped up and took the shot," Bower recalls. Bure voiced no objections. "A few days later I asked him to autograph a couple of prints for me. He had a big grin on his face. He said to me, 'Hey, Ralph, are you working for *Playboy* now?'"

The photo was a huge hit. More than 4,000 extra copies of the paper were sold that day and Bower received a lot of mail from appreciative females. As one woman noted in a letter to the editor, "I think you should have a photo of a nearly nude Canuck on page one every day. It would do wonders for your circulation. It certainly does wonders for mine. Yow!"

Although rarely mentioned in the sports pages, the sexuality of male athletes has always been an essential ingredient in their appeal to the female audience. In Bure's case, the attraction is magnified because he projects an androgynous allure, the way actor James Dean did. He appeals to both men and women. A few hockey players in the past have possessed this quality. Author Roy MacGregor, citing the young Wayne Gretzky as an example, told me: "I've always thought that Gretzky resembled Princess Diana. You could see it especially in his downcast eyes and shy smile. It was a very disarming quality. Bure has the same appeal. It cuts across all kinds of levels."

One of those levels was Bure's appeal to the gay community. Daniel Gawthrop, a Vancouver freelance writer who made no attempt to conceal his sexual persuasion, was responsible for introducing the topic in a piece entitled "Sex Sells Like a Rocket" that appeared in the *Vancouver Sun* in March 1992. Ruminating on Bure's exotic magnetism, Gawthrop extolled the Russian's "fawn-like features, rose-petal lips and bedroom eyes" and pronounced him "drop-dead gorgeous."

Such descriptions made Canucks management uneasy. Gawthrop

was subsequently denied requests for an interview with Bure, a point that was noted in an article about Bure's following in Vancouver's gay community that was published in Toronto's *Globe and Mail* during the 1994 Cup finals. According to Gawthrop, Bure was attractive to gays not only because of his striking looks, but also because of his "Rudolph Valentino mystique."

Gawthrop's message that NHL hockey—and Bure—had a following beyond the stereotypical fan featured in beer commercials got greater exposure than he had anticipated thanks to a line in the *Globe and Mail* article in which Gawthrop stated: "I'm just as Canadian as anyone on *Hockey Night in Canada*, but nothing I've ever worn in drag could possibly equal the sheer campiness of Don Cherry's wardrobe." A bemused Cherry read the remark on the air during the Western Conference finals and asked cohost Ron MacLean to translate the word *campiness*, which MacLean described as meaning "sort of tacky cool."

In the aftermath, various other North American papers, including the *Village Voice* and the *LA Weekly*, published articles on the subject. The attention led some people to conclude that since Bure appealed to gay men, then he, too, must be gay, or at least bisexual.

Homosexuality in hockey had always been a strictly taboo subject in the mainstream media, despite the fact that locker-room culture is infused with latent homosexual undertones. Even the language of the game is ripe with innuendo, an aspect capitalized on to humorous effect by a renegade Vancouver sports publication called *The Bum Report*. Although in the context of homosexuality its name might suggest otherwise, *The Bum Report* was supposed to represent the voice of the average fan, the bum in the bleachers. The paper often published top-10 lists on various subjects. One of its most popular collections were "the homoerotic sayings of Tom Larscheid," a Canucks radio commentator, whose inadvertent double entendres were plentiful enough to supply material for several top-10 lists. Some samples are:

- I was with Pavel before the game and he says his groin has never felt better.
- Carson has such good hands. A lot of the guys have told me they'd like to be able to play with him.

- Don't you just love to see the big guys play the body. I know I do.
- Kirk McLean is so fundamentally sound. Look at how erect he is in the net.
- There's Sather, with that grin on his face, relaxing behind the bench, hands in his pockets, enjoying himself.
- This Gelinas is a good-looking player. It's no secret that a lot of coaches in the league would love to have had him.
- Sometimes all you have to do is look at Gretzky and he goes down.
- Pavel Bure plays with such speed that his linemates can't keep up to him. If only he could play with himself out there, that would really give the fans a show.

Although the Canucks were uncomfortable addressing Bure's sexual allure in either the gay or straight communities, they did realize they had a player with a unique persona. As part of Bure's new US$25-million contract, the club had acquired the marketing rights to his image and likeness. According to the deal, the team would earn the first $500,000 from selling Bure's rights, with a 50–50 split taking effect past that point. The team believed it could eventually recoup a fifth of its overall investment by selling the photogenic Russian's marketing rights.

To help make this a reality, a New York–based talent agency, J. Michael Bloom and Associates, was hired to develop marketing vehicles for Bure. Projects considered included a pictorial biography; a video about his life and times; a bit part in a new Mighty Ducks hockey movie; a hockey-equipment advertising campaign with Canstar based around a "Pavelocity" slogan; endorsements for Nike, Coca-Cola and General Motors; and even a Bure candy bar.

None of these endeavors bore fruit. In fact, nothing of any significance was ever accomplished in terms of marketing the NHL's flashiest player, due largely to Bure's lack of interest in becoming a public-relations tool. Although the Russian Rocket was a dedicated athlete, he was always a reluctant superstar.

According to Glen Ringdal, who was head of the Canucks' sales-and-marketing department at the time, the problem was twofold. On one hand, the club had overestimated Bure's commercial appeal. "We couldn't attract any major advertisers," Ringdal admits. Bure's potential as a pitchman for hamburgers and soft drinks was compromised by his imperfect English and his lack of a national profile in the United States, where NHL games still ranked lower in the television ratings than tractor-pulling contests.

The other factor was Bure's uncooperative attitude. "Pavel always resented our ability to make money off him," Ringdal says. "His position was that he was paid to play hockey, nothing else." Bure's resistance to the club benefiting financially from what he did away from the rink became a source of considerable frustration for management.

Ringdal cites one example in which Bure attended a sports memorabilia show in Hawaii where he was paid to sign autographs and then kept all the proceeds for himself. "We never saw any of that money," Ringdal says, "and we should have. It was ours. We owned him."

Of all the proposed commercial ventures, the book project came closest to reality. Several Vancouver publishers competed for the privilege of launching Bure's authorized biography. One bid was made by Raincoast Books, which enlisted a writer and offered Bure a US$60,000 advance—an enormous sum for a Canadian publisher—in return for the Russian's agreement to devote a couple of hours to interviews. But the deal broke down over Bure's involvement in promotion. Raincoast wanted the Canuck winger to do at least five public appearances to accompany the book launch, but he refused to do more than two and was reluctant to venture outside British Columbia. Raincoast's publicity request seemed a minor imposition for someone often accused of being driven by mercenary instincts.

Bure's unease with the trappings of celebrity was evident in his dealings with the media. Beat reporters who were assigned the task of getting postgame quotes described Bure as simply apathetic rather than rude. According to their contracts, players are supposed to make themselves available for 10 minutes after a game. Bure would participate, "but as soon as the time limit was up," says *Province* sportswriter Jim Jamieson, "you could see his eyes glaze over. A moment later he would be gone in a wisp of smoke."

Although Bure's game was full of vibrant expression, none of it carried over into his commentary. His quotes were so bland and clichéd they would never have been used if they had been uttered by any other player.

As the *Sun*'s Mike Beamish once noted, "His greatest sin, as far as the contingent covering him is concerned, is that Bure is not only uncommunicative and boring, he works at being uncommunicative and boring."

Bure was especially uncooperative when asked to explain why he was in a slump. His usual response was caustic disdain. If pressed, his English would deteriorate suddenly. This quality irked many reporters, who felt that professional athletes had an obligation to face the music, even when the tune was sour.

In Russian interviews, Bure was more articulate, but not any more revealing. In an article in *Argumenty i Fakty*, Russia's most popular newspaper, Bure was described as "thinking 10 times before he said anything to a journalist."

Bure's distrust of the media's motives had a basis. Some reporters were perpetually looking for negative things to say about him. But as he admitted in an interview in the Russian edition of *Playboy* in 1995, "In the overall picture I am glad that my name remains in the newspapers. Even if some information is far from the truth, it would be worse if they completely stopped writing about you. What would be terrible would be indifference."

Some of Bure's reticence was simply due to his personality. Although he could be engaging and humorous with friends, he was ill at ease with strangers. During the spring of 1995, he admitted to Tony Gallagher of the *Province*: "I feel very nervous when I am by myself here. In Russia I went out alone all the time, but here I don't like it. Even when I go out to the grocery store I like to have someone with me. In the four years since I've been in Vancouver, I've never been out to dinner by myself. I like having someone with me when I go out, whether it's my mother or father or a friend."

This need to keep the outside world at bay wasn't limited to the media or the public. With the exception of Gino Odjick, Bure wasn't particularly close to anyone on the Canucks. Reporters who covered the team on a daily basis viewed him as a loner. "On the road, he was always the guy by himself with a book," says Iain MacIntyre of the *Vancouver Sun*. Bure's eclectic reading habits alone set him apart from the majority of his teammates. He had a fascination for history, biographies and personal memoirs. At one point, Bure revealed to an interviewer that he was reading a biography of Cardinal Richelieu, the 17th-century French prelate and statesman. Of special interest to him were the events and major political figures of modern Russian history. He also had a weakness for political thrillers and detective novels and cited the work of Edward Topol, James Hadley Chase and Alexandre Dumas, the author of *The Three Musketeers*, as particular favorites.

In one of his rare moments of self-revelation, Bure spoke with freelance writer Ron Spence about the two-sided nature of fame: "I've read a lot of books about kings and queens. Sometimes the queen would say, 'I don't want to be the queen, I just want to be normal girl.' You know she could do whatever she wants. The normal girl would look at the queen riding by in her carriage and say, 'Oh, I want to be the queen.' That's what I was always thinking about when reading these books. Queen wants to be normal girl and normal girl wants to be queen. I think if they changed they wouldn't like it again."

This duality, this push and pull between extremes, is central to Bure's character. He is always flickering between sun and shadows, exuberance and melancholy, East and West. The deep paradoxes make him hard to know, but keep everyone interested.

As was his custom, Bure had retreated to Los Angeles after the 1994 playoffs to recharge his batteries. In the fall, however, he returned to new living quarters. He had purchased a $1 million home on Vancouver's exclusive Southwest Marine Drive. The 6,000-square-foot mansion, shielded by a high hedge and an iron gate, came equipped with an outdoor swimming pool, a hot tub and a waterfall. But typically, even this venture into domesticity had a bizarre twist. Three days before the sale was finalized Bure stopped by to view his new purchase and found the place occupied by a crew from the television show *The X-Files*. They were using his house to film a murder scene.

Bure's much-publicized contract had vaulted him into third place on the NHL wage scale, behind Wayne Gretzky and Mario Lemieux. Unlike those two veterans, though, Bure was only 23. It was, as he noted, "Huge money." Too huge for Pat Quinn's liking. The deal had been finalized with Arthur Griffiths without Quinn's blessing. According to one rumor, the Canucks GM had been so outraged by the size of the contract that he had threatened to quit. Whether or not that was true, it was safe to say that Bure's contract had complicated Quinn's job. The Russian was now earning more than the club's other top six forwards combined: Linden, Ronning, Courtnall, Adams, Gelinas and Momesso.

All of those players, as well as Brown and Hedican, were among more than a dozen Canucks who were either entering the option year of their contracts or who were restricted free agents. After reaching the Stanley Cup finals, they were all seeking upgrades. Early indications suggested that the negotiations were going less than smoothly. Courtnall had been offered no increase on the US$650,000 he made the previous year. Ronning was considering going to arbitration to get market value. Linden and the team were millions apart on a new deal. The grinding process was wearing thin on some players.

Momesso, whose US$500,000 salary was below the league average, told Mike Beamish of the *Sun*: "The year before the excuse was that they lost money. This year it's because they gave it all to Pavel. Each year it's something different. Pavel's a different case. We understand that. But for the rest of us it's been a lot harder than we thought. A lot of guys are pissed off. Even Trevor's having problems. Imagine. It doesn't make sense to me."

Although such financial squabbling was typical of Quinn's regime, it wasn't unique to Vancouver. Economic clout was shifting to agents and players, who seemed to consider renegotiating contracts in midstream to be standard business procedure. Mark Messier was the most high-profile example. The Rangers' captain, who was under contract for two more years with New York at US$2.6 million per year, evidently had a clause in his contract that permitted him to reopen bargaining if the Rangers won the Stanley Cup. Messier wanted the club to boost his salary to US$6 million per year to join Gretzky at the top of the heap.

Although money issues had become increasingly paramount in the off-season, hockey fans could usually find relief with the start of the hockey year, but in 1994–95 there would be no escape. NHL team owners were determined to institute a salary-cap system to put the brakes on escalating salaries, an innovation the NHL Players' Association was unwilling to consider. On October 1, 1994, with talks at a standstill, the owners took drastic action, closing their arenas and locking out the players.

Although the owners obviously felt they had to draw a line in the sand, the timing of the lockout was ill-advised. The dramatic 1994 play-offs had taken hockey's popularity to new heights at a moment when other professional sports were struggling. Major-league baseball was paralyzed by a bitter strike that had wiped out the last half of the 1994 season. The NBA had just suffered through a dismal 1994 playoffs, featuring on-court brawls that had spread into the stands, outrageous refereeing gaffes and perverse, pugnacious behavior by owners, shenanigans that had prompted the *Los Angeles Times* to declare that the sport had descended to the level of "mud wrestling."

None of this mattered to NHL team owners, who believed the solidarity of the NHLPA would dissolve once the reality of unemployment sank in. Instead, both sides stood their ground. When it became clear the lockout wasn't going to end quickly, several players vented their frustrations on Gary Bettman, the league's commissioner. Chicago Blackhawks defenseman Chris Chelios told a television interviewer: "If I was Gary Bettman, I'd be worried about my well-being. Some fans, or who knows, maybe a player, might take it upon himself to do something. I don't know what it is, whether it's the short-man complex or what, but he's the problem."

Although Chelios's outburst was clearly over the edge, his view of Bettman as the villain was shared by many in the NHLPA and by the public at large. The 42-year-old former New York tax attorney was perceived as a tourist in hockey country, a hard-line numbers guy imported to fatten the owners' bottom line. Bettman's appearance and mannerisms didn't help. He had the supercilious smile and stiff-necked haughtiness of an uppity maître d' who won't seat you unless you slip him some folding green. In comparison with the mournful, knitted-brow expression of plodding NHLPA president Bob Goodenow, Bettman's demeanor seemed about as trustworthy as a pit viper.

While the owners were bleating about financial hardship and insisting on the need for a mechanism to curb the growth of players' salaries, no one in management was suggesting any restrictions be put on executives' earning power. In December, when the details of Quinn's contract were revealed at the annual general meeting of Northwest Sports Entertainment, the Canucks' parent company, it was clear how handsomely he had been rewarded. In 1993–94, Quinn received a base salary of $788,600, plus a stunning $326,000 in playoff bonuses, and another $151,000 in "other compensation," for a grand total of $1,265,600. Kirk McLean was the only Canucks player whose salary (US$1.1 million) exceeded Quinn's pay, and McLean received no playoff bonuses from the club. Quinn, who had just signed a five-year contract extension as president and general manager, would earn even more in 1995, with a base salary of $1,023,500 and an added $460,000 in bonuses.

As winter set in and the lockout turned to permafrost, a number of NHL players began looking for somewhere else to play. Wayne Gretzky organized a European tour by a team of NHL All-Stars. Others found work in leagues in Switzerland, Germany, Finland and Sweden. In November, Bure joined a group of former Soviet stars who agreed to return home to play a series of exhibition games against Russian teams. The NHL Soviet team included Igor Larionov and Sergei Makarov of the San Jose Sharks; Viacheslav Fetisov, Valeri Zelepukin and Sergei Brylin of the New Jersey Devils; Valeri Kamensky of the Quebec Nordiques; Alexei Kasatonov of the Boston Bruins; Nikolai Borschevsky of the Toronto Maple Leafs; Vladimir Malakhov and Darius Kasparaitis of the New York Islanders; Alexei Kovalev, Sergei Nemchinov and Sergei Zubov of the New York Rangers; Sergei Fedorov of the Detroit Red Wings; and Alexander Mogilny of the Buffalo Sabres.

The tour was organized by Fetisov with the sponsorship of Sun Microsystems, a California-based computer company with a strong presence in Russia. In persuading his countrymen to return home, Fetisov's toughest task was alleviating their fears about security, specifically the threat from organized crime. The New Jersey defenseman arranged to have all the players assigned bodyguards and for the team bus to be chaperoned by rifle-toting soldiers. The precaution, unimaginable anywhere else in Europe, was routine in the new Russia.

For Fedorov and Mogilny, who had been branded as defectors just a few years before, it was an uneasy homecoming. Neither player had a passport—both had lost them when they defected—and their citizenship was in question. But both players had been assured by Russian officials that all had been forgiven and they would be issued documents upon arrival. The pair flew back to Russia together. "From New York to Helsinki, no problem," Fedorov told the *Detroit Free Press*. "But from Helsinki to Moscow we were most nervous. We were shaking. So many thoughts were coming to us." Their fears proved unwarranted. The returning players were treated like VIPs. No one held a grudge. At an official reception, Russian Deputy Prime Minister Oleg Soskovets declared, "The past is forgotten. They came to an absolutely new society."

Bure, Mogilny and Fedorov were reunited as a line for the five-game charity tour. The final game in Moscow was attended by high-ranking Russian government officials, including President Boris Yeltsin. "It was a great feeling. The three of us never thought we would play together again," admitted Fedorov, who had to refamiliarize himself with the larger dimensions of the international ice surface. "Huge ice. Can you imagine? Over there [in North America] you can lift your head up and see your partners right away. Here, you need binoculars."

"We scored so many goals every game," Bure said. "It was even better than I thought."

Viktor Tikhonov watched his former protégés perform and wondered what might have been. "They were amazing," he said. "They do everything right." They're artists of the highest class. You get a sense watching them that they can do anything."

The outpouring of affection for the returning Soviet stars was one more reflection of the dramatic changes that had occurred in Russian society since Mogilny, Fedorov and Bure had left for the West. Even the Russian hockey league had undergone a radical metamorphosis. Central Army's jersey now bore the cartoonish imprint of a grinning penguin, symbolic of a new joint-venture marketing agreement between Central Army and the NHL's Pittsburgh Penguins. The penguin was perched on a star, just beneath the logo of Iron City beer, the Penguins' major sponsor.

Describing the scene at the Moscow Ice Palace at a game in the winter of 1994, Jeffrey Lilley wrote in *Sports Illustrated*:

Garish advertisements, pitching everything from Clark bars to Apple computers, lined the boards. "We Will Rock You" was being blasted through the P.A. system to the hyped-up crowd of Muscovites, who were merrily guzzling Iron City beer from Pittsburgh. And when the

CSKA team was introduced, the players took to the ice like performers in the old Moscow Circus. Lights were dimmed, drum rolls sounded and each player was ushered in by spotlight.

In truth, it was a wonder Central Army still existed. The former goliath had fallen into dire financial straits after the fall of the Communist regime when the government stopped funding the team. A Georgian businessman named Nugzar Natchkhebia acquired control of the team and promptly sold off the club's best players to the NHL. Central Army plummeted to the basement of the league, and attendance dropped from near capacity to an average of 300 per game. To raise cash, the club rented the front of the arena to a Mercedes car dealer and transformed the Ice Palace into a disco on nongame nights.

In a bid to save the team, Tikhonov and several Red Army officers flew to Montreal in February 1993 for the NHL All-Star Game, where they convinced Pittsburgh Penguins owner Howard Baldwin to bankroll a joint-venture marketing agreement. With investors Mario Lemieux, actor Michael J. Fox and Disney chairman Michael Eisner, Baldwin formed a group called Penguin Army International Ltd. that put up more than US$1 million to buy a 50-per-cent interest in Central Army and a management contract to run the Ice Palace. Corporate sponsors were brought onboard, luxury suites were sold at the arena and special promotions were arranged. The gimmickry worked. Attendance increased by tenfold, and enough money was generated to increase the players' annual salaries from US$3,000 to $12,000 and to acquire free agents. Gradually Central Army climbed out of the red.

The partnership lasted about two years. By the spring of 1995, the Russian mafiya had taken control of Central Army, and Baldwin, although he claimed he hadn't been threatened, got skittish and withdrew from the deal. ESPN reported that the Penguins lost US$800,000 on the venture. Western sponsors also began pulling out as mobsters toting sawed-off shotguns under their leather trench coats forced out the paying customers and appropriated the luxury suites at the arena.

The NHL lockout ended on January 12 when the owners and players signed a new six-year collective bargaining agreement. Although the owners failed to get the salary cap they wanted, they were able to implement a rookie salary cap and an agreement that there would be no unrestricted free-agency status for players until age 32, and age 31 in the last three years of the deal. The players, on the other hand, obtained very little, and many were bitter about the entire process.

There would be a 48-game season, but because of the truncated schedule, teams would only play other clubs in their own conference. Restoring the fans' confidence was now the NHL's theme song. In Vancouver, the campaign got off to a rocky start. Bure had returned to Russia in late December and, according to his agent, Ron Salcer, due to a "serious grievance" concerning his contract, he wasn't coming back anytime soon. Salcer claimed the Canucks had reneged on a promise to pay Bure during the lockout, as specified by the terms of his guaranteed contract. The amount owing was US$1.7 million. Salcer said there were only four exceptions in the contract that would allow the Canucks to cease payment: suicide, voluntary retirement, conviction of a criminal act and withdrawal of his services. "Bure did not withdraw services on October 1," Salcer said. "He was locked out."

Salcer noted that this dispute wasn't an isolated incident, but merely the latest in a series of logjams with Canucks management: "It took almost two years to work out a new contract for Pavel. It seems there is always a glitch. It's never-ending. We had to fight for almost three months to get his signing bonus [US$1 million]. After about 25 letters and phone calls, we finally got it. Pavel is really frustrated."

In response, Canucks chairman Arthur Griffiths said, "It is our view that Pavel, like all players, will not get paid under this situation. Needless to say, we've had many lawyers look at this. Our interpretation is that he is not entitled to his pay. The only way Pavel gets paid is if a party that has binding authority on this interprets that he does."

Bure's holdout ended four days later, after a 15-minute long-distance telephone conversation with his father. As a compromise, the Canucks offered to put the disputed money in escrow and continue discussions to find a solution. Bure was expected back in Vancouver in time for the season opener against the Dallas Stars on January 20. "I'm sure every-one is happy about his return," Canucks assistant GM George McPhee said. "It's probably driving Pavel crazy staying away, because he's a competitive kid and he doesn't want to be perceived to be this kind of person because he's not. For now, everyone is happy. I think everyone wins in this situation."

There was a brigade of reporters and camera crews waiting at the Vancouver airport on the night of Bure's arrival. Some of them were there to check out a loopy rumor about the Russian's physical appearance—he was said to have ballooned to 225 pounds. All attempts to get the first photos of the waddling Moscow doughboy were frustrated when Bure was whisked out a special passage normally reserved for royalty and heads of state to help them avoid the media.

Camera crews did manage to corner Bure briefly when he showed up for practice the next day wearing an NHLPA jacket. The first question was about his weight. "Do I look like I weigh 225 pounds?" Bure asked incredulously. "I'm the same as always—180."

The Russian refused to discuss his contract difficulties. "We had some problems and hopefully it will all be worked out" was all he would say. Asked how he felt after his 20-hour flight from Moscow, he replied, "I feel great because I'm going to play hockey soon and it's my life and my job. I heard the fans were upset and that's why I'm here. I want to make the fans happy."

It would prove a tougher task than anyone had anticipated.

# Lost in Space

*There is plenty of room at the top, but not enough to sit down.*

FRED SHERO, FORMER NHL COACH

L ABOR STRIFE AND THE MONEY spat with Bure had derailed much of
the momentum generated by Vancouver's run to the 1994 finals. The
Canucks had lost more than 1,000 season subscribers, a drop attributed
not only to the lockout, but also to a steep hike in ticket prices. At an average price of $57, Vancouver now had the second-highest-priced tickets in
the NHL, next to St. Louis. Passing along the cost of players' rising salaries
to fans only increased the growing sense of public disillusionment.

After coming up one win short of the Stanley Cup, Quinn had moved
upstairs, handing over the head coaching job to assistant Rick Ley. Taking over from a figure who cast as large a shadow as Quinn wouldn't have
been easy under any circumstances, but Ley inherited a troubled team at
a troubled time. An added complication prevented him from assuming
his duties behind the bench for the first three games: he had been suspended for failing to restrain Gino Odjick during a preseason brawl in
September, so, assistant coach Ron Smith had to take his place.

The Canucks opened against Dallas. The game held an added element of curiosity because of the bad blood that had been generated between the two clubs during the previous season's playoffs and Shane Churla's vow to seek revenge on Bure. Despite the threats, no hostilities occurred. Instead, the teams skated to a lackluster 1–1 tie. Vancouver's lone goal was scored by rookie center Mike Peca, his first in the NHL.

Bearing no resemblance to the team that had reached the Cup finals, the Canucks followed with three sluggish, error-ridden performances, losing 7–1 to St. Louis, 6–3 to Detroit and 6–2 to Toronto. Vancouver didn't even score an even-strength goal until the 15:15 mark of the third period of their third game when Bure notched his first of the season. "We've been brutal so far," Jyrki Lumme admitted.

Before the next game in St. Louis, the players held a team dinner in the cause of unity. Bure picked up the $3,500 tab, earning an ovation from his appreciative mates. The food must have been good. The Canucks turned in a physical, committed effort and won 3–1 for their first victory of the season. Ley expressed relief. "Our players knew it was a must game and I think they were feeling the pressure of four games without a win," he said. "They have pride in themselves. They didn't get to the Stanley Cup finals just through luck."

Ley's optimism was premature. In their next game with Toronto, the Canucks raced out to a 4–1 lead, but after Bure shot high on a breakaway early in the third, the team suddenly unraveled and allowed the Leafs to pump in three straight goals. Four days later Chicago came to town and stomped the Canucks 9–4. Kirk McLean was lifted midway through the second period after being beaten six times on just 15 shots. It was the first time in three years that a Vancouver goalie had been replaced in mid-game, and the nine goals were the most the club had allowed in one game since 1984. The disgruntled paying customers booed the Canucks off the ice.

Ley was asked if he thought his players were distracted by their contract squabbles and the rude reception from the fans. "If these things are entering their minds before they step on the ice, they had better find a new line of work," the new head coach said. "They're getting paid a lot of money to put the Canucks uniform on. People pay big bucks to see them play and have a right to boo them or be unhappy. If they get off their asses and start playing good, the people will be behind them."

The Canucks rebounded four nights later in a fight-filled game against the visiting Winnipeg Jets, winning 5–1. The violence was sparked when Peca nailed Jets superstar Teemu Selanne with a bone-jarring check at center ice. Although only five foot 11 and 175 pounds, Peca was a devastating open-ice hitter, and the force of the collision could be heard in the upper reaches of the arena. A dazed Selanne had to be helped off the ice; Peca also went to the dressing room and didn't return. Jets captain Keith Tkachuk accused Peca of being afraid to come back onto the ice. In fact, the rookie had fractured his cheekbone and would be sidelined for several weeks.

With just two wins in nine games, the Canucks' stumbling start was the subject of much media analysis. Bure, who had displayed only brief flashes of intensity, was now out of the lineup with the flu. *Toronto Sun* columnist Al Strachan suggested the Russian's absence had more to do with his unhappy state of mind than any virus. "Bure has told the team he has not the slightest intention of returning next season and would actually prefer to be traded this season," Strachan wrote. "Bure has told his Russian friends that he despises assistant general manager George McPhee. He doesn't particularly like coach Rick Ley and is no great fan of Pat Quinn, but he does at least respect his hockey knowledge." The influential hockey columnist also claimed that the vast majority of those in the Vancouver media were reluctant to confront the issue because they were all "Bure apologists."

Meanwhile, the search for a center for Bure continued. Only eight games into the season, Linden, Peca and Ronning had all taken turns with the Russian Rocket. Most fans couldn't understand why it was so difficult to find someone who complemented Bure's game. Murray Craven, who was awaiting an arbitration hearing to determine his free-agency status, attempted to explain the unique challenge involved in playing with Bure to *Vancouver Sun* reporter Elliott Pap: "The biggest thing is that nobody ever played with a player like Pavel before. Very few players have his speed and it's not like you can look back and use your experience. He basically goes with the puck until he gets a scoring chance. He likes to circle up high [in the opposition's zone] and if you find yourself deep and he turns it over, you can get caught. He's always thinking offense—that's what he's paid for—so you always have to be conscious defensively."

In the Russian system, wingers were trained to be the attack players on a line, to be constantly thinking offense. It was the center who carried the brunt of defensive duties. Not surprisingly, Bure's greatest success had come when he played with Larionov and Semenov, two left-handed, Russian-trained centers who could read his moves and who were defensively aware. In 1993–94, Bure had clicked with Craven, another left-handed center who was solid defensively. But Vancouver had inexplicably deemed all three players to be expendable.

On February 15, Quinn made a bid to find a pivot for Bure, acquiring center Josef Beranek from Philadelphia in exchange for Shawn Antoski. Beranek was a Czech rather than a Russian, but he was at least familiar with the European hockey style. Beranek played on a line with Bure in his first two games with the club, a 3–1 loss to San Jose and a 2–2 saw-off versus Anaheim. Bure scored once against the Mighty Ducks, but he misfired on a half-dozen other chances, including a two-man breakaway with Geoff Courtnall.

On February 22, the Canucks met Winnipeg for the first time since Peca's concussion-inducing hit on Selanne. Prior to the game, NHL vice president Brian Burke warned the two teams against resuming their feud. Vancouver dominated, outshooting Winnipeg 46–21, but were stymied by goalie Nikolai Khabibulin and lost 4–1. There were no fireworks until the end of the game when a shoving match ensued. Jets tough guy Tie Domi began haranguing the Canucks, vowing retaliation. "Don't dress Bure in the next game," he shouted at Rick Ley, his threat picked up by a television microphone and relayed coast-to-coast.

In the Canucks' next two games, versus Dallas and San Jose, Bure showed signs of emerging from his slump, accumulating five points. In the Sharks contest, the little Russian was voted the first star for the first time in the season. Although the Canucks played better in early March, they were running into injury trouble. Lumme was knocked out of the lineup with bruised ribs after being checked by Courtnall at practice and Brown was sidelined with a broken wrist after being slashed in a game against Detroit.

On March 7, a news conference was held that would have far-reaching consequences for Vancouver. Arthur Griffiths announced he was selling a majority share of the Canucks, his recently acquired NBA franchise, the Vancouver Grizzlies, and his new stadium, General Motors Place, to Seattle cellular-phone tycoon John McCaw Jr. Although on paper Griffiths would retain the titles of chairman and CEO of Northwest Entertainment Group, the purse strings of the entertainment conglomerate were now under American control.

Griffiths had been forced to sell when he couldn't cover the $350-million debt he had accumulated with construction of the new stadium and the cost of purchasing the NBA franchise. Precisely what percentage of shares McCaw now owned or how much he had paid for them wasn't revealed.

McCaw didn't attend the news conference, which was evidently typical behavior. The entire McCaw clan shunned the public spotlight and rarely consented to interviews or even to having their photos taken. They had the money to protect their privacy. McCaw and his three brothers—Bruce, Craig and Keith—were among the richest people in North America. In August 1993, their company, McCaw Cellular Communications, had been bought by AT&T for a stunning US$12.6 billion.

On March 10, Quinn made another deal, sending restricted free-agent holdout Murray Craven to Chicago in exchange for Finnish forward Christian Ruutu. No one believed the Canucks were getting equal value in the deal. It was simply a cost-cutting move.

On March 14, Peca rejoined the team after missing 14 games with his fractured cheekbone. As fate would have it, Vancouver was in Winnipeg that night to face the Jets, who had vowed to get revenge on Peca for his hit on Selanne. Asked about the confrontation, Ley said, "Mike's a quality guy and he accepts this as a challenge and he'll meet it straight on."

Peca crushed Dallas Drake on his first shift with a clean but devastating bodycheck, stood up to the Jets' attempts at intimidation and set up Linden for the tying goal in the third period. The rookie's performance exhibited both courage and leadership, and Ley was suitably impressed. As he noted in his postgame comments, "You don't find character guys like that on trees."

With no points in his last nine games and only nine goals in 29 games overall, Bure was once again on the firing line. According to unofficial statistics, he had had 15 breakaways and had scored on just two of them. Not only was his scoring touch missing, his explosiveness on the attack was lacking. Bure claimed his muscles "felt lazy," possibly due to the lingering effects of a flu he had contracted earlier in the season. His critics claimed he was sulking.

It was only a matter of time before Don Cherry tossed a grenade Bure's way. Typically Cherry chose the moment when he could do the most damage. His blast was detonated while the *Hockey Night in Canada* crew was in Vancouver to telecast the Saturday-evening game between the Canucks and the Red Wings on March 25. In his "Coach's Corner" segment, the bombastic commentator blamed Bure for the Canucks' woes, called him "greedy" and said that his contract had created dissension on the team. Cherry also repeated the story from the previous spring about Bure's threat to withhold his services "in the seventh game" of the playoffs if the Canucks didn't come up with a new contract.

The segment aired between periods of the first game of the *Hockey Night in Canada* doubleheader between Toronto and Winnipeg. Cherry's comments lit a fuse under Quinn, who asked for a chance to rebut the charges during the second intermission of the Red Wings–Canucks game. When Quinn came into the television studio, he was livid. Bystanders said the big Irishman was on the verge of throwing a punch at Cherry. On camera, a visibly upset Quinn told interviewer Ron MacLean, "I know there is some prejudice in his [Cherry's] game. It's part of his shtick, but he slandered the young man. The boy did not threaten to sit out the seventh game, the first game or anything else."

Quinn, who had previously avoided comment on the boycott story because he felt a response would only lend it credibility, hoped he had finally put the rumor to rest. In truth, he only succeeded in raising its profile. As *Vancouver Sun* columnist Archie McDonald adroitly pointed out, "When you deliver a steaming rebuke to Don Cherry on national television and then threaten to knock the starch out of his shirt collar even Blue [Cherry's dog] wants to know what's going on."

Bure admitted he had watched the "Coach's Corner" segment, but tried to shrug off the incident, noting, "Would you comment on the clowns in the circus?" But judging by his peevish performance in the Detroit game, in which he was ejected for spearing Keith Primeau in the second period, his nonchalance was a sham. The only other time Bure had been tossed from a NHL game for using his stick as a weapon was Game 3 of the 1994 Cup finals, immediately after the appearance in the Vancouver papers of Tony Gallagher's account of the blackmail rumor.

In a strange footnote to the episode, Cherry claimed that a few hours after the game as he sat having a cold one in the lobby of his hotel, a waitress brought over another beer to his table, compliments, she said, of Vladimir Bure. Cherry responded by ordering Vladimir "three vodkas." Why Pavel Bure's father would be buying Cherry a beverage after he had just maligned his son on national TV is open to speculation.

After being blanked 2–0 by Calgary the next night, the Canucks held a players-only meeting to vent grievances. On the basis of their 9–13–8 record and their uninspired play, it was conceivable they might not even qualify for the playoffs. The club promptly reeled off three straight wins and a tie. But Quinn, sensing that more adjustments were needed, shook up the team by making four deals at the trade deadline, sending Greg Adams to Dallas in return for Russ Courtnall, trading Jiri Slegr to Anaheim for Roman Oksiuta, trading Gerald Diduck to Chicago for Bogdan Savenko and a third-round draft pick, and acquiring goalie Corey Hirsch from the New York Rangers for Nathan Lafayette.

Quinn admitted the Adams deal was a hard one to make. The classy veteran had been with the team for eight years and was a proven playoff warrior, but he had gone 16 straight games without a goal and looked as if he was wearing down. That same week the club also inked Kirk McLean to a five-year contract extension for US$12 million. The signing left only two core players without new deals: Trevor Linden and Geoff Courtnall.

Oksiuta, a Russian who had played with Bure on the 1989 and 1990 Soviet junior national teams, was immediately given a whirl as Bure's newest center, his seventh pivot in 35 games. In his first game, he scored a goal and set up Bure for the game winner in a 4–2 win over Calgary. Three nights later the Canucks hammered Anaheim 5–0 at the Coliseum as Bure counted a hat trick, his first multigoal game of the year.

But instead of continuing the roll, the Canucks fell 6–4 to the Oilers in a game in which the team failed to retaliate after Oilers defenseman

Bryan Marchment attempted to take Bure out with his knee in the first period. The Russian had barely leaped out of the way at the last second, getting cartwheeled in the process. "We didn't respond and that may have been the turning point in the game," admitted Ley, whose two enforcers, Gino Odjick and Tim Hunter, were out with injuries. "Marchment was intending to get Pavel's knees. Pavel was the only one who responded to it. We still have or should have enough physical presence to handle situations like that."

The lack of support from his teammates seemed to have a negative effect on Bure. He made a coverage error that led to a key goal by Dallas in a 2–2 tie on April 17, and it was his defensive lapse the next night that enabled Jeff Norton to score the game winner in a 4–1 loss to St. Louis. His plus-minus was now the worst on the team.

On April 22, the Oilers and Marchment returned to Vancouver, and once again the Edmonton bullyboy tried to low-bridge Bure in the first period. This time the Canucks met the challenge. Dana Murzyn fought Marchment, Jassen Cullimore duked it out with Shayne Corson, and Scott Walker took on Jason Arnott. Bure gained revenge by leveling Marchment with a crunching cross-check and played one of his most stirring games of the year, recording four assists, while Russ Courtnall erupted for three goals and two helpers in a 6–1 Vancouver win. "For the first time in a long time, we played a solid 60 minutes," Ley said. "When the shit hits the fan and you play like that, that's when you become a team."

Al Strachan used the game as a springboard to launch another attack on Bure in the *Toronto Sun*, saying it proved that when the Russian was motivated—in this case by his dislike for Marchment—he could dominate the opposition. The implication was that Bure was so good he could somehow win games by himself, a claim that ignored the contributions of his teammates. This sort of criticism was typical of Bure's detractors, who held him up to absurd expectations and then scolded him when he didn't deliver. Bure had become a lightning rod for the Canucks' fortunes. He was given too much credit when the team performed well, assigned too much blame when the team played poorly.

The Canucks finished the shortened season by beating St. Louis and Calgary and tying San Jose to give them an 18–18–12 record, exactly .500.

In the 6–4 victory over Calgary, Vancouver rallied from a 4–2 deficit, outshooting the Flames 22–2 in the third period and scoring four consecutive goals. It marked the first time all season that the Canucks had won a game they had trailed in entering the third period. The comeback was keyed by the line of Bure, Linden and Geoff Courtnall. Bure warmly embraced Linden when he scored to tie the game at 12:50 of the third. The gesture was intentional.

The night before, in the latest installment of his Bure-bashing crusade, Don Cherry had run a highlight on the *Hockey Night in Canada* telecast that appeared to show Bure snubbing Linden after the Russian scored earlier in the week against Chicago. It was, Cherry insisted, proof of a rift between the two Vancouver stars. "I didn't know about Cherry's highlight until Trevor told me," Bure said. "I just laughed. It's funny how people make up stories. We told each other before the game if we score, me and Trevor will go to the middle of the arena and hug each other. Maybe even kiss."

In the Canucks' last game against San Jose, Bure took a brilliant cross-ice pass from Russ Courtnall and scored on a short-handed rush to finish the season with 20 goals and 23 assists for 43 points. That left him 27 points behind Jaromir Jagr and Eric Lindros, who had tied for the league lead. A dozen players scored more goals than Bure. It certainly wasn't a banner year for the $25-million man. Even so, he led the Canucks in goals for the fourth straight year and in points for the third year running and was voted the team's most exciting player for the fourth time.

By finishing sixth in the conference, the Canucks would meet the third-place St. Louis Blues in the opening round of the playoffs. The series meant a rematch with Mike Keenan, who had bolted from the Rangers after winning the Stanley Cup, despite having four years left on his contract, to sign a long-term deal with St. Louis as GM and coach. Keenan had claimed he had been within his rights to leave the Rangers because the team had been one day late with his playoff bonus.

A more plausible scenario had Keenan and New York GM Neil Smith cooking up the late bonus payment in order to give Keenan an escape hatch. Cup or no Cup, neither man was willing to endure another season together. In the aftermath, NHL commissioner Gary Bettman fined Keenan US$100,000 and suspended him for 60 days for creating an "unseemly spectacle," but allowed him to remain with the Blues.

As he had done in New York, Keenan had bolstered his team by adding several veterans, including Al MacInnis, Guy Carbonneau, Adam Creighton, and four former Rangers, Glenn Anderson, Esa Tikkanen, Greg Gilbert and Doug Lidster. And, as he had in New York, Keenan also feuded with his star players, benching and then trading Craig Janney, blasting Brendan Shanahan for his work ethic and questioning the conditioning of goalie Curtis Joseph. St. Louis had improved under Keenan, but it hadn't been accomplished smoothly.

The Canucks were given little chance against the Blues. Martin Gelinas, Jeff Brown and Dana Murzyn were all nursing injuries. With Murzyn and Brown hobbled, the trading of Diduck and Slegr had left the team precariously thin on defense. Behind Dave Babych, Jyrki Lumme and Bret Hedican, the club had only rookies to call on.

Game 1 was decided in the first period when referee Paul Stewart whistled the Canucks for five minor penalties. Brett Hull and Creighton scored on the power play, and those were the only goals the Blues would need. Bure, playing with Linden and Russ Courtnall, was held to just two shots by the Blues' combo of Creighton, Tikkanen and Hull. On one of those shots, taken after the Blues' big line had left the ice on a line change, Bure scored the Canucks' lone goal.

Trailing 2–0 in Game 2, Vancouver got on the scoreboard with 39 seconds left in the first period when Momesso cashed a rebound. The goal jump-started the club's slumbering offense, and Vancouver stormed back to win 5–3, led by a hat trick from Russ Courtnall. Bure potted the last goal midway through the third on a short-handed breakaway. "It's a great, great builder for our team," Hedican said. "We just dug down deep tonight and threw everything we had at them. We know our fans will be there for us now. I hope to see a lot of those white towels back in Vancouver."

Not only were the towels flying in Game 3, so, too, were the Canucks' forwards, aided in large measure by the Blues' undisciplined play. After Hull scored just 20 seconds into the game, Denis Chasse took a five-minute penalty for kneeing. Lumme and Courtnall scored on the power play, and the Canucks never looked back, going on to hammer the Blues 6–1. Bure and Ronning picked up three assists each. Momesso, who potted two goals, said afterward, "I feel like we're getting that feeling again. I was looking at the guys on the bench and there was a lot of enthusiasm. Pavel was flying, and when he gets going like that, it lifts our whole team."

Vancouver opened the scoring in Game 4 when Bure beat Joseph on the Canucks' suddenly potent power play. Skating like the Bure of old, he supplied most of Vancouver's offense in the first period, collecting six of the team's 10 shots. The Canucks' intense forechecking was reminiscent of their play against the Rangers in the Stanley Cup finals the previous spring. Late in the period, Linden supplied a highlight reel for the ages by smashing defenseman Jeff Norton through the Plexiglas in the Blues' end, sending an explosion of fragments in all directions.

But the Blues were able to counter the Canucks' aggression by pressuring Vancouver's vulnerable defense into turnovers to even the series with a 5–2 win. Shanahan, playing on a line with rugged rookies Ian Laperriere and Denis Chasse, did most of the damage, scoring three goals in four minutes and 16 seconds during the second period.

Game 5 was a wildly entertaining, if sloppily played, game. The Canucks blew four leads, including a 3–1 second-period advantage and a two-goal edge in the third, before finally winning 6–5 with an overtime marker by Ronning. Bure started things off with a bang by weaving through and around two St. Louis defenders and snapping a shot high over Joseph's left shoulder. The goal seemed to unnerve the goalie, who was pulled by Keenan in the second period and replaced by backup Jon Casey after he allowed an 80-footer by Ruutu to skip past him. But the Blues suffered a more serious setback when Shanahan got tangled up with Odjick and fell awkwardly, breaking his ankle.

The Blues' undisciplined performance on the power play had hurt them badly again. Bedeviled by the speed of Bure and Russ Courtnall, St. Louis had now allowed Vancouver to score five short-handed goals in the series. Tikkanen, one of the Blues' key performers, had been held pointless and was minus six. "Esa Tikkanen has been a disappointment," Keenan said. "I'm baffled. I've never seen him play this poorly in playoff hockey."

Tikkanen answered Keenan's attack with an inspired effort in Game 6. The Finn set up Hull for the first two goals of the night and then scored himself to put St. Louis up 3–0 early in the second period. After that point, the Canucks were never in the game. McLean was pulled and replaced by Kay Whitmore with Vancouver trailing 6–2 at the end of the second. Up until then, McLean had played every minute of every Vancouver playoff game since 1992. The final score was 8–2, the most goals ever given up by the Canucks in a postseason game.

With Vancouver's overworked defense corps wearing down, it was imperative to get off to a fast start in Game 7, and the team did just that, scoring on its first two shots, a power-play goal by rookie defenseman Adrian Aucoin and a spectacular short-handed effort by Bure, who steamed past defenseman Bill Houlder, faked Joseph out of position and tapped in a backhand. It was Vancouver's sixth short-handed goal of the series, equaling the all-time playoff record. No one could have imagined going into the series that the Blues' power play would prove their undoing. They had only allowed two goals with the man advantage the entire regular season, the fewest of any team in the NHL.

St. Louis came out with a vengeance in period two, outshooting the Canucks 25–7, but McLean was a tower of strength. The Blues beat him only once—a wraparound effort by Basil McCrae at 13:36. A few minutes later Geoff Courtnall restored the two-goal gap on a five-on-three power play. Early in the third, Ronning increased the lead to 4–1, but the Blues fought back on goals by Chasse and Hull to make it a one-goal game with five minutes left. They were still trying to get the equalizer when Bure scored an empty-netter with 21 seconds remaining to bring down the curtain.

It was Bure's seventh goal, a franchise record for one series. He had also added five assists to set a team record for points in a series. If Bure was still unhappy about his unresolved dispute with the club over back pay, it wasn't evident in his play. "Money is only one side of it," Bure said after the series with the Blues. "Pride is the other side. If I didn't play well during the regular season, it wasn't because I wasn't trying. Every game I tried hard because I have pride."

The Canucks advanced to meet Chicago in the conference semifinal. The Hawks, who had outlasted Toronto in seven games in the other quarterfinal series, were likely to present a stiffer challenge than St. Louis. In addition to All-Star goalie Ed Belfour, the Hawks boasted the toughest, most experienced defensive corps in the conference.

Vancouver started fast, outshooting Chicago 12–4 in the first period and taking a 1–0 lead. But after that they ran out of gas. The Canucks were outshot 26–15 the rest of the way and had few good scoring chances. The Hawks tied it in the third and then won in overtime when Joe Murphy scored on a power play at 9:04, with Russ Courtnall off for tripping.

Chicago had shut down Bure with a team defense in Game 1 and, according to ex-Canuck Murray Craven, that was the only effective method: "I watched Mike Sullivan shadow Pavel in the Calgary series in 1994, and it doesn't work. You have to use five guys. You can't turn it over in the neutral zone when he's out there. Low-percentage plays against Pavel will kill you."

The Hawks got an emotional boost in Game 2 from the return of Jeremy Roenick, who had been out of the lineup for seven weeks with a bad knee. But the individual who had the most impact on the final result was referee Paul Stewart. Midway through the second period, with Chicago leading 1–0, Bure blasted home a rising shot from the point. Stewart waved it off, however, saying that Linden's toe was in the crease. It was the game's turning point. The Canucks never scored again and lost 2–0.

Game 3 was clearly a must-win situation for Vancouver. "We have to play harder on offense," Linden admitted. "We have to dump the puck in more and we have to get to their defense. We have to force them to move the puck before they want to and create some turnovers."

Russ Courtnall put the Canucks on top in the first period, scoring a breakaway goal while killing a penalty, but Patrick Poulin replied for the Hawks 15 seconds later. The game remained tied until 12:34 of the third period when Courtnall scored again on a breakaway. The Canucks still led with less than a minute left when Linden failed to control a loose puck in the Vancouver end. Chelios passed to Roenick, trapping several Canucks near the blueline, and Roenick alertly relayed it to Craven, who beat McLean from the edge of the crease. The Canucks protested that Craven was in the crease before the puck arrived, a claim that appeared to be supported by the televised instant replay, but referee Don Koharski refused to seek assistance from upstairs.

Both teams had chances to win early in overtime: Linden and Peca hit posts, McLean stoned Tony Amonte on a breakaway and Joe Murphy rang one off the iron. The game ended at 6:22 when the Canucks turned the puck over to Chelios at the blueline and he walked in and wired a shot past McLean.

With their season on the line, the Canucks finally managed to create some offense in Game 4, pulling out to a 3–1 second-period lead. But the Hawks clawed back on goals by Diduck and Roenick to force another overtime. Bure, who had been held scoreless in the series, was injured early in the third period and didn't return. Once again, the game winner was scored by Chelios, who broke into the Vancouver zone after taking a pass from Denis Savard and beat McLean low to the glove side at 5:35 of sudden death, to seal the 4–3 victory.

Although the Canucks had been swept in four games, the overall margin of defeat was tiny. Three games had been decided in overtime, and in each of those games Vancouver had led entering the third period. Still, it was hard to imagine the Canucks advancing any farther, even if they had squeezed past the Hawks. Their defense had been critically weakened by injuries, and Bure had suffered damaged ribs and wouldn't have been available in the next series.

It was a dismal ending to the Canucks' last season at the Pacific Coliseum, but unlike the sadness that had accompanied the passing of many of the NHL's other old arenas, nostalgia over the Coliseum's demise didn't run deep. There were no Stanley Cup banners to pack up and few memories of past glory. For most of its 26-year existence, the Coliseum had been a palace of pain. General Motors Place, the new arena the Canucks would move into in 1995–96, meant a fresh start, and in the eyes of many, the promise of a brighter future.

The formerly close relationship between Bure and Canucks coach and GM Pat Quinn soured during the negotiations on Bure's 1994 contract. The five-year US$25-million deal made the 23-year-old Russian one of the NHL's highest-paid performers. MARK VAN MANEN/*VANCOUVER SUN*

*Right, inset:* Bure autographs a photo of himself for a young admirer during a goodwill visit to a Vancouver hospice for children with cancer. GERRY KAHRMANN/ *PROVINCE*

*Right:* This infamous front-page *Vancouver Sun* photo of a topless Bure undergoing a pinch test in 1994 sold a lot of newspapers and inflamed the hormones of many female readers. RALPH BOWER/*VANCOUVER SUN*

*Below:* Bure and his girlfriend, Dahn Bryan, share a quiet moment while sitting courtside at a Vancouver Grizzlies–Chicago Bulls basketball game at GM Place in December 1995. IAN LINDSAY/*VANCOUVER SUN*

*Above:* A July 1995 trade reunited Bure and Alexander Mogilny, former teammates on Moscow's powerful Central Army club. Here the two high-flying Russians are pictured wearing World War II Soviet aviator uniforms during a 1995 photo shoot for a Vancouver Canucks team poster. COLIN PRICE/*VANCOUVER SUN*

*Above, right:* Bure and his pal, Gino Odjick, were no strangers to the nightlife scene. When the Canucks opened their 1997–98 season in Japan, the pair prowled Tokyo's neon-lit streets. GERRY KAHRMANN/*PROVINCE*

*Facing page:* Canucks conditioning coach Pete Twist had Bure skate with a parachute to strengthen the muscles around his surgically reconstructed right knee during the winter of 1996. CHRIS RELKE

*Facing page, inset:* Number 96 proved to be an unlucky number for Bure. After switching to the digits in 1995–96, he suffered two consecutive injury-plagued campaigns. In 1997–98, he returned to his old number 10 and a season of good health. LES BAZSO/*PROVINCE*

*Above:* Bure's scoring attempt is foiled by Czech Republic goalie Dominik Hasek during the 1998 Olympic gold-medal game in Nagano, Japan. BRUCE BENNETT/BRUCE BENNETT STUDIOS

*Facing page, inset:* Bure escorts his mother, Tatiana, out of GM Place after the 1998 All-Star Game in Vancouver. MARK VAN MANEN/*VANCOUVER SUN*

*Right:* Bure seems to embrace the crowd at Vancouver's GM Place after scoring his final goal as a Canuck during a game against the Toronto Maple Leafs on April 19, 1998. COLIN PRICE/*PROVINCE*

*Following page:* Bure's trade to the Florida Panthers in January 1999 ignited a frenzy of Pavelmania in the Sunshine State. JIM McISAAC/BRUCE BENNETT STUDIOS

CHAPTER FOURTEEN

# Ninety-Six Tears

And while the sun and moon endure
Luck's a chance, but trouble's sure.

A. E. HOUSMAN, "THE WELSH MARCHES"

AS TRADES GO, it had the look of a daylight mugging. On July 8, 1995, just moments before the Vancouver Canucks made their first selection at the NHL Entry Draft, it was announced the team had traded that pick (12th overall), along with center Mike Peca and junior defenseman Mike Wilson, to the Buffalo Sabres for Alexander Mogilny.

In exchange for some unproven young talent, the Canucks had acquired one of the league's most dangerous offensive threats. The 26-year-old Mogilny was lightning-quick and pure poison around the net. In 1992–93, playing with center Pat LaFontaine, Mogilny had scored 76 goals, the fourth-highest total in NHL history. A slow recovery from a broken leg suffered in the 1993 playoffs, coupled with the loss of LaFontaine to a knee injury in 1993–94, had prevented Mogilny from duplicating that performance, but the Canucks, who would be inheriting his US$3.7-million contract, obviously felt he had the potential to do it again.

Although Quinn accepted the kudos at the time, in 1998 he would tell Toronto's *Globe and Mail* that the push to acquire Mogilny had come from the "suits" in upper management. Orca Bay, the corporate entity that now controlled the Canucks, wanted to create a box-office buzz. "We were coming off a disappointing season, the lockout year, and they said we needed an attraction," Quinn said. "That's why we went out and traded for Alexander Mogilny. With Pavel Bure, we had two-thirds of the great Soviet line—something we could sell."

As soon as the trade was announced, requests for season tickets began to pour in. Even the city's jaded sportswriters had trouble containing their enthusiasm. "As fire sales go, it had the look of Dante's inferno," the *Vancouver Sun*'s Mike Beamish gushed. "By the time the smoke cleared the Buffalo Sabres were left with second-degree burns and the Canucks had claimed the insurance payoff."

The usually laconic Mogilny appeared equally thrilled. "I'm incredibly excited," he said. "Going from Buffalo to Vancouver. It's so beautiful out there. And to be playing the kind of hockey they want to play there instead of in our conference is exciting to me. It was so boring to play that [defensive] way."

Mogilny and Bure were expected to be reunited on a line, a sobering prospect for opposition teams. Commenting on the prospect of skating alongside Bure, Mogilny said, "To have a friend you've played with before at Pavel's level means a lot to me. It will be the same as it was before, only we are better players now."

Maybe the only person in Vancouver not completely enraptured with the trade was coach Rick Ley, whose repeated calls for an improved work ethic and team defense had fallen on deaf ears in 1994–95. Ley had frequently accused his team of lacking heart, and heart was the aspect of Mogilny's game that had come under fire in Buffalo. It was felt the stylish Siberian rarely pushed himself to the limit. Maddeningly inconsistent, he could be overpowering one night and invisible the next.

In truth, the team Quinn was assembling appeared to share little in common with Ley's blue-collar character. There was a lot of spit to Ley, but little polish. His personality was as gruff and blunt as his puglike face. "With his broad, flat forehead, he looked," the *Vancouver Sun*'s Iain MacIntyre wrote, "more like a villain from *The Rockford Files* than a 1990s

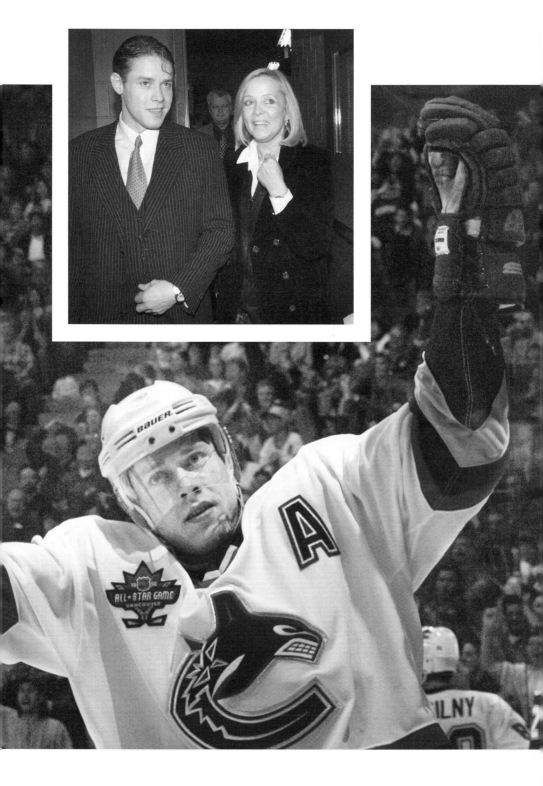

coach." Glib quotes and pop psychology weren't Ley's forte. In postgame Q-and-A sessions, he appeared as comfortable as a murder suspect.

During his 13-year career in the NHL and WHA, Ley had been known as a tough plugger whose determination far exceeded his talent. A highly successful minor-league coach, he had held one previous head coaching job in the NHL, with the Hartford Whalers from 1989 to 1991. Ley had been fired after his second year in Hartford after clashing with Ron Francis, the Whalers' captain and star player, a conflict that had led to Francis being shipped to Pittsburgh in a disastrous deal.

Quinn had been gradually altering the character of the Canucks since the 1994 playoffs, sacrificing size and toughness for speed and creativity. His strategy had been prompted by the league's avowed determination to modify the game to encourage offense. The latest edict from head office was a crackdown on interference fouls in 1995–96. To emphasize its commitment, the NHL had even coined a new term for such infractions. Players who hooked, held or otherwise illegally harassed their opponents would be ticketed for "obstruction."

The rule modification had been introduced after another season in which defense had dominated, and several teams, most notably the 1995 Stanley Cup champion New Jersey Devils, had employed a stifling checking system known as the neutral-zone trap. Quinn believed the popularity of the trap was the result of lax officiating. As he explained, "Interference had been permitted all over the ice and it basically caused some changes in our game. You saw so many trap teams last year because no one could get in to forecheck. You had to run through a picket fence. So then a coach says, 'You can't get there, so let's sit back.' It slowed our game down and got us back to a style played in the '60s and '70s—a stand-still game."

Mogilny arrived in Vancouver in early August, took up temporary residence in Bure's home and began twice-a-day workouts with Pavel and Vladimir. By the time training camp rolled around, he was in superb shape. Although Mogilny was initially the focus at training camp, the spotlight abruptly switched to Bure when he revealed he had changed his uniform number from 10 to 96. Pat Quinn had long opposed his players wearing high digits because it suggested an emphasis on the individual that he felt was at odds with the team concept. However, since

Mogilny had been permitted to wear his customary 89, there was no reason to deny Bure 96.

There was a great deal of conjecture as to why Bure had made the switch, speculation inspired because Bure, in his typically cryptic fashion, offered no explanation. The story offered by the team—that 96 represented the year Bure was to become a Canadian citizen—was nonsense. Bure had requested 96 when he first joined the Canucks in 1991, long before the question of citizenship was an issue. The real reason was connected with his exit from Russia.

High numbers were usually adopted by European players to mark significant dates. Czechoslovakian Jaromir Jagr picked 68 to commemorate the memory of the Soviet invasion of his country in 1968. Mogilny chose 89 to mark the year of his defection to the West; Fedorov had adopted 91 for similar reasons. Bure, who landed in North America on September 6, 1991, simply followed suit, but with his own personal twist. Since 91 had already been claimed by Fedorov, Bure substituted the digital representation of the month and day of his arrival in the West: 9/6.

There was nothing new about players changing numbers; the practice had a long history among hockey superstars. The NHL's three most famous number 9s—Maurice Richard, Gordie Howe and Bobby Hull—all began their careers with different numerals on their backs. Richard initially wore 15. He switched to 9 to celebrate the birth of his first child, a daughter who weighed nine pounds. Howe first wore 17. He changed to 9 to improve his sleeping arrangements. In Howe's era, players were allotted berths on trains according to their jersey numbers and the lower berths were bigger. Hull switched three times. He first wore 16, then 7, before claiming 9 in his sixth season.

But all this occurred before souvenir sales of replica jerseys became big business. Bure's switch annoyed a lot of people, especially parents who had shelled out $150 to buy their children suddenly out-of-fashion replicas of his number 10 Canucks jersey. Some believed, incorrectly, that the switch was inspired by greed—that Bure would directly profit from the number swap. In fact, revenues from jersey sales were divided between the NHL Players' Association, NHL teams and retailers.

A dispute over numbers was also the root of another controversy at camp—the absence of captain Trevor Linden. Contract talks between

Linden and management had dragged on for a year. The two sides were said to be US$200,000 apart, a pittance by NHL standards. A number of Canucks were frustrated by the impasse, but only Jeff Brown spoke publicly about it. "The biggest thing that Trevor has against him is he loves it here in Vancouver and wants to stay," he said. "If the situation was different, you'd see something different happen. You don't think that management knows he wants to stay here? They've got him over a barrel."

A few days later, after two other high-profile restricted free agents — Calgary's Theoren Fleury and Winnipeg's Teemu Selanne — signed for US$2.4 million and US$2.7 million respectively, setting a benchmark for the category, Linden and the Canucks finally agreed on a three-year deal at US$2.4 million per annum.

Early in training camp, Bure and Mogilny played together on a line with Mike Ridley. But the expected magic didn't materialize. Mogilny, like Bure, normally played on his off wing, the right side. Forced to switch to the left side, he seemed lost positionally and confused about his role on the line.

When the exhibition season began, Mogilny was skating on right wing with Ronning and Oksiuta. Beranek centered a line with Bure and Russ Courtnall, while Ridley was between Linden and Gelinas. Fourth-line grit would be supplied by feisty rookie Scott "The Wild Thing" Walker, Alek Stojanov, Gino Odjick and returning veteran Jim Sandlak. On defense, the veteran core of Lumme, Babych, Brown, Hedican and Murzyn would be supplemented by youngsters Jassen Cullimore, Adrian Aucoin, Leif Rohlin and Dean Malkoc. In goal, Kirk McLean was backed up by rookie Corey Hirsch.

By all accounts, this was the most talented team the Canucks had ever assembled. With a payroll of US$26 million, it was certainly the most expensive. Expectations were high. Management had indicated that .500 hockey would no longer be acceptable, a welcome message to the fans who would be filling the high-priced seats at General Motors Place, Vancouver's $160-million state-of-the-art sports palace.

The arena had its official opening on September 19 with a concert by rock star Bryan Adams. Bure and Odjick, who were in attendance, joined Adams onstage to sing backup on a version of "Cuts Like a Knife." The first hockey game at GM Place was played on September 23, as the

Canucks defeated Anaheim 4–3 in a preseason encounter. Although the jury was still out on the team, the arena was deemed an artistic success. However, Orca Bay's initial pleasure at the favorable reviews the stadium received was soon replaced by anger and frustration when sportswriters dubbed GM Place "the Garage," a moniker that management felt lacked the proper sense of decorum.

The Canucks got a scare at the Garage during their second-last preseason game against Calgary. Late in the match, Ron Stern cross-checked Bure, who retaliated by dropping his gloves. Several players joined the fray and began tussling. Bure emerged from the scrum doubled over in pain, clutching his right arm. While trying to throw a punch at Stern, he had connected with the helmet of teammate Alek Stojanov and had dislocated the index finger on his right hand. Fortunately the mangled digit appeared worse than it actually was. "I almost puked when I looked at it," Bure told the *Vancouver Sun*'s Elliott Pap. "It was so ugly. I thought, 'I'm done for the rest of my life.'" Still, it would be several weeks before Bure regained full use of his hand.

Vancouver opened the season with a 5–3 home-ice loss against the Detroit Red Wings before a sellout crowd of 19,024. Ridley got the club's first regular-season goal at the new arena, scoring on a power play at 5:48 of the second period. The Canucks had put forth an honest effort, but seemed befuddled by the disciplined precision of the Red Wings.

Rick Ley was the one who was befuddled after the next game against Los Angeles. Vancouver streaked out to a 5–1 lead in the second period, but then collapsed, allowing the Kings to pump in six straight goals before rallying late in the third to earn a 7–7 tie. The two teams combined for an incredible 95 shots, 49 by the Canucks and 46 by the Kings. Bure scored twice, while Mogilny added a goal and three assists.

Blowing a four-goal lead is a rarity in the NHL, but Vancouver nearly managed it two nights later against San Jose. After surging to a 6–2 lead, the Canucks surrendered three goals in five minutes in the third period and were in danger of squandering the two points until Mogilny scored his third goal of the game with three minutes left, as they held on for a 7–6 win.

The Canucks followed with improved efforts in a 3–3 tie with the Kings and a 5–1 win over the Mighty Ducks. With two goals against Anaheim, Mogilny now had seven goals and 11 points in five games. But the sloppy defensive play resurfaced on October 21 against Edmonton, a game in which Vancouver was outshot 21–5 in the second period and lost 6–4. In a bid to send a message, Ley benched defenseman Jeff Brown for the last half of the game.

Brown, the team's highest-paid blueliner, watched the next game, a 5–2 loss to the Rangers, from the press box. He seemed confused by his benching. "I don't know what's going on," he told reporters. Ley claimed that Brown had been told he wasn't working hard enough, but Brown insisted Ley hadn't said a word to him.

The next night the Canucks downed New Jersey 4–2, and Brown was a healthy scratch again. The veteran reacted angrily, sounding off in a radio interview: "I'm not 19 years old where I have to sit and take all this shit. I'm upset by it. I'm hurt by it. I'm embarrassed by it and I certainly don't deserve it and that's the bottom line." Brown claimed he was merely a scapegoat and that Ley wouldn't "have the guts" to bench Bure, Mogilny or Linden for playing poorly.

His assertion had more than a little truth to it—he wasn't the only player who was struggling—but the defenseman had never been a favorite of management. Ley and Quinn's distaste for him had increased when he opted to sit out several games in the 1995 playoffs with a sprained knee rather than play through pain, even though the team was hurting on defense. Brown had further angered Quinn with his candid comments regarding Linden's contract negotiations. There was also a persistent but unconfirmed rumor that Brown had caused a rift in the team by getting involved with Kirk McLean's wife. If that was true, then it was no surprise the team was behaving like a dysfunctional family.

While Brown clearly wanted out of Vancouver, another high-profile player indicated he wanted to join the team. Igor Larionov, who was on the trading block in San Jose, had named Vancouver as his first choice as a destination. "My concern is I've got two years to go on my contract and to have a chance to win a Stanley Cup," the 35-year-old noted. "I think I could do it with those two Russian guys in Vancouver."

Acquiring Larionov would solve the long-standing problem of finding Bure a compatible center. It also raised the intriguing possibility of creating an all-Russian line, a concept no NHL team had adopted yet.

But the Canucks, who were leery of Larionov's age and durability, made no serious overtures to San Jose, which eventually dealt the wily Russian to Detroit for winger Ray Sheppard on October 24.

The trade paid major dividends for Detroit. The addition of Larionov allowed Detroit coach Scotty Bowman to assemble not just an all-Russian line, but a five-man Russian unit composed of Larionov, wingers Sergei Fedorov and Viacheslav Kozlov, and defensemen Viacheslav Fetisov and Vladimir Konstantinov. The Russian quintet's fluid and artistic play became the talk of the hockey world in 1995–96, as Larionov enjoyed his most productive NHL season and the Red Wings logged a league-record 62 wins.

Brown rejoined the lineup on October 28, as the Canucks returned home from a four-game road trip and dropped a 4–1 decision to Winnipeg. Brown and Ley had declared an uneasy truce. They had agreed not to speak to each other except in practices. Brown's spot in Ley's doghouse was next occupied by Russ Courtnall, who was benched after he made three glaring defensive errors in a 4–4 tie against Toronto. Courtnall had fallen a long way in a short time, having begun the season skating with Bure on what was billed as the team's top line.

Another player feeling the heat was Gino Odjick, who had suddenly lost his mean streak, a change in demeanor he attributed to his new-found sobriety. After a seven-day drinking binge at the conclusion of the previous season, Odjick claimed to have had a near-death experience that caused him to take stock of his life. "On the seventh day," he said, "my heart started beating real fast and then my left arm went numb. I felt my spirit leave my body." Publicly admitting he was an alcoholic and that he had been indulging in drinking binges since the age of 12, Odjick had embarked on a 500-mile walk during the summer, a journey of healing through Alberta and British Columbia, to warn aboriginal youth about the dangers of drugs and alcohol. Now that he was living a slower, less volatile lifestyle, Odjick was finding it difficult to summon the anger that allowed him to be a menacing force on the ice. The Canucks, although supportive of his sobriety, were running out of patience with his docility.

On November 4, as Vancouver began a three-game road trip in Calgary, Ley reunited Bure and Mogilny on a line with Beranek. Bure responded by notching his first goal in seven games in a 4–4 tie. In the next game against the New York Islanders, the Russian chemistry experiment suddenly clicked. Displaying dazzling speed and puck movement, the trio fired 14 shots on goalie Jamie McLennan in a 5–2 victory. Bure had a sensational night, scoring one acrobatic, defense-splitting goal and setting up two others, while Mogilny chipped in with a goal and two assists. "It was probably the first game this season where I really had fun," Bure said.

After the game, Ley noted: "As I said all summer, there is no reason why Pavel and Alex can't play together. I split them up late in camp because it wasn't working, but maybe I didn't give it long enough. I sat down and talked to both of them last week about retrying it and I got a good feeling about it."

Buoyed by the sweet sound of Russian music and riding a five-game unbeaten streak, the Canucks journeyed to Chicago to meet the Blackhawks on November 9. Once more the Windy City proved to be a killing ground for the Canucks, who lost 5–2 despite directing 51 shots at Hawks goalie Ed Belfour. But more troubling than the loss was a knee injury Bure suffered in the first period when he was decked by defenseman Steve Smith. After lying in pain on the ice for nearly a minute, the Russian hobbled to the bench and didn't return.

Bure wanted to stay in the game, but 24-year-old rookie trainer Mike Burnstein insisted on a trip to the dressing room, where he asked the Chicago doctor to examine Bure. The knee seemed quite firm. The doctor's diagnosis was a sprain. He prescribed "10 days maximum" rest and relaxation.

But when Canucks team doctor Ross Davidson, whose medical specialty is reconstructive knee surgery, examined the videotape of the injury, he suspected something far more serious. The results of magnetic resonance imaging (MRI) confirmed his suspicions. Bure had torn the anterior cruciate ligament (ACL) in his right knee. Surgery was required, and Bure would be sidelined six to nine months.

The news that Bure would miss the rest of the season sent shock waves through Vancouver. A season that had begun with such glowing optimism was rapidly becoming a nightmare. Looking for a positive angle, Quinn suggested that perhaps the loss of Bure would inspire the players to renew their commitment to team defense. The other question, the one nobody wanted to address, was the injury's long-term effect on Bure. For a player whose game was based on explosive speed and agility, healthy knees were imperative. When Bure came back, would he be the same player?

The high incidence of ACL injuries in athletics masks their severity. The ligament provides mobility and stability to the knee. Once severed, it can't be sewn back together and must be reconstructed with tissue taken from a different part of the patient's body, with artificial tissue or with tissue from a donor. In Bure's case, Davidson used tendon removed from the Russian's hamstring muscles.

Only 10 years before, surgeons had to open the entire knee to repair torn ligaments, but by using an arthroscope—a steel cylinder the thickness of a soda straw with a powerful light and a tiny camera encased in its tip—it is now possible to peer inside the knee and make repairs without major trauma. Inserted directly into the joint, the device functions like a microscope, relaying magnified images to a television screen mounted above the patient's hip. To repair Bure's injury, Davidson drilled a couple of tiny holes through his knee joint at the site of the torn ligament. He then took the harvested tendon, pulled it through the tunnel in the knee and laced it through the center of the old ligament. The ligament would serve as an internal splint around which the old ligament would hopefully heal. Titanium screws were used to attach bone plugs at each end of the graft to the knee.

Prior to the advent of the arthroscope, the knee had to be kept immobile in a plaster cast for three months after surgery. Because of the resulting atrophy of the muscle, it would be four or five months before an athlete could walk without the aid of crutches. With the arthroscope, rehabilitation can begin almost immediately. A week after his operation Bure was able to move around. Within a few weeks, he began an exercise program designed to regain a range of movement and strengthen the muscles around the knee. Under the guidance of Canucks strength-and-conditioning coach Peter Twist, and his father, Vladimir, Bure set off on the long road to recovery.

With Bure out of the lineup, Vancouver promptly hit the skids, winning only one of its next eight games. The pattern became distressingly familiar—score early and collapse late. After absorbing a 7-2 pasting at the hands of the lowly San Jose Sharks on November 25, Ley seemed a beaten man. "There were a lot of turnaways, there were no hits, there were no takeouts, there was nothing," he said glumly.

Three days earlier Ley had ripped his players after they blew a two-goal lead in the third period against Dallas, saying, "We've got too many guys looking for the headlines. I've never been a part of a team this selfish. I feel like slitting a few throats." After the Sharks debacle, the only throat Ley looked intent on slashing was his own. Asked if he had given the club a tongue-lashing, he replied, "No, it would only be a waste of time."

Time was something Ley was fast running out of. With a record of 6–11–6, the Canucks had slipped to 10th in the conference. They had only one win at home and had allowed 84 goals, second most in the NHL. The Vancouver media, which two years before had campaigned for Quinn to hand over the coaching reins to Ley, were now clamoring for Quinn to replace Ley.

On Sunday, November 26, they thought they had gotten their wish. On its 11:00 P.M. Vancouver broadcast, UTV's *Sports Page* reported that Ley had been fired. Primed by the scent of blood, a mob of journalists descended on the Canucks' practice on Monday morning, only to discover Ley was still in charge. George McPhee, the Canucks' assistant GM, assured everyone that Ley's expiry date hadn't been reached yet. "Rick's our coach and we're going with him." The firing, McPhee said, was a media-created fantasy.

UTV sports director Paul Carson tried vainly to defend the station's erroneous report. Carson claimed that on Sunday afternoon he had received information from a source "very high up in the Canucks' hierarchy" that indicated Ley was going to be fired within a matter of hours. According to Carson's source, Canucks chairman Arthur Griffiths had ordered Quinn to ax Ley and step behind the bench for the team's next game. In order not to lose the scoop, Carson said a decision had been made to run the story before the Canucks made the firing official. Carson believed the station's report had caused the club to change its mind: "I'm absolutely confident that Ley was about to be canned and that Ley himself knew it. But we caught them with their pants down and they had to back off. Now it's just a matter of time. It is going to happen."

Whatever the Canucks' true intentions regarding Ley, the confusion indicated that not everyone in management was on the same page. Despite previous assurances that McCaw's increased share of ownership wouldn't affect day-to-day hockey operations, the chain of command had changed. Quinn now had to entertain personnel suggestions from deputy chairman Stanley McCammon and CEO John Chapple, the two executives McCaw had brought in from Seattle to run the business. Behind the scenes, McCammon had been pressuring Quinn to fire Ley for weeks.

In a 1999 interview with the *Vancouver Sun*'s Iain MacIntyre, Quinn admitted, "The first indication to me how much things had changed was when they wanted to make the coaching change with Rick. That was when it dawned on me that I didn't run this anymore. It shoved a stake in our hearts. When I first went there I was given total control. When the ownership amalgam happened that was no longer the case. I saw mom-and-pop become a big corporation. The money people came in and along with them came a lot of other people with opinions about how the business should be run. There were a lot of conflicts there."

Virtually ignored in the furore over Ley's status was the arrival of forward Esa Tikkanen from the New Jersey Devils in exchange for a second-round draft pick. But even this seemingly innocent transaction became an object of dispute when Tikkanen failed his physical. He was discovered to have degenerative arthritis in his right knee. It would take six weeks to sort out the assorted legal and medical issues before the Finn was cleared to play.

Damaged goods was also the label being applied to another Canucks newcomer. Mike Ridley was suffering from chronic back problems that would eventually knock him out of action for four months.

After Ley's false firing, the team pulled out of its death spiral, winning back-to-back games for the first time in the season. In an effort to make life easier for Ley, Quinn finally traded Brown on December 19, sending him to Hartford in exchange for minor-league forward Jim Dowd and journeyman defenseman Frantisek Kucera. Some of the Canucks weren't sad to see him go. One unnamed player called Brown "the laziest son of a bitch he'd ever seen." Still, it wasn't a popular move among the fans. Brown had been the quarterback of the power play, and at the time of the trade he had the best plus-minus on the club.

In February, Bure began to skate for the first time. His typical routine involved a 60-minute on-ice workout composed of regular practice drills—shooting, passing, give-and-gos and transitional breakouts, as well as resistance skating using harnesses, parachutes and weighted vests. The on-ice drills were followed by 60-minute sessions in the gym that included riding the stationary bike and weight work to strengthen the muscles around the knee and maintain his overall conditioning.

It was lonely, boring work, but Twist says Bure handled it well. Contrary to the popular perception of Bure as a petulant problem child, Twist found him very positive and accommodating. "He is one of the most coachable athletes I've ever worked with, very hardworking, very cooperative and respectful. He didn't skip on anything," Twist says.

While working with Bure, Twist noticed that his skating mechanics were quite different than those of most North American players. "Most players skate on their inside edge and push off at a 45-degree angle, but Bure starts on his outside edge and rolls over to his inside edge and pushes back straighter on his stride than the typical North American player." As a result, Twist says, "he gets more power and force in his stride to get up to top speed quicker."

In a game composed of quick stops and starts, it was Bure's acceleration, not his pure speed, that made him such a dynamic force. "Other players would beat him in a race around the rink," Twist notes. "It's his ability to get up to top speed in a short distance that sets him apart."

In February, the Canucks gave Bure a few days off. He flew to Los Angeles, accompanied by his new girlfriend, Dahn Bryan, a model and aspiring actress who had a small role in the Jackie Chan film, *Rumble in the Bronx*. Bure was photographed sharing an ice-cream cone with Bryan in the book *A Day in the Life of the* NHL. The pair had a stormy relationship. They would break up and then get back together again several times in the next few years.

In February, Bure tried to relieve his tedium by purchasing a new car: a candy-apple-red Ferrari F355. The high-powered vehicle, like Bure himself, had a lot of power under the hood. It could go from zero to 100 miles per hour in 11 seconds, had a top speed of 183 miles per hour and was priced at US$130,000.

During Bure's rehabilitation, Arthur Griffiths arranged for him to attend seminars with James Hoggan and Associates, a Vancouver public-relations company. The object was to help the Russian feel more comfortable in dealing with the media. According to the firm's vice president, Nancy Spooner, Bure was an enthusiastic and willing student.

Late in the season, the *Province* arranged with the Canucks to have sportswriter Jim Jamieson and photographer Gerry Kahrmann spend a day with Bure in an attempt to humanize their enigmatic superstar. Jamieson began the day by watching Bure work out, and from there they were to visit Ronald McDonald House, a residential facility for families whose children are undergoing cancer treatment. The trip had been set up by Orca Bay in order to demonstrate Bure's commitment to charity work in the community. "The first thing he asked us," Jamieson says, "was 'How do you get to this place?' He'd never been there."

Once they did arrive, Bure slipped easily into conversation with the children. "He was great with the kids," Jamieson recalls. "A couple of the young boys cuddled up next to him on the couch. They were just awestruck."

In the afternoon, Jamieson accompanied Bure to the airport in his Mercedes to drop off his agent, Serge Levin, who had been visiting him. "Although I had covered the team and known Pavel for five and a half years, I'd never actually ever been in public with him," Jamieson says. "I thought it would give me a chance to see how people reacted to him." They walked into the terminal and sat down in the cafeteria and waited 45 minutes. While they waited, Bure signed souvenir photos of himself for Levin to take back to Los Angeles. "Not a single person recognized him," Jamieson says.

The loss of Bure had less negative economic impact on the Canucks than one might imagine. The team's insurance policy provided a rebate of nearly US$3 million on Bure's salary, and the club continued to draw well at the new arena. By the end of the year, the Canucks recorded 28 sellouts and set a new franchise record for attendance, with 729,629 spectators.

Led by the scoring of Mogilny and Linden and the goaltending of rookie Corey Hirsch, who had supplanted McLean as the team's top netminder, the Canucks inched up the standings into fourth place. But after opening March with three straight wins, the wheels suddenly came off. The team lost eight of their next 10 games, including six in a row, and were outscored 42–22. The slump coincided with Mogilny's sudden inability to find the net. After scoring 51 goals by February 29 and appearing to be a lock to shatter Bure's franchise record of 60 goals, he notched only four more in his last 19 games.

On March 28, Vancouver's record stood at 29–32–15. They ranked seventh in the conference but were falling fast. The howling for Ley's head began again in earnest. Quinn, who was worried not only about the possibility of the club not making the playoffs, but about his own job security, finally acted, gassing Ley and taking over as head coach with six games left in the season.

Ley's firing coincided with the appearance of Bure practicing in full gear for the first time since his injury. Was it possible he would be back in the lineup before the end of the season? "We're in the homestretch as far as his readiness is concerned," said Twist, who claimed a playoff return was realistic. Bure pronounced himself 90-per-cent healthy: "Maybe I'll play late season, maybe I'll play in the first round of the playoffs, maybe not. Now I don't know. It's dangerous. I want to play, but if I rush it I could reinjure it."

The speculation about Bure rejoining the club had been fueled by the remarkable recovery of two other players felled by torn ACLs. Bob Bassen of the Dallas Stars, who had his knee repaired on October 11, had just re-joined the Dallas Stars, and Uwe Krupp of the Colorado Avalanche, who had surgery on October 6, was now practicing with his team.

In Quinn's first game behind the bench, the Canucks defeated Chicago 4–2, their first win over the Blackhawks in 14 games, dating back to the 1993–94 season. But the optimism sparked by the victory quickly faded as the Canucks won only two more games in their last five, barely scraping into the playoffs by a single point on the strength of a 5–0 win over Calgary in their final game.

Despite the club's struggles, several players had turned in stellar performances. Mogilny led the team with 107 points, only three short of Bure's club record. His 55 goals was third-best in the league, behind only Mario Lemieux's and Jaromir Jagr's totals. Linden added 33 goals and

47 assists for 80 points, the highest number of his career, and Martin Gelinas hit the 30-goal mark for the first time.

By virtue of their seventh-place finish, the Canucks drew the Colorado Avalanche in the first round of the playoffs. The Avalanche was a formidable foe. Well stocked with such gunners as Joe Sakic, Peter Forsberg, Valeri Kamensky and Claude Lemieux, Colorado had shored up its one weak spot—goaltending—by acquiring Patrick Roy from Montreal in a crucial midseason trade.

Any hope of Bure returning for the playoffs was dashed on the eve of the Colorado series when it was revealed that his knee hadn't passed the strength test. "He's deficient, especially in the hamstring area," Quinn said. The news, while disappointing in the short term, removed any pressure that Bure might have been feeling from the team to return, a possibility that had the potential for disaster.

Despite Colorado's edge in talent, the Canucks mounted a determined challenge, getting solid goaltending from Hirsch, who played the entire series after replacing McLean in the second period of Game 1, and strong efforts from Mogilny and Linden. But ultimately, Vancouver was unable to overcome its lack of depth behind the blueline. The trading of Brown and an injury to Babych left Vancouver's defense corps even more threadbare than it had been the previous year.

Even so, the Canucks nearly pulled off the upset. They were six minutes away from taking a 3-2 lead in the series when referee Paul Stewart, the Canucks' playoff nemesis, handed Ridley and Murzyn penalties 30 seconds apart late in Game 5. Avalanche captain Joe Sakic knotted the score 4-4 on the five-on-three power play and then notched the winner in overtime. The sixth and deciding game of the series was almost as close, with the Avalanche prevailing 3-2 on a Sakic goal at 17:18 of the third period.

Colorado's fast-skating juggernaut rolled over Chicago, Detroit and Florida to capture the Stanley Cup. Afterward, Avalanche coach Marc Crawford admitted Vancouver had given his club its toughest series. With a healthy Bure in the lineup, things might have been different. That thought and the anticipation of the Russian Rocket's return to action were the lone consolations left for the team's supporters in the ruins of a shattered season.

# CHAPTER FIFTEEN

# Season of Shadows

*It is better for the sheep to have the wolf as an enemy than as his friend.*
RUSSIAN PROVERB

WHILE RECOVERING from his knee injury, Bure had begun pursuing interests outside hockey. One was a plan to resurrect his family's historic watchmaking business, which had closed in 1917. His partner in the venture was a 47-year-old entrepreneur named Anzor Kikalishvili. In an interview with Associated Press, Kikalishvili described the project in altruistic terms: "Bure has such a strong personality, a sense of history and a self-made fortune on the ice. It's marvelous that he is investing his hard-earned money into restoring the old Russian trademark."

Like his ancestors, Bure planned to have the watch parts made in Switzerland, then shipped to Moscow and St. Petersburg for assembly. A limited edition of 50 gold timepieces, replicas of the old company's last model, had already been made. Priced at US$30,000 each, they were luxury items, which was in keeping with tradition. The Russian royal family had always worn Bure watches and used them as awards for service to the crown. Bure had presented the first three models to President Boris Yeltsin, Prime Minister Viktor Chernomyrdin and Moscow's mayor, Yuri Luzkhov.

At the same time as Bure was attempting to restore his family's legacy, Orca Bay majority owner John McCaw had launched a plan to revive his hockey team's flagging fortunes. He was intent on making Wayne Gretzky a Canuck.

Gretzky had parted company with the St. Louis Blues after only a half season. On July 1, he became an unrestricted free agent and began shopping his services to interested bidders. By mid-July, only two suitors were left: the New York Rangers and the Canucks. After meeting with McCaw at his retreat in Sun Valley, Idaho, Gretzky seemed to be leaning toward Vancouver. A meeting was scheduled at McCaw's Seattle offices to hammer out contract details. The deal came together so swiftly that Quinn had to be called back from a vacation in Singapore.

Discussions began at midday on July 18. The two sides were still dickering at 11:30 P.M. when Gretzky returned to his hotel, leaving his agent, Mike Barnett, and his lawyer, Ron Fujikawa, behind to continue talking with McCaw, Quinn, deputy chairman Stanley McCammon and George McPhee. Around midnight, the Canucks upped their offer to three years at US$5 million per year. Barnett and Fujikawa took the proposal back to Gretzky. After a brief discussion, they agreed to sleep on it and decide in the morning.

But at 1:30 A.M. Canucks management phoned Barnett and told him it wanted a decision immediately. The team was concerned that Gretzky intended to use its offer to lever a better deal from the Rangers. Barnett woke Gretzky again to inform him of the ultimatum. Irritated by the hardball tactics, Gretzky told everyone to go back to sleep. By the next morning, Vancouver's offer was off the table. Gretzky flew back to Los Angeles and signed a two-year deal for US$10 million with the Rangers the next day.

Precisely why the Canucks became so suspicious of Gretzky's intentions was unclear. Asked why the team refused to wait until the morning, Quinn told the *Province*: "We felt a decision should have been forthcoming. It wasn't, so we decided to withdraw. We had a timetable." Gretzky insisted he was serious about the Vancouver offer, so much so that he hadn't even booked a round-trip flight back to Los Angeles. Whatever caused the breakdown, the deal that would have brought the Great One back to Canada mysteriously disappeared in the Seattle night.

Bure wasn't around to offer an opinion on the Gretzky affair. He was in Moscow, preparing to play for the Russian team in the 1996 World Cup tournament, which was to begin in late August. Ideally the Canucks would have preferred Bure to test his rebuilt knee at training camp under the eyes of the team's medical staff, but the winger was eager to play for his country. He first suited up with his Russian teammates on August 14. *Toronto Star* reporter Alan Adams, who was in Moscow covering the team's preparations, was amazed by the cavalier attitude toward Bure's well-being. "If Pat Quinn had been there, he would have blown a gasket," Adams says. After a cursory medical examination, coach Boris Mikhailov threw Bure into a practice without even giving him a chance to warm up.

Afterward, Adams interviewed the Russian Rocket in his chauffeur-driven limousine. Bure refused to talk outside the arena because he was worried about his safety. He had reason to be concerned. A few weeks before, Vladimir Bogash, an official of the Central Army hockey club, had been gunned down in broad daylight outside the team's offices when two men pulled up in a Mercedes and pumped nine bullets into him. He was the second Russian hockey official killed in a gangland-style slaying in two months.

The deaths were part of a clandestine struggle for control of the Russian hockey league. High-ranking officials had formed alliances with mobsters, and disputes were now being settled with machine guns. Hockey wasn't the only Russian sport infected by violence. Soccer had experienced similar problems. In October 1995, Alexander Bragin, president of the Ukrainian team Shaktyor Donetsk, and five bodyguards were killed by a car bomb that scattered body parts around the stadium before a game. In 1997 Larisa Nechayeva, the woman who was the business brains behind Spartak Moscow, Russia's top soccer club, was shot to death at her dacha.

Underworld involvement in Russian hockey had escalated in 1993 after the Russian government, in an effort to prevent the financial collapse of the Russian Ice Hockey Federation, granted the organization the right to import consumer goods without paying taxes. The tax break became an attractive moneymaker for hockey officials, who used it to import hundreds of millions of dollars' worth of duty-free vodka, cigarettes, cars, computers and electronic equipment, which were then resold. However, instead of the proceeds being reinvested in the league and youth hockey programs, most of this money simply disappeared.

In 1997 Valentin Sych, president of the Russian Ice Hockey Federation, said of his senior rivals in the organization: "They're the biggest thieves. All they are concerned with is lining their own pockets. Our hockey is now so corrupt I don't see how we can ever clean it up." Two months after uttering those words Sych was cut down in a hail of gunfire as he drove to work. Six men were eventually tried and convicted of carrying out the murder. Also arrested and charged, but later released because of insufficient evidence, was Robert Cherenkov (Bure's former coach with the Russian national junior team), who had been the president of a hockey league composed of teams from former Soviet republics. Cherenkov's league had been shut down in 1995 and replaced with an exclusively Russian league led by Sych. According to one of the conspirators, former hockey referee Alexander Artemyev, it was Cherenkov who had initiated the plot to eliminate Sych.

Sych's death wasn't mourned by Russian hockey players. One of the old bosses, he was reputed to have been a former KGB man. As the Detroit Red Wings' Viacheslav Kozlov told the *Detroit Free Press*, "He was a bad guy, corrupt. That is why somebody killed him. It is not a surprise to me."

The turmoil had a distracting effect on the Russians' World Cup team. Players were divided over who should oversee and coach the squad. Fetisov and some of the other veterans criticized Bure for refusing to sign a petition calling for the ouster of officials they considered corrupt. Bure replied, "I don't belong to any groups or opposition. I do not sign petitions. I believe I should work—play hockey. Petitions to the federation or to Olympic committees do not interest me."

As it turned out, Bure didn't play in the tournament. Six days before Russia's first game he suffered a bruised kidney in an exhibition match against Team USA. The mishap would sideline him for three weeks.

Although hockey fans were disappointed, Canucks management was pleased, since it eliminated the risk of Bure damaging his knee during the tournament, which was eventually won by the American team.

Bure skated for the first time with the Canucks at training camp on September 12. The team was counting heavily on his full recovery and a return to his former dominance. Despite Vancouver's earliest playoff exit in four years, Quinn had done little to address his club's deficiencies. Worse, he had lost Cliff Ronning, the team's best offensive center, to free agency. Claiming it couldn't afford his US$900,000 salary, the club didn't even bother to make Ronning a qualifying offer. The center quickly signed a three-year deal with Phoenix for US$3.75 million, with Vancouver getting nothing in return.

The Ronning decision had other consequences. When it appeared Mike Ridley might be forced to retire because of back problems, the club re-signed Josef Beranek, a player it had earlier deemed a liability, for US$500,000. When Ridley did return, the Canucks sent Beranek to the minors. Beranek went home to the Czech Republic, but because he had a one-way contract, he continued to collect his NHL salary while playing for Petra Vsetin in the Czech elite league, until he was traded to Pittsburgh in March.

Vancouver entered the 1996–97 season with center ice manned by Linden, Ridley, Mike Sillinger and Russian Alexander Semak, claimed on waivers from the New York Islanders. Semak's salary was US$735,000. For the amount the Canucks were paying Semak and Beranek, they could have re-signed Ronning.

Quinn's only major off-season move was the hiring of new coach Tom Renney. A successful junior coach with the Kamloops Blazers in the Western Hockey League, Renney had piloted the Canadian Olympic team to a silver medal at the 1994 Olympics and the Canadian national team to a silver medal at the 1996 World Championships. Renney represented a 180-degree departure from Ley. Young, personable, stylishly dressed and media-friendly, he had an academic air to him that was enhanced by his habit of tossing around words such as *cognizant* and *reciprocal*. As if he were a New Age guru, Renney had inspirational sayings painted around the Canucks' dressing room, such as "Master technique but let the spirit prevail." Renney had rejected offers from

Toronto and Phoenix to take the job with Vancouver. When asked why, he said, "I wanted to identify myself with longevity."

The one item missing from Renney's résumé was professional experience. What he did have, however, was a defensive system, something the Canucks had often been accused of lacking. Renney called it the "weak-side lock." Despite the technical name, it was a simple concept. When the opposition had the puck, the job of the Canucks forward on the far side of the ice (weak side) was to lock up the opposing winger, enabling the strong-side defenseman to plug the lane nearest the puck carrier without worrying about giving up an odd-man rush. In the system the Canucks had used previously, the third forward was positioned closer to the middle of the ice between the two forecheckers and the two defensemen.

Bure, who declared his knee 100-per-cent healthy, seemed to be a new man at training camp, full of enthusiasm and more self-assured and relaxed. He said that the long rehabilitation process had sharpened his appreciation for hockey. Although he was now wearing a large brace on his rebuilt right knee, he didn't appear too troubled by the encumbrance.

Bure emphatically announced his return during a preseason game with Boston when he drew ovations with a couple of whirlwind shifts and scored a goal that would still be running on highlight packages six months later. While killing a penalty during the first period, Bure picked up the puck near center, engaged the afterburners and sped away from defenseman Ray Bourque. As he cut in from the right wing on Bruins netminder Scott Bailey, Bure pulled the puck into his skates, freezing Bailey, then, in one balletic motion, kicked the puck back up to his stick and swept it into the net. The scoreboard replay of the goal drew as many cheers as the real thing.

After the game, John McKeachie, a Vancouver TV sportscaster who is infamous for his long, convoluted questions, cornered Bure and launched into a word-tumbling jabber about the goal that finally concluded with McKeachie saying, "I guess what I'm trying to get at is would you ever try a move like that in an NHL game?"

A quizzical Bure stared back at McKeachie and said, "I just did."

At the next practice, all the Canucks players were trying to duplicate Bure's move. Renney joked to reporters that he had taught the Russian the maneuver. "And I only had to show him once," Renney deadpanned.

Vancouver opened the season with a 3–1 victory against Calgary at GM Place on October 5. Although no one realized it at the time, it was the most significant game the Canucks would play in 1996–97. During the third period, as Bure carried the puck wide past Flames defenseman Todd Simpson, the rookie gave Bure a hard push, sending the Russian crashing into the end boards. Bure managed to break his impact by sticking out his arms but still hit the boards with his head.

Although Bure left the ice under his own power and finished the game, the collision left its mark. The first indication that all was not well came in mid-October when the winger missed two practices. Renney explained that Bure had a headache and had been experiencing "those little black spots" for a couple of weeks. "The doctors said to keep him away from contact and any real exercise for a few days," Renney said. "It's just precautionary. He doesn't need any tests or anything. I don't know how much it's bothering him, to tell you the truth."

Bure, who appeared pale and watery-eyed, denied it was his head, but rather his stomach that was the problem. He felt nauseous. Although no one raised the issue, he appeared to be exhibiting the symptoms of a concussion.

Despite feeling ill, Bure played the next night, as Vancouver scored a convincing 6–1 victory over Dallas. The victory evened the team's record at three wins and three losses. The early impression was positive. The Canucks were playing a sounder defensive style and, with a little luck, their record could have easily been five and one.

But the enthusiasm was erased in the next game as the 1996 Stanley Cup champion Colorado Avalanche trounced the Canucks 9–2 in Denver, pumping nine goals past Kirk McLean on just 22 shots. Despite the shellacking, Renney remained upbeat, telling perplexed reporters that "the beauty of losing like this is that it camouflages nothing."

Four days later Colorado visited Vancouver in a return match. Although the Canucks played with more effort, they lost again 4–1, allowing three unanswered goals in the third period. Afterward, Linden said, "I'm not going to point fingers, but I expected more out of our group. We need more guys onboard giving 100 per cent."

Rather than criticize his players, Quinn, who had been repeatedly taken to task by the media for failing to upgrade his roster, fired a volley at his tormentors. "You guys are fixated with the fact there hasn't been a lot of changes," Quinn told reporters. "How much change do you have to have happen? How many faces do you need to wheel in and out? There comes a time when you have to say, 'We're going to work with what we've got.'"

Quinn's message seemed to strike a responsive chord as the Canucks reeled off four straight victories against Pittsburgh, Anaheim, Edmonton and Calgary. It was their longest winning streak in three years. Bure, whom Renney had shifted to a line with Linden and Gelinas, was a force in all of the wins.

During the contest with the Flames, Todd Simpson had renewed hostilities with Bure, tackling the Russian, rubbing his glove in his face, knocking his helmet off and body-slamming him to the ice. Bure responded by flooring Simpson with a roundhouse right. Later in the game, Simpson jumped Bure from behind and was given a match penalty for a deliberate attempt to injure. Afterward, Bure tried to play down his run-in with Simpson, preferring to focus on the team's win.

At the next day's practice, the Russian Rocket found himself again trying to play down a story, but this one had more sinister implications. ESPN, the U.S. sports channel, had reported that Anzor Kikalishvili, Bure's business partner in his watchmaking venture, was a Russian mob boss involved with drug dealing, money laundering and extortion. ESPN also revealed that Bure's connection with Kikalishvili extended beyond watchmaking. Bure was vice president of sports for Kikalishvili's company, the Twenty First Century Association, a supposedly nonprofit Russian corporation designed, among other things, to promote athletic events and competitions. According to the FBI, the company was actually a mafiya front worth at least US$100 million in illicit funds, with interests in real estate, hotels, banks and casinos. Bure's golden halo had suddenly assumed a darker hue.

Sitting in the Canucks' dressing room, surrounded by two dozen reporters and bathed in the hot glare of television lights, Bure patiently answered questions for 30 minutes. He admitted his business connection with Kikalishvili and described the Georgian as an influential figure in Russian sports. Bure said he had known Kikalishvili for two years. "I really don't think he's involved in crime," Bure said. "You can point to anybody and say he's a bad person. I don't believe rumors because I've heard so many about myself that aren't true. It's what friendship is all about. You don't give up on somebody because someone says he's bad."

The other Canucks players, unsure of what to think about the commotion, tried to make light of the situation. "Don't wind your watches, boys," Kirk McLean cracked. "They may explode."

Bure sounded completely sincere, but some of what he said was completely unbelievable. When asked if there was a serious problem with the mafiya in Russia, he claimed to know nothing more than what he had seen on TV. As for the issue of extortion of Russian hockey players, he said he had no firsthand knowledge of it.

When teammate Alexander Mogilny was asked by reporters about incidents of extortion of Russian players by crime figures, he stretched the bounds of credulity to absurd lengths, saying, "Why talk about it? It doesn't exist. There is no such thing." Mogilny, of course, had been the victim of an extortion attempt in 1994.

In a 1997 interview with the Russian publication *Sport Express*, Vladimir Bure elaborated on the connection with Kikalishvili, admitting he had known him for 20 years. They had first met, Vladimir said, when Kikalishvili worked in Komsomol, the Young Communist organization. According to Vladimir, Kikalishvili "later introduced me to the highest echelon of leaders in the Soviet Union. Even today, he is still close to many of the top politicians in the country."

One of those top politicians was Yosif Kobzon, a wealthy Russian-Jewish singer, businessman and politician, who was known as "the Frank Sinatra of Russia," more because of his association with mobsters than for his voice. Bure had often been seen in Moscow in the company of Kobzon's daughter, Natalie, prompting much speculation about the seriousness of their relationship. Kobzon had fanned the gossip by referring to Bure as his "son-in-law." In Russian interviews, Bure denied any romantic interest in Natalie, saying, "I am more a friend of the father than the daughter." Exactly what was the basis of Bure's friendship with the 57-year-old Kobzon remained unexplained.

Kobzon, like Kikalishvili, was a person of interest to law-enforcement officials. In 1995 he had been denied entry into the United States because of his suspected criminal ties. Kobzon seemed to revel in his roguish reputation. He had earlier publicly admitted his friendship with Otari Kvantrishvili, a notorious crime boss who was killed by a sniper as he exited a Moscow bathhouse in April 1994. Kvantrishvili was an unusual hoodlum who combined gangster activities with public service. An Olympic wrestling coach with the Dynamo Sports Club, he had founded several charitable foundations, including one for the families of murdered police officers. Kvantrishvili eventually created his own political party, Sportsmen of Russia, which was better financed and organized than some legitimate political parties in the Russian parliament. The mourners at his funeral included a who's who of celebrities from sports, entertainment and politics. As Kvantrishvili's widow sobbed on Kobzon's shoulder, Russian television, which covered the proceedings, played the theme from the movie *The Godfather*.

In May 1999, Kobzon narrowly escaped death himself when he showed up late for an appointment at his corporate offices in Moscow's Intourist Hotel. A bomb, set to an automatic timer, exploded shortly before his arrival, destroying the entire floor. After surveying the damage, Kobzon declared, "This means God exists."

A day after the ESPN story broke, Pat Quinn said the Canucks were doing some "fact-finding to see what truth there is, if there is any, in this matter." Quinn also said he had spoken to Bure about the allegations. This marked the third time Quinn had asked Bure to end his relationship with suspected criminals. By any accounting, it revealed a troubling pattern. If Bure hadn't been such an extraordinary talent, it is likely Quinn would have long since traded him.

Trading appeared to be a common response of NHL teams whose Russian players were linked with crime, even if they were merely victims. Alexei Zhitnik, Viacheslav Fetisov and Vladimir Malakhov, who had all reportedly been targeted by extortionists, were traded within a year after their predicaments became public. Oleg Tverdosky, a 20-year-old defenseman with Anaheim's Mighty Ducks, was another Russian NHLer who was shipped out following an extortion incident, although the details of his case weren't revealed until two years after it occurred. On January 30, 1996, four thugs had kidnapped Tverdosky's mother outside her apartment in the Ukrainian town of Donetsk. Shortly afterward, Tverdosky received a photograph of her in handcuffs and a ransom demand of $200,000. When her abductors attempted to transport her to Moscow on a train to make the cash exchange, she was rescued by Russian police, who stormed the train and arrested the kidnappers. A couple of days after the rescue, Anaheim dealt Tverdosky to Winnipeg.

For his part, Bure resented Quinn's meddling in his private life. Although he said nothing at the time, he described his chat with Quinn to a Russian interviewer in 1999: "The general manager called me up. I was told to end the friendship. I replied that if Kikalishvili is charged with narcotics, prostitution or arms dealing, then I will publicly renounce our friendship. 'Okay,' the manager told me, 'tomorrow we will phone you with proof.' Three years have gone by now. And still no phone calls regarding proof."

In fact, neither Quinn nor the NHL was pursuing an investigation of Kikalishvili. There were no league rules governing who an NHL player could have as a business partner. If consorting with criminals was a felony, then the NHL would have had to drum Wayne Gretzky out of the league. The Great One was the bosom buddy and business partner of Bruce McNall, owner of the Los Angeles Kings and chairman of the NHL's board of governors who, in March 1997, began serving a six-year prison sentence for defrauding various banks and investors out of US$250 million.

The flap over Bure's alleged mob ties blew over as suddenly as it had begun. Without the time, resources or inclination to pursue the story further, sports reporters treated it like another hockey game, abandoning it as the Canucks dropped a 4–2 decision to the St. Louis Blues and left on a four-game eastern road trip. But at least one journalist didn't let it go. A year later Robert Friedman, a New York–based investigative reporter, would reveal more details about Kikalishvili and the Russian mob's penetration of the NHL.

While the Canucks were out of town, Arthur Griffiths quietly sold the rest of his shares to John McCaw, making Orca Bay Sports and Entertainment a wholly American-owned enterprise. Griffiths insisted he had made the decision to sell voluntarily. Still, it was a shocking reversal of fortune. The man who just two years before had owned the entire operation had been reduced to the humble status of an employee.

Griffiths's declining role in the company had become evident when, one by one, most of his management appointees had lost their jobs and been replaced. Griffiths hadn't made a public appearance in connection with the team in many months. He was expected to be on hand in August when Orca Bay held a news conference to announce Vancouver would host the 1998 NHL All-Star Game at GM Place. When he failed to show, Orca Bay president John Chapple explained that Griffiths was trapped in a traffic jam.

With the exception of a 6–1 loss to Montreal, a game in which the Bure brothers met for the first time, the Canucks played solid hockey throughout November. After rallying from a 2–0 deficit to defeat the Rangers 5–3 on November 23, Bure said the team was playing with a determination that reminded him of the 1994 playoffs. "It's the first time I've had the feeling since those playoffs," he said. "You enjoy coming to the rink, you think you are going to win and that's what confidence is all about."

But confidence is a precarious commodity, and with the Canucks perched in fourth place in the conference at the end of the month, it suddenly slipped away. The slump was set in motion by a sudden plague of injuries. By early December, six regulars were out of the lineup, including Linden, who suffered strained knee ligaments against Philadelphia on December 1, an injury that ended his NHL-leading ironman streak of 482 consecutive games.

Bure, who hadn't scored a goal in eight straight games since the Canucks' victory against the Rangers on November 23, wasn't playing with his characteristic boldness. He appeared tentative and was shying away from physical contact. In response to inquiries about Bure's sub-par play, Renney said Bure had damaged his shoulder in the November 23 game with the Rangers and was playing hurt. Renney also noted the Russian was still struggling to adapt to the team's new system: "Pavel is a conscientious guy. All he wants to do is the right thing. He needs encouragement. I think he's a great kid."

A week later, after Vancouver suffered a 6–1 whipping at the hands of Colorado, Renney abruptly changed his tune, singling Bure and Mogilny out for not providing leadership. "You expect your best players to step up in a time like this and I don't think we saw that. I can accept results like this if the effort is there, but I'm not sure it was for some of our key people."

In the next game against Dallas, Renney shifted winger Esa Tikkanen to center between the two Russian snipers. Although the Canucks lost 2–1, Bure skated better than he had in weeks. Two nights later in St. Louis the line erupted for 13 points as the Canucks demolished the Blues 8–0. Bure notched two goals and three assists, equaling his personal high for points in an NHL game, while Mogilny recorded a hat trick and an assist and Tikkanen added four assists. The lifeless performance by the Blues signaled the end for coach Mike Keenan, who was fired four days later.

In the intoxication of victory, Tikkanen pronounced the two Russian wingers to be better than his former Edmonton linemates, Wayne Gretzky and Jari Kurri. "More powerful these two guys," the Finn said. "Their speed, everything. It is just amazing. I'm getting more excited, coming to the rink like a young kid again. I want to keep it up."

Mogilny was less sanguine. "Next game we'll be horseshit and you'll be back asking why," he told reporters.

Perhaps clairvoyance was one of Mogilny's unrecognized talents. In their next game, a 2–1 home-ice loss to the New Jersey Devils, the Canucks were stunningly inept, recording a paltry eight shots on net. That was five shots fewer than the franchise record and only one shot more than the all-time NHL low of seven, set by the Washington Capitals in a game against the Philadelphia Flyers in 1978.

The Devils had frustrated the Canucks by clogging the neutral zone, slowing the pace and forcing them to play in tight quarters in the corners and along the boards. This sleep-inducing brand of hockey was precisely the sort of thing the new obstruction rules had been designed to eradicate. Unfortunately enforcement of the rules had fallen by the wayside. As Mario Lemieux noted, "Early last year, when they were calling the clutching and grabbing, it was fun to be able to skate and make plays. It was more like the hockey I grew up playing. A couple of months later, it went back the other way. Now, it's the same old boring hockey."

A 5–3 home-ice loss to Philadelphia on December 31 left the Canucks with a dismal 3–9–1 record for the month. They had slipped to ninth in the conference. In a move calculated to irritate management, Mogilny spoke out, saying the team needed a legitimate first-line center. "I like it here and I want to stay, but we need help. Everybody knows it all starts with strength up the middle. If it doesn't change, then I hope when they make a trade it's me."

Mogilny's comments were widely perceived as mischief-making, but he was merely stating the obvious. With Linden out, the Canucks had nothing but doughnut lines—they all had holes in the middle. After posting three points in 18 games, Semak was now occupying a permanent seat in the press box, leaving the Canucks' sagging middle staffed by Ridley, Sillinger and converted wingers Esa Tikkanen and Dave Roberts.

Rents in the fabric were beginning to show. On January 10, during a 5–3 win over Hartford, Mogilny and Renney engaged in a heated exchange on the bench that Bure had to break up. A few days later Tikkanen, unhappy with the lack of progress on a new contract, went public with his request for a trade.

Bure, who had managed to avoid any verbal hassles with management, got into one off the ice with David Duchovny, the star of *The X-Files*. The incident reportedly occurred when Bure and his girlfriend, Dahn Bryan, arrived at Quattro on Fourth, a restaurant in Vancouver's Kitsilano neighborhood. Duchovny, who had also dated Bryan, was sitting nearby. Bure and Bryan began quarreling when the Russian jealously sniped at her about her relationship with Duchovny. After Bryan bolted to the bathroom in tears, Duchovny walked over and said to Bure, "Why do you have to be such an ass?" The two men almost came to blows.

Despite the undertow of discontent, the Canucks pulled out of their tailspin. Bure, who had rediscovered his shooting eye, notched nine goals and seven assists in a 10-game stretch from January 1 to January 23 as the club went 8–4–1 for the month and climbed back into the playoff race.

When Linden returned to the lineup on February 1, Vancouver was in sixth place in the conference and looked capable of moving up in the tightly congested standings. On February 6, Renney put Bure on a line with Linden and Gelinas, and the trio led the Canucks to a 7–4 upset over the powerful Detroit Red Wings. Bure picked up four assists in the game, tying his career high. But in the next game Vancouver meekly succumbed 4–2 to Toronto, one of the league's doormats, provoking Renney to attack his players for their lack of intestinal fortitude. "Our physical play was nonexistent. It was absolutely zero. That's straight guts and a willingness to pay a price to win a hockey game. There are no shortcuts to winning. It's straight up-the-pipe guts."

On February 22, two days after he again insisted his weak-side lock system wasn't an issue of contention, Renney abandoned the system and reverted to the more conventional 2–1–2 format. Quinn, who had been conspicuously silent throughout the winter, announced he still believed the Canucks could win the Stanley Cup, a statement that was greeted with general amazement.

Bure, who had scored just two goals in his last 13 games and had been demoted to the third line, appeared to be only a shadow of his former self, yet when asked on February 28 if he was hurt, he told Elliott Pap of the *Vancouver Sun*: "There are no problems. There are no injuries. None." Bure's statement was backed up by trainer Mike Burnstein, who noted, "There is nothing wrong with Pavel. He is fine."

In fact, there was very little fine about either Bure or the team. The dressing room was badly divided and the players, who had grown tired of Renney's complex X-and-O sessions and theoretical dissertations at practice, had begun tuning out their coach. The extent of the trouble wouldn't become apparent until late in the season when several players complained anonymously to Iain MacIntyre of the *Vancouver Sun*. Contradicting Renney's image as a communicator, they told MacIntyre the man was inflexible and unwilling to listen and rarely conferred with assistant coaches Glen Hanlon and Stan Smyl. They also claimed Renney had been overly assertive, instituting a ban on beer on team flights, scheduling tough practices after losses during long road trips and refusing to give praise or extra ice time to his best players.

If Quinn was aware of the dissent, he didn't let on. During the first intermission of the telecast of a game with Colorado on March 3, he brazenly vowed the team would make the playoffs. The Canucks went on to lose 5–1, for their 11th defeat in 15 games. Bure, after another inconspicuous night, left the game in the third period after taking a bodycheck from Aaron Miller.

Afterward, Bure admitted what many had suspected—that he had been playing hurt. He said he was suffering from whiplash and would be out of action until the condition cleared up. "It goes back to the first game, but the last couple of months it's been getting worse and worse," he said. "It's my whole upper body—my chest, my neck, my spine, my arms, everything. I have pain 24 hours a day, even when I'm lying down. The last six or seven weeks the pain's been awful."

Bure agreed he probably should have taken some time off, but that after missing 62 games the previous season with his knee injury, he didn't want to sit out and had decided to try to play through it. Bure said the extent of the injury had been concealed so that other teams wouldn't be able to target him.

The unanswered question was: Why had it taken the team so long to remove him from the lineup? Renney insisted, "At no time did we ask him to play when he thought he couldn't. He left us with the impression that he could play." Still, it was difficult to understand why, after it became apparent that Bure was suffering, someone in management didn't order him to rest. Considering the problematic nature of neck injuries, there was no way Bure was going to improve if he continued to absorb abuse.

The confusing signals from the team about the injury would cause some to question if Bure was actually in distress as much as he claimed. The timing of his withdrawal from the lineup, just as the Canucks began to fall out of the playoff race, prompted further suspicion.

On March 8, the Canucks finally made a trade, sending Tikkanen and Russ Courtnall, the two players accused of being major malcontents, to the Rangers in exchange for Sergei Nemchinov and Brian Noonan. Tikkanen, elated by the move, fired a parting shot at Renney, declaring him "the worst coach in hockey."

The acquisition of Nemchinov, a solid two-way center, had the potential to help the team, but once again Quinn was stuck with damaged goods. Nemchinov's bruised ribs proved more problematic than the Canucks' GM was led to believe by the Rangers. He wouldn't be cleared for active duty until the end of the month and ended up playing only six games.

The initial word on Bure was that he would be out for two weeks, but when he failed to respond to treatment, the prognosis was ominously changed to indefinitely. The Canucks won only one of their next eight games after Bure left the lineup, a performance identical to what had occurred the year before after he blew out his knee. The slide effectively destroyed any realistic hopes of making the playoffs.

The Canucks finished with a rush, losing only once in their last 10 games. The streak saved Renney's job, but it still left the team five games under .500 and four points shy of a playoff berth. It was the first time in seven years that the club had failed to qualify for the postseason.

As the season wound down, an emotional Quinn made a speech at a Vancouver Board of Trade luncheon, in which he blasted his players for blaming Renney rather than looking in the mirror. "Players making threats about their salaries and what would happen next season when they're free agents put themselves ahead of the team environment." He also admitted the debacle was ultimately his responsibility: "I may have missed the boat in assessing this team."

One team that hadn't missed the boat was Detroit, which won the Stanley Cup for the first time since 1955, dismantling the Philadelphia Flyers in the finals in four straight games. The victory silenced the team's critics, who had complained that the Red Wings would never win the Cup with their "Russian Five." In the summer, Larionov, Fetisov and Kozlov took the 35-pound trophy home to Russia and posed for pictures with it in Red Square. The surreal episode ended with the three hugging and kissing the Cup on the doorstep of Lenin's tomb. It was as if they were dancing on the graves of the past.

CHAPTER SIXTEEN

# Fear and Loathing

*The fish rots from the head down.*

RUSSIAN PROVERB

MOSCOW, LONDON, PARIS, AMSTERDAM — Bure was seen in all these great cities following the end of the 1996–97 season. The jet-setting Russian arrived back on the West Coast in early June to have his ailing neck examined by team doctor Ross Davidson. Although it had improved, he was still complaining of stiffness after workouts. While in Vancouver, Bure made an appearance at the official unveiling of the Canucks' new uniform.

Orca Bay had replaced the club's skate logo and black, gold and white colors with a killer-whale crest and a blend of blue, black, red and white. A killer whale also happened to be Orca Bay's corporate logo. The company had been tempted to dump the Canucks' moniker altogether and simply rename the team the Orcas. From a marketing standpoint, having a team called the Canucks was problematic. Johnny Canuck, the 1940s comic-book hero the club was named after, may have been a popular figure in his time, but to the team's American owners his legacy was an irritation. At Orca Bay headquarters, "Canuck" was referred to as a "disconnect"—corporatespeak for something that can't be tied to any easily marketable image.

The uniform makeover was merely an appetizer for Orca Bay's next major marketing initiative. Faced with the challenge of stirring up fan interest in a team that was rapidly sinking under the weight of inertia, management set out to sign 36-year-old free agent Mark Messier, a player who had the word *winner* stamped in capital letters on his forehead.

Messier, the New York Rangers' captain and icon, had become available after he spurned a Rangers offer of two years at US$10 million, calling it "insulting." Several teams made bids for his services, but Vancouver was the most persistent. Negotiations began at Messier's family compound at Hilton Head, North Carolina, on July 20, and ended six days later aboard John McCaw's yacht in the sea off San Francisco. All of the brass—McCaw, McCammon, Chapple and Quinn—were on hand for the occasion. Late that afternoon Messier agreed to a three-year US$20-million contract, with fourth- and fifth-year options that could push the total package to US$30 million.

At a news conference in Vancouver on July 28, a grinning Messier pulled on one of the Canucks' new Free Willy jerseys and thrust up his arms in victory. The next day the club sold more than 100 season-ticket packages, most of them to new customers. The fiercely competitive Messier was perceived as the perfect antidote for the Canucks' woes. "He'll make those Russians dance," Oilers GM Glen Sather clucked.

McCaw denied Messier's signing was an act of revenge for the Rangers' grabbing of Gretzky from the Canucks the previous year. Instead, he said it was an indication of the team's commitment to winning the Stanley Cup. "The value is huge. If he increases every player's performance by 10 per cent, we've made a very good investment."

The euphoria over Messier's signing completely ignored the risks involved. Not only was Messier 36, it had become clear to New York hockey reporters that he was no longer the dynamic force of former years. He took some nights off, he was often hobbled by injuries and he had been physically overpowered by Philadelphia's Eric Lindros in the 1997 playoffs.

Messier was asked if his contract included being named captain of the Canucks. "Everybody knows Trevor Linden is the captain of Vancouver and that he's done a tremendous job being captain," Messier said. "There is no reason to change that, so it never came up."

Although the Canucks had failed to re-sign center Sergei Nemchinov, who returned to the Rangers, and had released Mike Ridley, Quinn finally had the big playmaking center he had long been seeking. The club had also bolstered its back line by signing highly touted Swedish defenseman Mattias Ohlund and two other free agents, defenseman Grant Ledyard and goalie Arturs Irbe. Mogilny had yet to sign a new contract, but the rest of the team seemed set, and it appeared the Canucks might open training camp without any distracting controversies.

But on August 26, *Province* columnist Tony Gallagher, citing the usual "anonymous sources," tossed a stick of dynamite into the calm by stating that Bure had met with Quinn and had asked to be traded. Gallagher also noted that Serge Levin, Bure's financial adviser, had been given permission to shop a deal around the NHL. Considering that Quinn loathed Gallagher and wouldn't have talked to him even if roasted over an open fire, it is reasonable to conclude that the details of the meeting were leaked by Bure's camp. But judging by Bure's reaction, it hadn't been done with his blessing.

Bure admitted to talking with Quinn but said the meeting was confidential. Did he want to be traded? Bure refused to answer directly. "Well, it's a business and there is nothing I can do about it," he told *Vancouver Sun* reporter Elliott Pap. "They can trade me. Wayne Gretzky was traded a few times. Today I'm a Canuck and I'm just getting ready for the season."

Levin confirmed Bure was seeking a trade, but that the request had nothing to do with money. "He is just looking for fresh air, a fresh opportunity and a strong team." Levin felt confident a deal would be completed before the season began. Bure, however, denied Levin had any authority to speak for him. A few days later he made that crystal-clear by firing Levin and Salcer as his representatives and replacing them with former NHL player and Queen's University law professor Mike Gillis, the agent who represented Markus Naslund of the Canucks and ex-Canucks Geoff and Russ Courtnall.

At the same time as he turfed his agents, Bure also dismissed his father as his personal trainer. Vladimir Bure told Pap that the split was due to "philosophical differences" and admitted, "Yes, I'm upset. It is not the happiest time in my life. I don't know what's happening in Pavel's life. He is my baby, but I understand he's 26 and has to make decisions by himself."

Vladimir's dismissal meant the end of his employment by the Canucks who, according to Levin, were paying him US$100,000 a year to serve as Pavel's personal trainer. Vladimir, who had a new wife and a two-year-old daughter, revealed he was opening a new business, a Russian restaurant that specialized in catering to private functions in Vancouver's Russian community.

The split between the Bures was likely inevitable. In some respects, it is surprising it didn't occur earlier. Few 26-year-olds would have been able to accept the regimented control Vladimir exerted over his son without rebelling. But the manner of the split, a complete severing of ties, suggested there was more involved than simply a dispute over Pavel's workout schedule, as Vladimir had indicated.

Salcer learned of his termination via a fax and claimed to have no idea why Bure had fired him. He said he felt betrayed. But one contributing factor was Salcer's inability to resolve the festering issue of the US$1.7 million Bure claimed the Canucks still owed him in back pay from the lockout in 1994–95. Although Bure's dispute had attracted all the headlines, he wasn't the only player affected. Two dozen NHLers had the same sort of guaranteed contracts. In three years, the NHL Players' Association had made no progress resolving the issue, but some players had been mollified by bonus payments and renegotiated contracts. *Vancouver Sun* columnist Greg Douglas reported that Jyrki Lumme, one of the players affected, had actually received his lockout pay from the Canucks, an act that enraged Bure. But according to Lumme's agent, Don Baizley, this isn't true. Lumme's contract dispute has never been settled.

Salcer and Levin would also have a parting of the ways. Levin claims Salcer never understood that Russian players require a different type of service than North American players. "Salcer pretends to be a genius, but he doesn't know hockey. He approaches contract negotiations like a math teacher."

Quinn steadfastly refused to comment on Bure's purported trade request, but sportswriters had no such compunction. Convinced the Russian would soon be moved, they began unloading on him. Neil Campbell of Toronto's *Globe and Mail* concluded, "For all his early promise, Bure has been a failure. Perhaps it's time for the team to face that and move on." Neal Macrae of the *Province* pronounced, "The magic Bure once had is gone." Gary Mason of the *Vancouver Sun* claimed there had "been emerging questions about Bure's commitment to hockey both on and off the ice," and that trading the Russian "would likely be applauded by the fans if the team came away with the right deal."

Not only were most of Vancouver's media confident that trading Bure would be prudent, they also agreed Mogilny was the superior of the two Russians and that he would be a better fit on a line with Messier. This assessment wasn't shared by other NHL teams. Quinn had tried to trade Mogilny in the summer but had found there was virtually no interest in him.

In the midst of this outbreak of Bure bashing, the Russian received support from a most unlikely source. Don Cherry, Bure's longtime nemesis, used his weekly column in the *Province* to mock the attitude of "Bure's fairweather friends." As Cherry observed, "Pavel gave you some beauty years and he's paid the price. Sure he's making good dough, but he always gave 100 per cent, not like a lot of guys who make the big ticket. He's a little guy who never backed down."

Perhaps it was Cherry's affection for the underdog or simply his sheer contrariness, but this marked the second time in recent months that the high-collared one had come to Bure's defense. The first occasion was in March 1997 when Cherry attacked the people who insinuated Bure was faking his neck injury. Bure had obviously taken note. Two months later, during a playoff game in Montreal, Cherry was studying the monitor in the empty television studio when he felt somebody's presence. As Cherry recalled in his column, "I looked around and Pavel was standing there in a long black top coat staring at me. I thought, 'Oh, boy! He's pissed about something. Okay, let's get it on.' But he stuck out his hand and said, 'Thanks for sticking with me, Grapes, when I was having a rough time.'"

Few Canucks commented on Bure's desire to leave the team. One who did was Martin Gelinas. "Most of the guys wonder why," he told the *Vancouver Sun*. "Obviously it's not the money. The sad thing is that he's going to miss a pretty special year here. I feel sorry for Pavel not to realize that."

Bure's hazy future remained an issue throughout training camp, although it didn't appear to have an adverse effect on the Russian, who was the best player, and once again, the best-conditioned athlete at camp. Renney immediately slotted Bure on Messier's wing. The former Ranger admitted he was impressed: "There's not anybody more skilled in the game. Pavel is just lightning-quick and an unbelievable passer."

During training camp, Gillis met with Quinn to try to resolve the contractual sources of Bure's discontent. Lockout back pay was only one of Bure's grievances. He also wanted the Canucks to return his promotional rights, and there was another wrangle with the team over taxes.

In order to avoid paying Canadian taxes on Ron Salcer's fee, Bure had arranged to have the Canucks pay the agent in US$250,000 annual installments over the course of his five-year contract. But in 1996 Bure discovered that the Canucks had added $340,000 to his 1996 earnings to cover payment for Salcer's fees. Bure was thus compelled to pay income tax on an extra $340,000 he hadn't earned. The Russian eventually took the matter to court, arguing that he had no idea the Canucks were paying his agent's fees and that the payment wasn't connected with his contract. The incident only further served to exacerbate the tensions between Bure and management.

Ironically, by firing Salcer, Bure had turned the tables on his agent. Salcer, who had been unable to get Bure the lockout back pay he felt was rightly owed to him, would now be faced with a similar problem— trying to collect agent fees from the Canucks for a player he no longer represented.

Gillis had advised Bure that it was in his best interest to continue to play for the Canucks while the issues were sorted out. The better he played, the more pressure they could exert on the team. Having invested so heavily in Messier, the Canucks desperately needed to get off to a good start, something that would be difficult to do without Bure. By the same token, a fast start would confirm Bure had recovered from his injury problems and enhance his trade value.

The Canucks kicked off the season with a home game, but they had to fly across the Pacific for the opening faceoff. The contest was in Tokyo, part of a two-game series with Anaheim's Mighty Ducks. The NHL had arranged the games to promote the participation of NHL players in the Winter Olympics in Nagano, Japan, in February. Bure, who had kept everyone in suspense about his intentions, showed up at the airport minutes before boarding.

In Tokyo, prior to the first game, Linden told his teammates he was relinquishing his captaincy to Messier. He had prepared a speech but, struggling with his emotions, had difficulty getting through it. Linden explained that surrendering the C was entirely his own decision and that he was doing it to eliminate the potentially distracting issue before the season began.

Bure also revealed that after two injury-jinxed years he was switching back to his old number 10. "I'm not superstitious," he said. "But the last two seasons have been bad memories." Playing on the Olympic-size rink at Yoyogi Arena was a tonic for Bure, who fired 11 shots on net and scored the winning goal in a 3–2 Canucks victory. He also scored in the second game, which Anaheim won 3–2.

Off the ice, Bure and Odjick remained inseparable. If anything, their relationship was even closer. When Odjick's wife gave birth to a son in 1998, they would name him Bure Odjick. The two players' affinity for each other continued to baffle reporters. Some felt they shared an attraction for the nightlife. There is no doubt they were both drawn to the dark side. Whereas the rest of the team stuck cautiously to Tokyo's main tourist haunts, Bure and Odjick vanished into the mazelike streets of Shinjuku, the city's most notorious red-light district.

The Canucks looked jet-lagged when they returned to face Toronto in their first game at GM Place on October 9. The listless game ended 2–2, with rookie Mattias Ohlund scoring a goal and an assist. The mood was much different two nights later when the Canucks hosted the Rangers. Although it was only the fourth game of the season, the head-to-head meeting between Messier and his former team and Wayne Gretzky lent the game a sense of heightened drama. Before a sellout crowd, Messier scored his first goal of the season to tie the score 1–1 on a nifty setup by Bure, but in the end it was Gretzky who stole the show. Capitalizing on numerous Vancouver miscues, number 99 notched three goals for his 50th career hat trick and added two assists as the Rangers routed the Canucks 6–3. Gretzky's third goal, a mesmerizing effort that saw him leave a trail of defenders sprawled on the ice before finally circling the Vancouver net and tucking the puck into the open goal, drew a thunderous ovation.

One could sense Gretzky had an extra incentive in the game. When asked if he had any hard feelings toward Canucks management as a result of its failed bid to sign him in the summer of 1996, Gretzky remarked, "I'm just disappointed with the fellow who kept saying that [agent] Mike Barnett negotiated in bad faith. A guy by the name of John Chapple."

Chapple wasn't around to respond to the dig. The Orca Bay president and CEO had been transferred to Seattle after clashing with deputy chairman Stanley McCammon. His replacement, Stephen Bellringer, the former president and CEO of BC Gas Inc., had no background in sports. But even Bellringer could see that Orca Bay's nose had been bloodied in this battle of free-agent heavyweights.

Upon returning from Japan, the Canucks played five straight home games, the most favorable start in club history, and yet they won only once, a worrisome sign. Arturs Irbe replaced McLean on October 21 for his first start in goal when the Canucks visited Dallas. Irbe had a terrific game, turning aside 29 of 30 shots, and Bure broke loose for a hat trick, his first in 30 months, as the Canucks won 5–1. The win evened the Canucks' record at 3–3–2. It was the last time they would be at .500 all year.

A 4–1 loss to St. Louis was followed by a 3–2 loss to Pittsburgh, a 5–1 loss to Detroit and a 3–0 loss to Chicago. Aside from Bure, who had six goals, no Canuck had more than three. Gelinas, the previous season's top goal scorer and team MVP, was out with a knee injury, and Mogilny was still a holdout. Messier appeared to be suffering from some strength-sapping disease. Despite logging plenty of ice time and playing on the first power-play unit, he had only 12 shots on net and two goals and one assist after 12 games.

When New Jersey crushed Vancouver 8–1 on October 30, reporters wondered aloud how much longer Renney would retain his job. "Are they trying to get me fired?" the Canucks' coach asked, referring to his players. "I don't know. You'll have to ask them."

Messier, sounding more like an administrator than a hockey player, said, "I came to Vancouver with an open mind. I am trying to learn what the problems are and what deficiencies we have. I'll evaluate that and take the steps necessary to turn the team around."

The slide continued with a 7–6 loss to Pittsburgh and a 5–3 loss to the Carolina Hurricanes—seven straight defeats and counting. On November 4, with the Canucks in Washington to face the Capitals, McCaw finally pulled the trigger, dispatching his hit man, McCammon, to Landover, Maryland, to do the deed. But contrary to expectations, McCammon fired Quinn and not Renney.

Back in Vancouver, Bellringer, who had been on the job for less than two months, announced Quinn's termination at a news conference. Bellringer didn't distinguish himself. Displaying the warmth of an icicle, he made a robotic and perfunctory speech that made scant mention of Quinn's contributions to the franchise. By the end of the day, Quinn's office had been cleaned out. Eleven years of memories sat packed in cardboard boxes in the corridor. Two days later Griffiths was asked to vacate the premises, too.

The Canucks' players reacted to Quinn's firing with disbelief. "I never thought they were going to fire Pat Quinn," Bure said. "He's a great human being. He's honest and well respected and he was always there for me. You could always talk to him like a friend. It seems like everything I've done and I have in the NHL is with Pat Quinn. I guess there will be a lot of changes now."

According to Bellringer, the decision had been mulled over for weeks, but if the team's ownership had a coherent plan, it wasn't apparent. Quinn was replaced by a committee consisting of Bellringer, vice president of hockey operations Steve Tambellini, head of scouting Mike Penny, and Renney. Renney's position in this strange four-headed beast was extremely shaky. Orca Bay was already seeking his successor.

Quinn, whose silence had been assured with a handsome severance package, offered little comment about his exit, although he did tell Province columnist Dave Randorf that he thought he had been fired because he had tried to trade Bure. Others believed Quinn had been gassed because he was about to oust Renney and assume the coaching helm himself. If Quinn had done that and the team had begun to win, it would have made it much tougher for management to remove him.

Renney bravely soldiered on as the Canucks' losing streak stretched to a franchise-record 10 games. The misery finally ended with a 5–2 win against San Jose on November 12, but it was too late for Renney, who was sacked the next morning. His replacement was Mike Keenan, hockey's prince of darkness.

Having given up on Quinn's patient approach, Orca Bay had opted for shock therapy. Once described by Brett Hull as "the sort of guy who will stab you in the back right to your face," Keenan was, depending upon who you talked to, either a misunderstood genius or a twisted despot. No one denied he was driven and intense. Earlier in his career, Keenan had been so demanding that he would bench players for one bad shift; if they made a mistake in practice, they didn't dress for the next game. When Chicago goalie Ed Belfour refused to answer a question after he was replaced during a game, Keenan grabbed him by the jersey and screamed at him. Another time, when Keenan felt a timekeeper had cheated his team out of precious seconds, he ran across the ice to throttle him. Denied this opportunity, he returned to the dressing room and tore down the bathroom stalls. Recounting Keenan's rages in a 1996 interview with the *Toronto Star*, former Blackhawk Jeremy Roenick said, "Sometimes between periods you'd have to cover up for fear of being hurt. He'd just go nutso. He'd be swinging sticks and tossing skates."

Despite having taken three different teams to the Stanley Cup finals and compiling one of the more impressive winning percentages in NHL history, Keenan had left a trail of burning bridges in every city he had coached in. At each stop the blazes had gotten bigger. In St. Louis, where Keenan had wielded the most clout of his career, things had really spun out of control. Functioning as GM and coach, he had wheeled and dealt with a maniacal zeal—82 different players wore the blue note during his two-and-half-year stint in St. Louis. Not content to simply move players, he also played musical chairs with the team's medical and secretarial staffs.

Discarding draft picks for veteran plodders, trading fan favorites Brendan Shanahan and Curtis Joseph, alienating Wayne Gretzky, feuding with superstar Brett Hull and spending US$25 million on free agents failed to bring the Blues a championship, but it did drive the fans away. Season-ticket renewals dropped to 85 per cent from 97 per cent, and attendance declined by 3,000 a game. By the time he was fired, the mood was so poisonous that the camera operators at the Kiel Center had been instructed not to show Keenan's face on the scoreboard because of the chorus of boos it provoked.

Mark Messier, however, who had won the Stanley Cup with Keenan in New York, was one of the coach's biggest boosters. "There have been some negative things about Mike in the media, but I can honestly say that my experience with him is all positive," said Messier, who allowed his role as captain would be to function as a buffer between Keenan and the team.

The same week Keenan was hired, the Canucks inked Mogilny to a four-year contract for an average of US$4.4 million per year. The contracts of Mogilny, Bure and Messier now accounted for half of the team's top-heavy payroll.

There was an immediate improvement under Keenan's lash. A 3–3 tie with Anaheim was followed by a 4–1 win over Carolina and a 4–2 triumph over Phoenix. The Canucks blew a late lead and lost 5–4 in overtime to Chicago, but then proceeded to win three straight road games against the Rangers, Bruins and Leafs.

It had been widely predicted that Bure and Mogilny would be the individuals with whom Keenan would clash. Instead, Keenan initially targeted Gelinas and Linden, who had always been considered two of the team's hardest-working players. Gelinas, who had just returned from a knee injury and was struggling to regain his form, soon found himself subjected to petty humiliations. Two games after Keenan's arrival, Linden pulled a groin muscle during a high-tempo practice. Keenan's reaction was to note that if Linden couldn't keep up, then maybe he wasn't in game shape.

After Linden left the lineup, Keenan put Bure and Mogilny on a line with Messier and gave the big three copious amounts of ice time, killing penalties and doing duty on the power play, and they responded. Bure scored five goals on the three-game road trip and even took some shifts at center for the first time in his career. In Messier's emotional homecoming against the Rangers, Bure played head-to-head with Gretzky in the first period and scored a key goal, as the Canucks gained a measure of revenge for their earlier loss to the Rangers.

The Canucks' suddenly inspired play drew raves from the media and the players themselves. Although Bure was still being evasive about his future with the team, his sparkling play suggested he had found some contentment. "He looks like he's enjoying going out there and burning guys, which is his game," defenseman Dave Babych noted. "I remember when he first came here he would turn it on and you could just see it in his eyes. He just loved to do what he wanted to do, which was to score goals."

Part of Bure's satisfaction was due to Gillis's success in negotiations with management. To appease Bure, the team had quietly paid him US$1 million of his lockout back pay, defying the league's opposition to any sort of compensation. Gillis had also shown more willingness than Salcer to answer Bure's critics. When *Province* sports columnist Kent Gilchrist referred to Bure as needing "near constant maintenance and being either injured and or underachieving," Gillis fired back. He said, "There is no substantive proof he's ever fudged an injury or underachieved when he's not hurt. He had one bad year when he had a soft-tissue injury last season. But if he's an underachiever, how do you explain the fact that he comes back to camp the following year as the team's best-conditioned athlete and perhaps the best-conditioned in the league? He's been at peak level since day one of training camp despite all the turmoil that has gone on with this team. For this he's called an underachiever?"

In an interview with Bob Marjanovich of *Sports Vue*, Bure acknowledged he was enjoying playing for Keenan because of all the ice time he was getting: "I'm always in the game. I feel like always playing and more importantly, I feel he trusts me. When you go on the ice, you can feel the energy go up when you know the coach trusts you." But Bure admitted that as well as everything was going he sensed it wouldn't last. "I feel like something big is coming. Usually every month or two something happens. I don't know what it will be next because I think I've had it all happen. I just think something is going to happen."

The Canucks' surge ground to a halt on December 4 when they blew a two-goal lead against San Jose and lost 3–2. Two nights later they were outgunned 6–4 by Colorado. Bure played his best game of the year in the losing effort, racking up a hat trick and an assist.

On December 8, the Canucks traveled to St. Louis for a fateful game with the Blues. Having been run out of town a year earlier, Keenan was eager to make a good showing. But instead of rising to the occasion, the Canucks played poorly. Linden, who had just rejoined the team after missing eight games with his groin injury, was ineffective, and Keenan replaced his line with an all-pluggers unit of Odjick, Sillinger and Steve Staios. By the end of the second period, with Vancouver trailing 4–1 and the crowd openly jeering him, Keenan's blood began to boil.

Some Canucks players revealed to Gary Mason of the *Vancouver Sun* what happened next. During the second intermission, Linden was going around congratulating the fourth-liners on their effort. At that point, Keenan walked into the room and shouted, "Sit down, you fucking idiot! Shut the fuck up! Just shut the fuck up! Who are you, anyway? What have you ever done?" The profane tirade continued for several minutes as Keenan berated Linden for not having any pride, saying it was he who should be leading by example rather than relying on others to do the job for him.

Keenan's tantrum killed any hope of a comeback. The club came out flat in the third period, managed only two shots on net and went down to a 5–1 defeat. Looking disorganized and dispirited, the Canucks stumbled through the rest of December, compiling a 2–9–3 record and falling into last place in the division.

It was difficult to find positives in the club's performance, but Bure continued to light it up. He finished December with 11 goals and six assists for 17 points in 14 games, the fourth-highest point total of any NHL player for the month, and netted his third hat trick of the season against Los Angeles. In the 21 games since Keenan had been hired, Bure had scored 28 points.

Early in January, Keenan had Linden ride the pine again, and this time he criticized his effort publicly, estimating that Linden was "probably playing at a 50-per-cent level." Several Canucks players disputed Keenan's evaluation, but only Lumme and Odjick were willing to speak on the record. Odjick told the *Vancouver Sun*'s Iain MacIntyre: "There is no use slandering Trevor or embarrassing a guy who has devoted his heart and soul to his team. I know for a fact that Trevor goes all out every time he laces on the skates. In the eight years I've been here, there's no player I respect more than Trevor Linden."

In the ensuing media firestorm, Messier backed Keenan, saying, "Unless we're willing to change the behavior that's been here a long time, things aren't going to change in the standings. Players have to make the commitment and change necessary to win."

At this point, Keenan wanted to trade Linden but encountered resistance from the management council. Instead, acting on Keenan's recommendation, the club shipped out McLean and Gelinas, two core players who also happened to be two of Linden's closest friends on the team. They were sent to the Carolina Hurricanes in exchange for goalie Sean Burke, forward Geoff Sanderson and defenseman Enrico Ciccone. The day of the trade, Carolina also dealt Jeff Brown to Toronto. In Vancouver, BCTV sportscaster Barry Deley suggested on the air that Brown had been moved "to clear the way for McLean," a veiled reference to the bad blood between the two players as a result of Brown's rumored affair with McLean's ex-wife. McLean angrily termed the entire story "a crock of shit."

The move failed to quell the chaos. The Canucks won only one of their next 12 games and players continued to anonymously leak details about angry confrontations between Keenan and his players. On January 30, in a long article in the *Vancouver Sun*, Gary Mason revealed more details of discord, describing an incident in which Donald Brashear challenged his coach to duke it out on the bench, and a heated verbal exchange between Odjick and Keenan that was sparked when Keenan sarcastically described Odjick as "one of Pat Quinn's boys."

The revelations didn't sit well with Messier, who kept tabs on what the press was saying by having clippings delivered to him daily. Messier sounded off in an interview with Mason, calling the leaks "completely gutless." He disputed that Keenan's tongue-lashing of Linden in St. Louis was extreme. "Sure, it's tough, but you have to be able to accept criticism and accept the truth." He also denied, as some believed, that he was a GM disguised as a captain. "My allegiance has always been toward the players. I have nothing to do with player personnel on this team or who's going where."

Messier's comments rang hollow. Rather than defend his teammates, he had been silent when Keenan began his verbal assaults, and contrary to his claim of noninvolvement in personnel decisions, Messier actually had considerable input on player moves. As early as training camp, he had talked to Renney about players he felt were of no value to the team. As Quinn told Toronto's *Globe and Mail* in 1998, "Messier was consulted by ownership on personnel decisions. When that happens it's deadly."

In fact, the entire episode was filled with duplicity, as Keenan himself, rather than his players, had actually been the source of some of the leaks. It appeared Keenan was actually attempting to foster a sense of paranoia and mistrust in order to increase his control. The tactic worked. Alarmed by the dissension, Orca Bay gave Keenan a promotion in late January that gave him the power to make trades. He had become the de facto GM.

Keenan quickly began an overhaul, making four deals in a span of two days in early February, trading Sillinger to Philadelphia for a sixth-round draft choice, dealing recently acquired Geoff Sanderson and a third-round draft pick to Buffalo for Brad May, picking up Peter Zezel from New Jersey for a fifth-round draft pick and trading Linden to the New York Islanders for defenseman Bryan McCabe, winger Todd Bertuzzi and a third-round draft pick.

Strictly on a hockey basis, it was possible to argue that Linden's departure was necessary. His play had declined under Keenan, and as long as Linden was around, Messier would never have the full support of the team. But it wasn't possible to justify Keenan's attacks on Linden's character. Linden had always been a class act, and his charitable work with terminally ill children and underprivileged youth had made him an admired member of the community.

Keenan was gracious in his comments about Linden after the trade, but behind closed doors he was cruel to the very end. Linden had been one of the players picked for the Canadian Olympic team. On January 26, he hurt his knee in a game against Phoenix. Believing the injury had ruined his dream of playing in the Olympics, he retreated to the trainer's room between periods and wept. Teammate Grant Ledyard found him there and tried to console him. As he did, Keenan walked in and angrily ordered Ledyard out.

At the feverish pace he was going, it appeared Keenan might conceivably trade the entire team within a week, but he was forced to stop as the NHL shut down in early February for two weeks for the Olympics.

Relieved to escape the Canucks' pressure cooker, Bure flew home to join his Russian teammates, only to encounter more turbulence. As had been the case during the World Cup in 1996, the Russian team was beset with turmoil. There were hard feelings toward the Russian players who had refused invitations to play for their country. Igor Larionov and Viacheslav Fetisov had originally been left off the list of invitees, then after they were included, declined to accept because they felt snubbed. Viacheslav Kozlov, Sandis Ozolinsh, Sergei Zubov and goalie Nikolai Khabibulin all opted out. One player who did show up, Sergei Fedorov, was thought to have joined the team less out of a sense of patriotism than a desire to spark his stalled contract talks with Detroit.

But unlike the World Cup, this time the Russians were able to overcome their differences and pull together. Many of the players later gave credit to the leadership of Bure, who had been named captain. His appointment, like Eric Lindros with Canada, signaled a changing of the guard to a younger generation.

Valeri Bure later described the Olympic competition to me as the best experience he has had in hockey. With their parents, wives and families in attendance, he said the atmosphere "reminded me of the old times back home as a kid when your parents came out to watch your games. In the NHL," Valeri said, "everything is a business. Everyone worries about how much money they make and how much ice time they are getting. In the Olympics, it didn't matter who made the most money. We had no jealousy about who scores the goals. All that mattered was the team. It was the pure joy of hockey."

When the tournament began, the prevailing view in the North American media was that the gold medal would be won by either the Canadian or American teams. Although it was true that Canada and the United States had the greatest number of NHLers, the analysis overlooked a key factor. The games would be contested on the wider international-size rink, a playing surface Europeans had grown up on. Skating, passing and puck control would be of paramount importance rather than physical play or cornerwork. Winning an Olympic gold medal also meant more to the European players than the North Americans, whose ultimate goal was to capture the Stanley Cup.

In an interview with CBC-TV, Vladimir Bure was asked what it would mean to him if his two sons won gold medals. Appearing to be close to tears, Vladimir said it would be the greatest day in his life. It would be a sad one, too, now that he was estranged from his family.

The Russian team went unbeaten through the tournament to reach the semifinal against Finland, while the Czechs upset the United States to qualify for the other semifinal against Canada. Led by their acrobatic goaltender, Dominik Hasek, the Czechs defeated Canada in a game of high drama. When the score remained deadlocked 1–1 after 60 minutes of play and a 10-minute overtime, the teams went to a shootout. Five players from each team were sent in one-on-one against the opposition's goalie. Canada's netminder, Patrick Roy, stopped four of the Czech shooters, but Hasek turned aside all five Canadians.

The Russia-Finland contest was equally exciting, but completely different in style. The game began with the Russians bursting into the lead on three goals by Bure. The first came on a scramble, but the next two were scored on Bure's signature play, the breakaway, one set up by a sharp lead pass from Dmitri Mironov, the second after Bure stripped Finnish defenseman Janne Niinimaa of the puck and scooted in to beat goalie Jarmo Myllys. But Finland fought back, evening the score with three goals in 13 minutes in the second period, only to have the Russians reply on a power-play goal by Alexei Zhamnov.

In the third period, Finnish forward Saku Koivu knotted the score again on a pretty give-and-go with Teemu Selanne. The Russians went ahead once more when Andrei Kovalenko put the puck in off a Finnish defender's skate. With the Finns pressing to tie, Bure finally delivered the dagger stroke, poking the puck free at the Finnish blueline and racing in to deke Myllys for his fourth goal. Bure capped off his stunning performance by firing a shot into the empty Finnish net with seconds left for his fifth goal of the game. The five goals gave Bure nine for the tournament, the most of any player.

Afterward, Russian defenseman Darius Kasparaitis pointed out the fatal flaw in the Finnish game: "You can't let Pavel have five breakaways in a game, because he's going to kill you."

The Olympic final pitted two historic rivals against each other. Although the end of the Cold War had thawed relations between the Czechs and the Russians, emotions still ran deep. Driving to the arena for the gold-medal game, the Bures sat together on the team bus. As reported in the *Globe and Mail*, Pavel turned to Valeri and said, "This is the best time there is—the waiting. Your adrenaline is pumping. That's what it is all about."

Many felt the Russians' nimble offense would prevail against the Czechs. But as they had demonstrated against Canada, the Czechs had mastered the art of team defense. Employing cohesive five-man units to prevent the breakaways and fast counterattacks that had spelled doom for the Finns, the Czechs repeatedly thwarted the Russians' attempts to crack their defensive shell. Whenever a shot did get through, Hasek, their Gumby-limbed phenomenon, was there to make the save.

After two scoreless periods, the specter of yet another shootout loomed. Then, eight minutes into the third, a rising slap shot by Petr Svoboda slipped through a thicket of skates and sticks and hit the mesh behind Russian goalie Mikhail Shtalenkov. With Hasek putting up a brick wall, the Czechs held on for a 1–0 triumph.

In the aftermath, Hasek received the lion's share of the accolades, but author Roy MacGregor, who was in attendance at the game, was even more impressed with Bure's performance. "I have never seen anyone play as well as Bure did that game," he says. "He didn't score, but he just seemed to be operating on a level above everyone else. And there were a lot of great players in that game—Jagr, Yashin, Fedorov. Every time Bure touched the puck a jolt of electricity shot through the building. He was just so much faster than anyone else." MacGregor believes that because the rink was larger and the ice was better in Nagano than in most NHL arenas, Bure's skills were allowed to shine: "Put Bure on that ice here and he'd be better than you could imagine."

Keenan continued his personnel purge after the Olympics, now dealing players who had been acquired in earlier trades. Sean Burke was sent to

Philadelphia for goalie Garth Snow, and Enrico Ciccone to Tampa Bay for Jamie Huscroft. Ciccone was sent packing when he complained about being scratched from the lineup before a game in Montreal, his hometown. Ciccone accused Keenan of having a "God complex."

That night in Montreal Bure scored his 40th goal of the season in a 2–2 tie. Messier, with 21, was the only other Canuck within shouting distance of him. The goal triggered a unique bonus clause. Bure's contract stipulated that if he scored 40 goals or 80 points, he would have to be paid the average of the top five NHL wage earners in the final year of his contract. If he scored 50 goals or 100 points, he would have to be paid the average of the top three. With salaries for stars such as Eric Lindros, Paul Kariya and Joe Sakic now pushing into the US$8-million range, Bure was looking at a substantial raise.

In a season so filled with rancor, Bure had been one of the few players to avoid a public dustup with Keenan, but in a game against Ottawa on March 20, the two finally butted heads. The *Province*'s Jim Jamieson reported that early in the second period, with the Canucks trailing 1–0 and Bure having an uninspired game, Keenan began needling the Russian, asking him if he was going to play tonight and calling him a "selfish little suck."

Bure shot back, "Fuck you! I've already played 69 games this season."

A few minutes later Bure scored the tying goal. When he came back to the bench, Keenan said, "Way to go, Pavel."

Bure, who was still incensed, told Keenan to "Fuck off!"

Three days later the Canucks sent Gino Odjick to the New York Islanders in return for defenseman Jason Strudwick. "He's my best friend and I'm really disappointed," Bure said. "Some people say he's not a great hockey player, but he's one of the toughest guys in the NHL and he got 15 goals when he played with me. He's a part of Canucks history."

History was fast becoming all the Canucks had left. When Babych was dispatched to Philadelphia for a third-round draft pick on March 24, only four players—Bure, Murzyn, Hedican and Lumme—remained from the team that went to the 1994 Stanley Cup finals. Odjick's departure only served to further isolate Bure, who had become increasingly reclusive, abandoning his home and moving back into his downtown apartment. On road trips, he spent much of his time alone, reading or working on his computer and rooming by himself.

Not long after his trade to the Islanders, Odjick fired a bitter broadside at Messier in an interview with the *Province*'s Tony Gallagher, saying, "He didn't break a sweat for the first 10 games and just waited for Tom Renney and Pat Quinn to be fired. They signed him to help us, but all he wanted was most of us out of there so he could bring in his own people. He talks to ownership all the time, and he's responsible for Keenan being here and he's part of most of the trades. Messier just wants to destroy everything so he gets the power. Everyone is brought in to play for Mark."

Messier refuted Odjick's charges, and in doing so took what appeared to be a backhanded swipe at Linden. "I think this is a lot more than Gino Odjick coming forward. I think there's a lot of people who don't have the courage or guts to say it to my face and they used Gino as a vehicle to do it. It shows you the kind of people who were here and why we needed changes."

Any fans who thought Bure's inspired play was a sign he had found inner peace received a rude awakening late in March when the media reported that the Russian had renewed his trade request. The news sparked a fresh round of debate among Bure's detractors and supporters. In the latter camp was *Province* columnist Bob Stall, who launched a campaign to convince Orca Bay to keep Bure with the Canucks. In a series of open letters to team owner John McCaw, Stall extolled Bure's talents and predicted dire box-office consequences if Orca Bay were to trade its charismatic star. As this sideshow played out, Bure promised to reveal the reason for his dissatisfaction at the end of the season.

Although the Canucks had played .500 hockey since the Olympic break, it was obvious that a playoff berth was out of reach. Official elimination came on April 6 when the Edmonton Oilers defeated Vancouver 3–2. The only remaining question was whether Bure would score 50 goals. On April 17, in the second-last game of the season against Calgary, he answered affirmatively, taking the puck in his own end, rushing through the neutral zone and blasting a drive past Flames goalie Dwayne Roloson. In the season finale against Toronto, he netted Vancouver's lone goal in a 2–1 defeat. After scoring, Bure circled around with his arms aloft. The marker gave him 254 goals in a Canucks uniform, eight shy of the club's all-time record, held by Stan Smyl. Bure had scored 254 in 428 games; Smyl netted 262 in 896 games. The Canucks ended the year with a 25–43–14 record. Their 64 points ranked last in the Western Conference.

Bure notched 51 goals, one behind league leaders Teemu Selanne and Peter Bondra, and placed fourth in scoring, with 90 points. They were impressive numbers in a season in which defensive hockey held sway, doubly so considering the off-ice distractions and his weak supporting cast. He also led the NHL in shots on net with 329, 157 more than the nearest Canuck. As Messier noted, "I think that shows you part of Pavel's character. I think it's been misunderstood how good a team player he is in that he's able to put that aside and come to the rink and play hard and feels he has an obligation to his teammates."

Vancouver fans voted Bure team MVP and most exciting player, and he won the Molson Cup Award for most game star selections during the season. But his accomplishments had been overshadowed by the organizational tumult. The Canucks had been awful, and Bure found himself accused again of not being a team player, as someone purely interested in his personal stats. The fabled Bure celebratory jump, so uplifting when the team was winning, now looked out of place. In a season of fear and loathing, his detractors found a new reason to criticize him: he enjoyed scoring goals too much.

CHAPTER SEVENTEEN

# Florida Sunrise

*What has puzzled us before seems less mysterious and the crooked
paths seem straighter as we reach the end.*

JOHANN PAUL FRIEDRICH RICHTER, GERMAN NOVELIST

BURE RETURNED TO RUSSIA without revealing his reasons for wanting
out of Vancouver, his future with the Canucks still uncertain. Although his hockey season was over, he continued to make news. In May
1998, *Details* magazine published an article by Robert Friedman, entitled "Power Play," about the Russian mafiya's infiltration of the NHL.
Bure's photo appeared prominently in the title spread above a shot of a
Russian mobster in handcuffs and beside a bull's-eye dripping blood.

Friedman's article had been inspired by a 15-month investigation
by a U.S. congressional committee into the Russian mafiya's growing
influence in the United States. One area examined by the committee
was the link between the Russian mob and Russian NHLers. According
to Friedman, the NHL refused to cooperate with the inquest. As the
committee's chief investigator, Michael Bopp, told Friedman, "We had
subpoena power and still doors were slammed in our faces at every turn.
The league just didn't want us poking around."

Friedman also probed the connection between Viacheslav Fetisov, Valeri Kamensky and a legendary Russian crime lord named Viacheslav Ivankov who, in 1995, was sentenced to a nine-year prison term for attempting to extort US$3.5 million from two Russian Wall Street bankers.

Ivankov had risen to the rank of a *vory v zakonye*, a "thief within the code," as the leader of a powerful gang in Vladivostok. His unimposing appearance—small, with a close-cropped beard and tinted glasses—belied his fearsome reputation. One of his specialties was said to be sealing plastic bags in the rectums of his victims with an oxyacetylene torch. After serving 10 years in a Russian prison for extortion and torture, Ivankov was released, reportedly because of some lavish bribes. In 1992 he was sent to North America with a mission to organize the Russian-Jewish mob in the United States.

Upon his arrival, Ivankov established an import-export firm called Slavic Inc. in Brooklyn that the FBI claimed was a front for a money-laundering operation. The man who signed the business-incorporation papers and who was listed as president of Slavic Inc. was Fetisov, then a member of the New Jersey Devils.

Friedman claimed that in 1994 Kamensky, who was with the Quebec Nordiques at the time, had enlisted the aid of Nordiques president Marcel Aubut to help him obtain a visitor's visa to Canada for Viacheslav Sliva, Ivankov's second-in-command. Sliva, whom police recorded discussing drug deals, death threats, extortion and money laundering with Ivankov and others, was later deported by the RCMP in 1997.

Friedman also described Kamensky as being close to Vatchagan Petrossov, another of Ivankov's associates, and a man the FBI has identified as a major player in the Russian mob in Denver, the city where Kamensky wound up after the Nordiques moved to Denver and were renamed the Colorado Avalanche.

As well, Friedman shed more light on Anzor Kikalishvili, Bure's business partner. Kikalishvili had come to the attention of U.S. law-enforcement officials in 1994 when he moved to Miami. Florida had become a burgeoning center of Russian mob activity in the mid-1990s as Russian organized crime groups began doing business with Colombian drug traffickers. In exchange for cocaine, the Russians were selling the Colombians military hardware such as combat helicopters and surface-to-air missiles. Undercover drug agents even stumbled upon a Russian scheme to sell a diesel-powered submarine to the Colombians. The plan was to station the craft in Panama under the guise of oceanographic research and use it to rendezvous with cocaine-laden ships in the Pacific Ocean.

Citing an FBI affidavit, Friedman alleged that during his stay in Miami, Kikalishvili was involved in the drug trade with the Colombians, in importing Eastern European prostitutes to the United States and in extortion. Friedman wrote:

> He bragged on one FBI wiretap that he controlled an army of over 600 men and started buying millions of dollars in real estate to establish a beachhead. In one instance, he warned the Russian owners of a Miami deli that if they didn't pay his demands of some half a million dollars, they could be found anywhere in the world and skinned like an animal. The couple fled the country.

In a telephone interview, Kikalishvili told Friedman the conversation with the deli owners had been taken out of context and that he had never been involved in any criminal activity and that he should be properly described as a "philanthropist."

After the *Details* article was published, Bure held a news conference in Moscow during which he denied any connection with the mafiya. "It's very easy for people to print all sorts of totally unfounded rumors about myself, but it's very difficult for me, or anyone else for that matter, to clear his name after such false information," he said. Kikalishvili, who appeared with Bure at the briefing, claimed such stories were part of a conspiracy by the American media to foster distrust between the United States and Russia.

But Friedman's story had hit a nerve. Shortly after it appeared, he received a Valentine's Day card. "It was easy finding a Valentine for someone like you," the card's cover stated. Inside was a handwritten, obscenity-laced death threat signed by Ivankov. The card had been mailed from a federal prison in upstate New York.

A month later Friedman got a call from an FBI agent named Michael McCall, who told him that another Russian organized crime figure, whose identity he refused to reveal, had taken a contract out on his life.

McCall said they were working on the case and asked the writer to keep quiet and "lay low" while the investigation was under way. But after eight months of feeling "like a billy goat on a stake" and frustrated by a lack of action on the FBI's part, Friedman went public with his predicament. He told his tale to the New York Times and asked for help from the Committee to Protect Journalists, which lobbies publicly and privately on behalf of journalists who are targeted because of their work.

At last report Friedman was still among the living.

In June 1998, Bure's name appeared on the front pages of Vancouver's newspapers in an entirely different context when police wiretap tapes revealed that his girlfriend, Dahn Bryan, was the niece of Gillian Guess. At the time, Guess was on trial for her role in obstructing justice in a murder case, a charge she would be found guilty of. Guess had been a juror in a trial of six men accused of the gangland murder of Jim and Ron Dosanjh. During the trial, she had become intimately involved with Peter Gill, one of the accused. Guess kept the affair secret and continued to serve on the jury, which eventually found Gill and the other five defendants innocent.

The police, who had learned of Guess's affair with Gill, put a wiretap on her phone in an attempt to gain incriminating evidence. When Guess went on trial in 1998, some of these wiretap tapes were played in court as evidence. In one conversation on March 2, 1996, Guess described an incident to her sister, Vanessa, in which Gill had taken her to a bar and then had gotten drunk and punched out a man who had been ogling Guess.

Vanessa Bryan responded, "Well, it sounds like him and Pavel should get together. He's obsessively jealous and he can't let go of the fact that Dahn dated David Duchovny, and it, I mean, it's before, I mean, they kind of overlapped, but I mean at the time, like Pavel wasn't anything serious to her."

In January 1999, Dahn Bryan made her own court appearance in Vancouver, testifying on behalf of a friend named Tannisah Kruse in an insurance dispute. Kruse was suing the Insurance Corporation of British Columbia after it refused to reimburse her for the loss of her missing 1992 Lexus. Kruse claimed the car had been stolen, but ICBC believed she and her boyfriend were running an insurance scam—an assertion the corporation failed to prove. One of the factors that made ICBC suspicious was that Kruse paid $22,000 of the vehicle's $31,900 price in cash, even though she was unemployed.

Bryan testified she had loaned Kruse $10,000 to buy the car. When asked how she happened to have that sort of cash on hand, Bryan explained she was Pavel Bure's girlfriend and that he kept her well provided for.

Late in June 1998 the Canucks finally clarified their management situation by hiring former NHL vice president Brian Burke as general manager. Burke said one of his priorities would be restoring a sense of sanity to the Canucks' hockey operation, which he caustically dubbed "the asylum." But Burke was handicapped in this task by not being able to hire his own coach. Orca Bay insisted on retaining Keenan.

Although Burke professed satisfaction with the arrangement, saying, "I'm thrilled to have Mike Keenan as my coach. It's not something that I am saddled with. It's something I have been blessed with," virtually everyone else expected trouble. Not only did their personalities appear to be totally incompatible, Keenan had far more hockey experience than Burke, a factor that was sure to stir up the latter's insecurity.

Burke's other major problem was settling Bure's status. The Canucks' GM admitted his intention was to try to keep the high-scoring winger in the fold. As he told reporters, "Our reluctance to trade this player should be obvious to everybody. We go to sleep at night dreaming of getting players like Pavel Bure."

The two men met on July 5, at which time Bure informed Burke that he wanted a trade and wouldn't play for the Canucks in 1998–99, even though he was still under contract for one more year. Burke asked Bure to give him some time to swing a deal. "I said give me a deadline. Give me until November. But he was adamant. I asked if there was anything I could do or say that would convince him to stay in Vancouver. He said, 'No.' I was very disappointed."

Bure went public with his trade request in August, telling reporters, "I'm not going to play for the Canucks for personal reasons. The reasons are my own and I don't really want to discuss them. I love the fans here and I love the city. I want to thank them for the seven years they supported me. But I really feel it's time to move."

Burke insisted he wouldn't be stampeded into making a poor trade. "I'm not operating with any artificial timetable and I'm not making any promises. If a trade is not made, he'd better have a good TV set." In September, when Bure made good on his vow not to report to training camp, Burke suspended him without pay.

None of this was welcome news for Keenan, who had the task of fashioning a contender out of a team that had finished last in the conference the previous year, without the services of a player who had figured in 40 per cent of the club's goals. An added complication was the fact that Canucks management, having lost $36 million the previous year, was now intent on cutting the team's payroll. Jyrki Lumme had been lost to free agency, and the Canucks' only off-season acquisition was journeyman defenseman Murray Baron.

In contrast to the hype of the past three years, Orca Bay made no grand promises for 1998–99. Ticket packs were being peddled with the slogan "New Grit," a phrase that could just as easily describe the fortitude required by fans to keep pushing through the turnstiles. The team's goal in 1998–99 wasn't a division title, nor even a winning season, but simply making the playoffs, the lowliest of objectives in the talent-diluted NHL.

Against all odds, Vancouver got off to a decent start, thanks largely to Garth Snow's sensational goaltending. Despite being outshot in 15 of their first 16 games, often by wide margins, the Canucks had an 8–7–1 record by mid-November. But the Bure situation continued to hover over the team like a dark cloud. Burke, who had vowed not to talk about Bure until he was traded, now seemed to do nothing but talk about him. The bidding war was heating up, he claimed. With each passing week, the number of teams supposedly involved in the pursuit of Bure gradually grew, much like Pinocchio's nose, from one, to two, to five, to six.

Heading the list were the New York Rangers, who were offering young goalie Dan Cloutier, winger Patrik Sundstrom and a draft pick. The New York Islanders were dangling their own contract holdout, Slovak sniper Zigmund Palffy, as bait. The Los Angeles Kings, flush with cash but struggling in the standings, were also in the hunt. Bure would be a useful gate attraction for the Kings, who were about to move into a swank new US$300-million arena the following year. The San Jose Sharks were supposedly trying to tempt Burke with center Patrick Marleau and a couple of other young prospects. The Philadelphia Flyers were also rumored to have entered the sweepstakes, although Flyers GM Bobby Clarke denied it, claiming Bure's sticker price was too extreme for the Flyers' budget.

By late November, with no solution in sight, Keenan was growing impatient. The Canucks had lost four of their last five games and were embarked on a hellish road trip. With Mogilny and Todd Bertuzzi, two of his best forwards, out with injuries, Keenan could sense his team's promising start swirling down the drain. On November 25, during a nationally televised game with Toronto, Keenan made what appeared to be a move to embarrass Burke into action. With 17 minutes left in the game and the Canucks down 3–1, he pulled Snow during a Canucks power play for an extra attacker. Neither team scored, but eight minutes later, when Toronto took another penalty, Keenan pulled Snow again. This time the Leafs scored into the empty net and coasted to a 5–1 win. Asked later to explain his motivation for the unorthodox move, Keenan said he felt he had to gamble because the team lacked the offensive talent to make up a two-goal deficit.

Despite the increasingly dire circumstances, Burke insisted he wouldn't make a trade until he was confident it was the right one and that he "didn't care if the club lost five games in a row." There was speculation that Burke was deliberately dragging his feet in order to punish Bure and to sabotage Keenan. Burke attempted to put this kamikaze theory to rest by stating he wouldn't hold Keenan accountable for the team's record until after the Bure trade was made.

Meanwhile, Bure had returned to Moscow and was practicing with his old Central Army club, or what was left of it. The team had split into two feuding factions. One faction was a privatized team coached by Viktor Tikhonov, the second was coached by Boris Mikhailov and controlled by the Russian defense ministry. Mikhailov's team was on the verge of collapse. It had been evicted from its home arena for failure to pay its bills and its players had gone without salaries for four months.

The contrast between the ragtag Russian players and Bure, who arrived for training each day with his chauffeur, was startling, and more than a little puzzling to Russians, who could no more fathom how he could walk away from a US$8-million salary than could hockey fans in North America.

Some Russians harbored the illusion that Bure might choose to remain in Russia and help to revitalize the country's ailing game. That belief gained support in December when Alexander Lukashenko, president of the neighboring republic of Belarus, offered Bure US$4 million tax-free to play for one of his republic's top teams. Burke dismissed the story as a ploy by Bure to increase the pressure for a trade. Although the offer was treated as comic relief in North America, it provoked a very different response overseas. Television footage of Bure exchanging warm embraces with Lukashenko, who was regarded as a ruthless dictator, offended many people.

Bure declined Lukashenko's invitation. His intent was to return to the NHL. Besides, playing for the dictator had its risks. In May, Lukashenko's son had shot the coach of the Belarus national team in a dispute over who would be on the team in its next international match.

Lukashenko wasn't the only controversial Russian politician Bure had been seen with in Moscow. He had also enjoyed a steam bath with ultra-nationalist leader Vladimir Zhirinovsky, a self-professed admirer of Adolf Hitler. As well, Bure had been seen in nightclubs with Yosef Kobzon and other reputed mob figures. Bure's questionable judgment in political leaders and his frequent appearances at casinos, nightclubs, parties and fashion shows provoked hostile commentary in the Russian media and a change in the popular perception of him. As the popular Russian tabloid *Argumenty i Fakty* noted, "The young millionaire seemed to spend little time at charity functions or fund-raising events for hospitals or orphanages. Instead, there are reports that Bure is noticed at a restaurant, or Bure was brilliant at a nightclub party, or he was spotted at a haute couture fashion show. Here he tasted this, there he played tennis, here he drank, there he had a bath."

The tabloid also criticized Bure for his high-profile appearances in "appalling" advertisements for the Twenty First Century Association,

Kikalishvili's mysterious show business and sports enterprise. "It's just too sad to watch him join our illiterate merchants in show business," the paper said. "Perhaps it's contagious; everyone in Russia gets this virus. So maybe it would be best for him to go back to Canada."

Back in Canada, the window on a Bure deal and the Canucks' season both appeared to be closing. On January 14, Burke announced that unless he had a deal by the 18th, he was going to take Bure off the market until the March 23 trade deadline. Told this by reporters, Keenan appeared stunned. In the 25 games since the disastrous road trip in late November, the Canucks had compiled a 5–16–4 record, an abysmal winning percentage of .230. "This franchise can't afford to miss the playoffs for a third straight year," said Keenan, implying that without help the cause would soon be lost.

But Burke was closer to a deal than anyone realized. At the World Junior Championships in late December, he and Florida Panthers general manager Bryan Murray had met in Winnipeg and opened up trade talks. On January 17, they reached an agreement. Burke announced the deal at a hastily called news conference at GM Place. Bure, Bret Hedican, junior defenseman Brad Ference and a third-round draft pick were headed to Florida in exchange for defenseman Ed Jovanovski, center Dave Gagner, minor-league goalie prospect Kevin Weekes, junior winger Mike Brown and Florida's first-round draft pick in either 1999 or 2000. Ironically Bure had been traded to the one NHL team, aside from Vancouver, he had never scored a goal against. Now he never would.

It wasn't exactly the franchise-saving deal many had anticipated, and Burke seemed to sense as much, admitting to reporters, "I didn't come here anticipating they'd plan a parade route for me." Although Burke tried to put a positive spin on the transaction, claiming, "We're ecstatic. We believe this is the best deal for our team for both right now and for the future," his solemn expression didn't match his words. If anything, the announcement had the smell of surrender.

Asked for a comment about Bure's departure from Vancouver, Pat Quinn, who was now coaching the Toronto Maple Leafs, told Ed Willes of the *Province* that he saw no point in dwelling on what went wrong. Instead, Quinn said he preferred to remember the good times. "He was such a bright light. I know a lot of people think he was more concerned with his points than the team's points, but knowing the kid, I don't buy that. He wanted to play well every night. He wasn't a floater."

Evaluation of the trade would take time. In dealing Bure, the Canucks had made an investment in youth, but one consequence was immediate. A week after the deal was completed, Burke fired Keenan and replaced him with Marc Crawford. In typical Canucks fashion, the firing was severely botched. The news was leaked to Gary Mason of the *Vancouver Sun,* and Keenan read about his dismissal in the newspaper while Burke was out of town negotiating with Crawford. Neither the coaching change nor the trade improved Vancouver's performance. The club continued to sink like a stone and ended the season in last place again.

Bure's trade to Florida caught most hockey observers by surprise and created fresh fodder for those with a conspiratorial bent. Florida was, after all, Kikalishvili's territory. Mafiya maneuverings aside, the three biggest reasons why Bure ended up in the land of alligators and flamingos were owner Wayne Huizenga's deep pockets, president Bill Torrey's sense that the team needed an image makeover and general manager Murray's appreciation of Russian artistry.

Torrey, who had built the New York Islanders dynasty of the early 1980s, recognized that the franchise had reached a crossroads. The Panthers had charmed southern Florida and made the Stanley Cup finals in only their third year of existence with a gritty, underdog team, but they had slipped since then, and the novelty had worn off. Having vacated downtown Miami and moved into a new arena in suburban Sunrise, the club desperately needed a fresh injection of excitement. Bure fitted the bill.

Murray was comfortable with the idea of a Russian as his star player. He had been the coach and general manager of the Detroit Red Wings during the early 1990s when Detroit began recruiting ex-Soviets such as Fedorov and Kozlov. He knew what they could do. He also knew Bure came with some baggage. But before making the deal, Murray had asked around and the answers had eased his concerns. "Things happen in young athletes' lives," Murray said. "You put them aside. They never happen again. If you deal straightforward with the athlete, if he's treated right, there won't be a problem. I'm not worried about the past in any way."

When Bure's mother heard the news, she broke down and cried for half an hour. "She cried and cried because she said she was so happy for me," Bure said. "She said she knew it was the hardest time of my life." Wearing a huge grin, the Russian Rocket bid farewell to Moscow at a press conference at an opulent Chinese restaurant in a neon-lit hotel.

On January 19, Bure flew to New York to join the Panthers. Because the team's regular physician, David Attarian, wasn't traveling with the club, Bure was given a physical by New Jersey Devils doctor Barry Fisher, who pronounced him fit, telling Torrey, "I've seen some athletes in my day, but this one is unreal."

The next day Bure finally did what he had long promised to do—he revealed the reasons behind his desire to leave Vancouver. In an interview teed up by his agent, Mike Gillis, he unburdened himself to the *Toronto Sun*'s Al Strachan and the *Province*'s Tony Gallagher. As Bure explained it, the seeds of his discontent were sown even before he joined the Canucks. He had taken a risk coming to North America and said he was nervous and uncertain when he arrived in Los Angeles in the fall of 1991. But instead of welcoming him, he felt the Canucks had been indifferent. "I was down there for two weeks before anyone showed up. It was really hard. I thought they'd be waiting for me when I got there, but there was nobody."

The sense of alienation increased after Bure won the Calder Trophy as rookie of the year in 1992. At the time, he said, the team agreed to renegotiate his contract. It took 17 months, but finally in November 1993, the two sides agreed on a new five-year $14.7-million deal. But Bure says that when he sat down to sign, he discovered that, contrary to his expectations, the Canucks had put everything in Canadian rather than U.S. funds. With the exchange rate, it meant a difference of about $3.5 million. He refused to sign and asked the team to trade him.

A month later, when he was mired in a slump, Bure says that someone in management, likely George McPhee, taunted him, saying, "You were lucky to get 60 goals" and that he would never do it again. Bure went on to count 60 goals that season. Once he regained his form, Bure says that management came back to him and apologized and said they wanted to patch up their differences.

The new relationship lasted only until the playoffs when the "lie" surfaced about Bure's threat to withdraw his services unless his contract demands were met. Of all his grievances, this one upset the Russian the most. "Somebody from [Canucks] management planted that story," said Bure, who noted that the contract had actually been agreed upon before the playoffs even started. "But the story was out all over and by the time it was denied by Pat Quinn and everybody else, it was too late. It looked like a cover-up."

Bure said that his five-year US$25-million deal was signed just before Game 3 of the Rangers-Canucks final. But Quinn, in an expression of his disapproval of the deal, wasn't present at the signing. Bure refused to put his name on paper until Quinn appeared. "I just felt like he didn't want to give me the contract," Bure admitted. Annoyed by Quinn's attitude, Bure said he was ready to pull out of the deal, but that Salcer convinced him to sign.

The rift widened after the season when the Canucks were three months late paying Bure's signing bonus, and it widened further after the lockout when the club refused to pay him his lost back pay. As the issue dragged on without resolution, Bure became increasingly frustrated. The matter wasn't settled until the fall of 1997 when Gillis became Bure's agent and negotiated a compromise payment of US$1 million.

After two injury-plagued years, Bure asked Quinn for a trade prior to the 1997–98 season, so he could get a fresh start somewhere else. Quinn agreed but asked him to start playing well to increase his market value, which Bure did. But before a deal could be made, Quinn was fired. Bure says he reconsidered his trade request after Keenan was hired, the team started playing better and his ice time increased, but soon after, the situation crumbled into chaos.

Bure denied that a dislike of either Keenan or Messier were factors in his decision. Keenan may have been a hard-nosed coach but, as Bure noted, "That didn't bother me. I played for Tikhonov, so that was nothing." In fact, Bure said Keenan was supportive. "I had 39 goals and a big bonus for 50. He called me into his office and said, 'Listen, don't worry about 50 goals. I'll get you 50 goals. I'll help you to do it.'"

For anyone who had closely followed Bure's career, these "revelations" came as no great surprise. The Russian's conflicts with Canucks management were part of the public record, although his indication that he wanted out as early as 1993 wasn't. If Bure's account of events was accurate, the Canucks had certainly made some boneheaded moves, but Strachan and Gallagher's role in detailing the Russian's complaints was puzzling. They were the two columnists most responsible for publicizing the Bure blackmail rumor in 1994. Strachan's flip-flop, in particular, was stunning. He had been a strident critic of Bure, and in 1995 had dismissed the majority of Vancouver sports reporters as Bure's "apologists."

Attempts to get a response to Bure's charges from the former Canucks regime proved futile. When approached by Florida writers, Quinn snapped, "I didn't hear what he said and I don't give a fuck." McPhee refused comment. Griffiths issued one brief statement in which he denied any role in leaking the blackmail rumor and objected to the insinuation that Bure's treatment had been anything other than first-class.

In Vancouver, many felt Bure's explanation was incomplete, that there had to be some dark secret he wasn't revealing. It appeared that most of his beefs centered around money, and how could you sympathize with a guy who had made more than $20 million in seven years? But the view that Bure's dissatisfaction ultimately came down to cash missed the point. It was clear from his complaints that money was only an expression of the real problem—Bure had never gotten the respect he felt he deserved from Vancouver's management. The team had repeatedly battled with him on contract matters, and when his heart and character had been questioned, as it had been with his neck injury in the spring of 1997 and after the 1994 boycott rumor, he didn't feel management had come to his defense quickly or vigorously enough.

This feeling of neglect was something Panthers GM Bryan Murray alluded to in an interview with Ed Willes of the *Province:* "I think it's important to Pavel that we allow him to be the most important part of the team. My understanding is that didn't always happen in Vancouver, but that's exactly what we need here. We want the guy to be front and center on the ice and he wants that."

Although Bure emphasized he had nothing against Vancouver fans, many of them weren't so forgiving. The Vancouver papers were filled with letters condemning the Russian for his ungrateful and whining attitude. Confusion had given way to bitterness. Good riddance was the prevailing sentiment. As the *Vancouver Sun*'s Iain MacIntyre noted, the reaction was similar to that of a jilted lover at the end of an affair. "Vancouver had Pavel Bure and he was the best the city ever saw. Now, Bure is gone, and who are we but the woman scorned?"

In Florida, the mood was buoyant. A blue-collar team of faceless pluggers now had a marquee talent. Murray said that after the deal was completed, Edmonton Oilers GM Glen Sather told him he had pulled off "the best trade in 10 years. You don't know this guy," Sather said. "He does things that don't happen with the puck very often. If you weren't on the West Coast, you didn't see all the things he can do. This is one special player."

But special players often require special considerations, and Bure's arrival had presented the Panthers with a dilemma. Florida had two games before the All-Star Game break, both in New York, one against the Islanders and the other against the Rangers. The club could wait and ease Bure into action after a week of practice or let him loose and see what he could accomplish on adrenaline. There was a risk involved with immediately inserting him into the lineup—Bure hadn't played an NHL game in nine months. On the other hand, he wanted to play and the Panthers needed the points. In the end, they opted for adrenaline.

Bure played his first game with Florida on an all-Russian unit with center Viktor Kozlov and rookie winger Oleg Kvasha. Although the club limited his ice time to 12 minutes, 15 fewer than Bure would normally get in a game, he scored two goals to pace the club to a 5–1 win over the Islanders. The next night against the Rangers he played nearly 20 minutes and scored again, beating Mike Richter on a breakaway as Florida won 2–1. Said Panthers captain Scott Mellanby: "Bure's like a shark out there. Waiting, waiting—boom, he takes off."

In his third game, Bure was even better, scoring three times as Florida tied Philadelphia 3–3. His first goal came when he slapped in a rebound, his second was a tip-in from the side of the crease and his third was a stunning bit of improvisation. After chasing down a lead pass deep in the Flyers' zone, Bure found himself near the boards to the far right of goalie John Vanbiesbrouck, fast approaching the redline. Scoring from that angle seemed an impossibility. Evidently Vanbiesbrouck thought so, too, as he began cheating slightly to his left, anticipating a pass from Bure to a teammate out in front. But instead of passing, Bure shot. The puck deflected off the back of Vanbiesbrouck's shoulder and into the net, a 35-foot flat angle bank shot into a six-inch gap between the Flyers' goalie and the post.

Bure made his home-ice debut for the Panthers against Montreal on January 27. The sellout crowd at the National Car Rental Center had been whipped into a frenzy by a five-minute video presentation of memorable moments from Bure's career. Leading up to his introduction, the narrator counted down from 10 and then boomed, "The Russian Rocket has landed." The crowd went crazy, as it did during the U.S. national anthem when the singer belted out the line "and the rocket's red glare."

There was less fire in Bure's game than there had been in the first three, but in the final period he got the rink rocking with a couple of sizzling shifts and set up Kvasha for the game winner as Florida skated to a 2–1 victory. In four games with Bure in the lineup, the Panthers had yet to lose and had moved up three places in the conference standings from 11th to eighth.

Bure met the media after the game dressed in a brilliant white suit. Asked about his Florida experience so far, he said, "It was a little weird for the first couple of days, but right now I feel totally comfortable. I don't think this could get any better. It's a great feeling—I was missing this feeling."

Dallas ended Florida's winning streak, but the Panthers quickly rebounded to defeat Toronto. In eight games, Bure had scored eight goals and three assists, figuring in 11 of the 19 goals Florida had scored in that stretch. He already had half as many goals as the Panthers' top scorer, Ray Whitney, had compiled in 46 games, and the club had climbed to within four points of the Carolina Hurricanes, who led the Southeast Division.

But trouble was on the horizon. In the Panthers' next contest with Pittsburgh on February 5, Bure was forced to leave the game in the first period with a knee strain. The club announced he would be out of action for at least a week. Although this was the same knee that required reconstructive surgery in 1995, the injury was said to be unrelated to that problem.

On February 8, the Panthers signed Bure to a long-term contract. The six-year deal was reportedly worth a staggering US$47 million. Bure was to be paid $3 million for the current year, $7 million in 1999–2000, $8 million in 2000–01, $9 million in 2001–02 and $10 million each in 2002–03 and 2003–04. The team also had an option for a seventh year at $11 million.

A week after suffering his muscle strain, Bure hadn't resumed skating yet, and the team had suddenly grown vague about his return. "I don't know how long it's going to be because I just don't have answers to those questions," coach Terry Murray said. In the interim, the Panthers had reverted to toothless tabbies, going 1–3–2 in six games and scoring only 12 goals.

It would be 20 days before Bure finally returned to action against Philadelphia. Although he was held off the scoresheet, the Panthers won 5–3. Two nights later Bure scored twice, including once on a penalty shot, as Florida staged a stirring rally to tie Detroit 5–5. On March 3, against Colorado, the Russian continued his hot hand, beating goalie Patrick Roy three times in the first two periods to spark the Panthers to a 5–0 lead. But Bure didn't return to the ice in the third. He had hurt his knee again in a first-period collision with Avalanche defenseman Adam Foote. With Bure gone, the Panthers collapsed and Colorado roared back to score seven straight goals.

Two days later Bure underwent arthroscopic surgery to repair torn cartilage in his right knee. The Panthers said he would be out for three weeks. But the truth was far more serious. During the procedure, it was discovered that Bure's anterior cruciate ligament was no longer functional. Another reconstruction was necessary, but Bure wanted to delay the surgery to the end of the season and attempt to continue to play with a brace. The team agreed to let him try. But after three weeks of intensive rehabilitation and limited skating, it became obvious the knee wasn't stable enough. On March 29, Dr. James Andrews, a world-renowned knee specialist, performed a reconstruction of Bure's ACL using a portion of his patellar tendon. He would be sidelined for six months.

It was devastating news for both Bure and the Panthers, whose playoff hopes quickly evaporated. But there was more fallout to come. On March 31, Panthers team doctor David Attarian told reporter Brian

Biggane of the *Palm Beach Post* that there had been problems with Bure's knee when he first examined him in Florida in late January, after only three games with the team. Attarian said his examination revealed that Bure's original reconstruction was already stretching when the Panthers signed him and that "set him up for a series of injuries."

According to Attarian, the muscle strain Bure suffered on February 5 might actually have been a partial tear of the ACL, although it wasn't until Attarian performed arthroscopic surgery on Bure's knee on March 5 that the torn ACL was confirmed. Attarian said he knew a second reconstruction was necessary, but that the club had opted to hide the severity of the injury. "A lot of information was never made public. We [Attarian, president Bill Torrey and GM Bryan Murray] felt it would be okay to conceal it if he was able to play safely."

The story caused a furore in Florida as radio talk-show hosts from WQAM attacked Attarian and Panthers management for their deception and reckless attitude toward Bure's health. Attarian called their accusations slanderous and also said the *Palm Beach Post* article had taken his comments out of context. "I never said he was destined to have a series of injuries," Attarian insisted. The *Post*, however, stood by its story.

Amid the accusations and denials, it was difficult to know precisely what to believe. A few things were clear, however. Bure had hit southern Florida like a meteorite, stirred up hockey hysteria, scored 13 goals in 11 games, propelled the Panthers into playoff contention and then had crashed and burned in a controversial ball of flame.

The operation to repair Bure's torn ACL was deemed successful and, according to Bure's physical therapist, Mary Ann Towne, the rehabilitation program was completed in less than seven weeks, five weeks ahead of schedule. Towne predicted it was reasonable to expect Bure would be 100-per-cent healed by training camp. Bure returned to Moscow in June to resume his normal workout regimen of bike riding, weight lifting and running.

By late summer, Bure was skating again. In mid-August, he attended a special training camp in Pompano, Florida, with 18 other Russian NHL players and displayed no sign of trouble with his surgically revamped knee. Bure was cautiously optimistic, saying he felt rusty and that his right leg needed more strengthening. As he admitted to the *Miami*

*Herald*, "I'm hopeful and I'll do my best, but you never know. We'll find out." Panthers president Bill Torrey was more definite: "I know what this guy is all about," Torrey told the *Herald*. "He'll be back, and he'll be every bit of the player he was before."

Torrey's confidence notwithstanding, Bure's fragile hockey future now depends on the resiliency of a three-inch band of tissue in his right knee. The Florida Panthers have 47 million reasons to hope he returns to action fully restored. But it is not only the Panthers who have a stake in his comeback. The NHL desperately needs players like the Russian Rocket. Runaway expansion, bad ice, an emphasis on size over skill, stifling defensive strategies and questionable officiating have combined to blunt the game's speed and beauty. Hockey's artistry is under siege. The magicians have become all too rare.

As a charter member in the NHL's fraternity of illusionists, Bure has carved out his own unique niche. His game is infused with a quality that is difficult to define, but easy to recognize. He provokes a visceral reaction. When he takes the puck and embarks on one of his maximum-velocity rushes, he can make the tiny hairs on the back of your neck snap to attention. With just a few flashing strides, he can bring 15,000 people to their feet, a levitation act that is limited to a privileged few. Invention and surprise are the touchstones of his art.

The sense of mystery that surrounds Bure's personality has only enhanced his allure. Although his associations with alleged underworld figures remain a contentious topic, and also pose a potentially dangerous situation for Bure, the subject is unlikely to detract from his hockey fame. If you score enough goals and sell enough tickets, all else fades to black.

Bure says he doesn't want to talk about the past anymore. It is a dead issue. At 28, he is only looking ahead. But hockey fans can't help but wonder. Is the scalding speed still there? Is his sorcerer's touch intact? In the end, as in the beginning, there is another curtain still to be parted, another riddle yet to be solved.

# Statistics

**SOVIET UNION/RUSSIA**

REGULAR SEASON

| YEAR | TEAM | GP | G | A | PTS | PIM |
|---|---|---|---|---|---|---|
| 1987–88 | CSKA Moscow | 5 | 1 | 1 | 2 | 0 |
| 1988–89 | CSKA Moscow | 32 | 17 | 9 | 26 | 8 |
| 1989–90 | CSKA Moscow | 46 | 14 | 10 | 24 | 20 |
| 1990–91 | CSKA Moscow | 44 | 35 | 11 | 46 | 24 |
| 1994–95 | Spartak | 1 | 2 | 0 | 2 | 2 |
| TOTALS | | 128 | 69 | 31 | 100 | 54 |

INTERNATIONAL

| YEAR | TEAM | TOURNAMENT | GP | G | A | PTS | PIM |
|---|---|---|---|---|---|---|---|
| 1988–89 | Soviet Union | WJC | 7 | 8 | 6 | 14 | 4 |
| 1989–90 | Soviet Union | WJC | 7 | 7 | 3 | 10 | 10 |
| | Soviet Union | WC | 10 | 2 | 4 | 6 | 10 |
| 1990–91 | Soviet Union | WC | 10 | 3 | 8 | 11 | 2 |
| 1997–98 | Russia | Olympics | 6 | 9 | 0 | 9 | 2 |
| TOTALS | | | 40 | 29 | 21 | 50 | 28 |

# NATIONAL HOCKEY LEAGUE

## REGULAR SEASON

| YEAR | TEAM | GP | G | A | PTS | PIM | PP | SH | +/- |
|------|------|----|----|----|-----|-----|----|----|-----|
| 1991–92 | Vancouver | 65 | 34 | 26 | 60 | 30 | 7 | 3 | 0 |
| 1992–93 | Vancouver | 83 | 60 | 50 | 110 | 69 | 13 | 7 | +35 |
| 1993–94 | Vancouver | 76 | 60 | 47 | 107 | 86 | 25 | 4 | +1 |
| 1994–95 | Vancouver | 44 | 20 | 23 | 43 | 47 | 6 | 2 | –8 |
| 1995–96 | Vancouver | 15 | 6 | 7 | 13 | 8 | 1 | 1 | –2 |
| 1996–97 | Vancouver | 63 | 23 | 32 | 55 | 40 | 4 | 1 | –14 |
| 1997–98 | Vancouver | 82 | 51 | 39 | 90 | 48 | 13 | 6 | +5 |
| 1998–99 | Florida | 11 | 13 | 3 | 16 | 4 | 5 | 1 | +3 |
| TOTALS | | 439 | 267 | 227 | 494 | 332 | 74 | 25 | +20 |

## PLAYOFFS

| YEAR | TEAM | GP | G | A | PTS | PIM | PP | SH |
|------|------|----|----|----|-----|-----|----|----|
| 1991–92 | Vancouver | 13 | 6 | 4 | 10 | 14 | 0 | 0 |
| 1992–93 | Vancouver | 12 | 5 | 7 | 12 | 8 | 0 | 0 |
| 1993–94 | Vancouver | 24 | 16 | 15 | 31 | 40 | 3 | 0 |
| 1994–95 | Vancouver | 11 | 7 | 6 | 13 | 10 | 2 | 2 |
| TOTALS | | 60 | 34 | 32 | 66 | 72 | 5 | 2 |

## KEY

WC   World Championships
WJC  World Junior Championships
GP   Games Played
G    Goals
A    Assists

PTS  Points
PIM  Penalties in Minutes
+/-  Plus/Minus Differential
PP   Power-Play Goals
SH   Short-Handed Goals

# Sources

Diamond, Dan, James Duplacey, Ralph Dinger, Igor Kuperman, and
 Eric Zweig. *Total Hockey: The Official Encyclopedia of the National
 Hockey League*. New York: Total Sports, 1998.
Edelman, Robert. *Serious Fun: A History of Spectator Sports in the
 USSR*. New York: Oxford University Press, 1993.
Fischler, Stan. *Hockey Stars Speak: In-Depth Interviews with the Game's
 Biggest Stars*. Toronto: Warwick Publishing, 1996.
Fischler, Stan, and Shirley Fischler. *Red Line*. Toronto: Prentice-Hall
 Canada, 1990.
Klein, Jeff Z., and Karl-Eric Reif. *The Death of Hockey*. Toronto:
 Macmillan Canada, 1998.
MacGregor, Roy. *The Home Team: Fathers, Sons and Hockey*. Toronto:
 Penguin Books of Canada, 1995.
MacGregor, Roy. *Road Games: A Year in the Life of the NHL*. Toronto:
 Macfarlane Walter & Ross, 1993.
MacSkimming, Roy. *Cold War*. Vancouver: Greystone Books, Douglas
 & McIntyre, 1996.
Martin, Lawrence. *The Red Machine: The Soviet Quest to Dominate
 Canada's Game*. Toronto: Doubleday Canada, 1990.